LOST DOG

LOST DOG

A LOVE STORY

KATE SPICER

EBURY
PRESS

3 5 7 9 10 8 6 4

Ebury Press, an imprint of Ebury Publishing
20 Vauxhall Bridge Road
London SW1V 2SA

Ebury Press is part of the Penguin Random House group of companies
whose addresses can be found at global.penguinrandomhouse.com

Penguin
Random House
UK

First published by Ebury Press in 2019

www.penguin.co.uk

A CIP catalogue record for this book is available from the British Library

ISBN 9781785039195

Typeset in 10.5/14 pt ITC Galliard Std
by Integra Software Services Pvt. Ltd, Pondicherry

Printed and bound in Great Britain by Clays Ltd, Elcograf S.p.A.

'This Be The Verse' by Philip Larkin, originally published in
High Windows, is reproduced here by kind permission of Faber &
Faber Ltd. Copyright © 1974, The Estate of Philip Larkin.

To anyone who knows what it is to love and be loved by a dog.

BEFORE

The clock barks twelve times and the day I decide to get a dog begins. I look up at my drug dealer's clock. The numbers are replaced by TV family favourites. It's Lassie's job to announce midnight.

What the hell is *that* doing here?

The heart of Tim's place is not the hearth or the kitchen or even the TV, it's a large marble-and-glass coffee table that must have been quite the natty thing in the eighties when Tim was a young man about town. Now the town comes to him, and hunched over his period monstrosity holding rolled-up notes, they sniff cocaine up into their respiratory system, where it is absorbed through the blood vessels in the mucous membranes, into the bloodstream where it shoots around the body and arrives at the brain. Boom, there's a big rush of dopamine. Delicious dopamine is the happy drug made in your own body. If only you can get enough of it, it makes life feel grand, even when you feel grim.

In this state time flew by. Every hour an echo from my innocence calls out more time past. More of my life, wasted. It seems Lassie has only just barked her warning that everyone should be in bed when Bagpuss starts his soporific yawning. It's 1 a.m. Sleepytime for kids. Not for Tim's visitors though, they felt talkative, perverse, horny, animated, they shouted, they confessed their truest darkest thoughts, they argued and pointed fingers at each other, one did a rigid hipped sexless sexy dance, they bonded for life and became fast friends – until, that is, the drug wore off and all that merriment is replaced by the urgent grubby desperate need for more cocaine. No one's your friend then, aside from Tim. Dear old Timbo.

Tim wasn't a dealer, not exactly; at first, he was very generous with his Tupperware full of finely milled snowy-white toot. This was no tawdry £30 pub dust. A gram of Tim's very moreish gak was £130. Hence he attracted a 'nicer' fiend, if there is such a thing. Eventually though, he just said no, and then you started paying him.

Sitting under the clock, now with the little hand on Mr. T, are two delinquent bankers. One is considered a genius of his speciality, the other is a more humdrum financial talent but far more handsome, if you go for that sharp-suit-and-slicked-back-hair kind of guy. They are bellowing at each other about LIBOR and complex financial transactions. Let's call them the Libores.

There's another woman here, a young one with coltish legs in a pair of knickerbocker-style leather shorts and a dainty singlet that shows the sides of her cute bee-sting tits. She's the brainy banker's girlfriend, not that he's paid any attention to her all night. Let's call her Chica. Tim is alternating his attention between the birds and the bankers. He is riveted by Chica's chat about her ambitions as an influencer. Which is a good thing, because she ain't letting anyone else get a word in edgeways. For now it feels like we are all getting on like a house on fire, though I'm experienced enough to know it's the drugs talking, and listening; I'm old enough to be her mother and, don't be fooled by the inky-black hair, Tim her grandfather. In the morning we will have nothing in common.

I sit with my head inclined to indicate that I'm all ears, though I'm not at all. I am just enjoying the anaesthetic escapism from a non-specific discomfort that throughout my whole adult life I have never quite been able to escape unless I am high, on what has changed over the years: drugs, sport, booze, love, work, they're all great numbing agents. Eventually though, I always land up back here.

The ashtray fills to overflowing and once an hour another snappy catchphrase from childhood falls through the gloom. It is dark everywhere in the flat except the coffee table, lit by an overhead lamp and our eager attention.

By four my mood is starting to seriously flag and I descend into a hunch-shouldered silence. What chat I've managed to edge in to Chica's self-absorbed monologue is grinding to a halt. The gas is running out.

I need more. Drugs.

There's a susurrant squeak of dead animal hide against Chica's delicious skin as her legs move on Tim's old white leather international playboy sofa. It sounds like guys making moves in old cars. This flat really is the land that time forgot. Specifically daytime. I cannot remember ever seeing the curtains open. I look up. This fucking clock really doesn't belong here. It belongs in a playroom, or a happy family kitchen, one bathed in sunlight and smears of biscuit.

Phil Collins is on Tim's mega-stereo with the big dials. Tim's got the drugs, and where there's drugs there's usually someone happy to have sex, but he's always struggled with the rock 'n' roll part of the equation. He is sitting, intent on Chica, now discussing monetising her Instagram account and advertisers and brands that will pay her for content. 'I'm sure you could attract a male audience too ...'

My cynicism is creeping back. Once, I had found it sad and offensive to my feminist principles, the sight of these younger women being slowly corrupted by the Tims of the world, older men with expensive drugs. Now I shrugged. The ordinary undoing of fortunate people didn't move me anymore. The French writer Huysmans said a 'heart is hardened and smoked dry by dissipation' and that sums it up better than I ever could. Nice girls move to London, nice girls get corrupted, and pretty willingly, from what I could remember of my own swift descent. I know it's meant to be a tragedy of gender inequality, but to me, it's cliché.

Chica, zipping through the lines like a pro and filling us in on her plans for a brilliant life, doesn't realise all this yet. She theatrically holds the phone above us. 'Selfie!'

No, no, no. No way. I can see the hollowed-out ocular sockets. Lack of focus in the eyes, the lifeless 5 a.m. skin, grey roots and the fuzzy jawline. I put my hands in front of my face.

'Come on! I can't believe you're the same age as my mum,' she says, excitedly.

'No!' I speak like I would to a dog about to steal a steak.

She still looks flawless. The satiny fabric of her smooth skin and her loose and easy slender body, her hair still a glorious reflection of her natural golden hope. Her beautiful eyes with only a mere hint of blue shadow underneath them stare intent and briefly hurt from her luminous dew-kissed face. 'Oh no, why?'

'Because even if by some miracle I look OK, I really don't like selfies. They're narcissistic, needy and embarrassing.'

'But there's this amazing filter I have,' she says, beetling away on her phone, scrolling. She tells me all about how many selfies she needs to post a day as a social media influencer.

'I don't think this is anything that should be documented in any way. You go right ahead, but me, uh-uh.'

Tim's offering to take the picture of her and she's reclining on his stupid white sofa, now doing something cute with her legs. She does a queer little pout and he shoots away. A real David Bailey. Yuck. He's arranging her hair. There's an #everydaysexism story right there. My great friend Timbo, the priapic sex pest with the massive bag of chang. What was it that first attracted you to pervy middle-aged Tim with a bit of a belly, weirdly too-black hair and a sandwich bag full of the most expensive drugs in London?

The smarter, less handsome LIBOR guy is still in his work clothes, but he's taken off his tie, undone his two top buttons. His oiled hair is flopping either side of his ashen face. He's barking at Tim across the powdered altar about how, despite appearances, 'You know, I'm an anarchist really. We need nothing short of a social revolution ...'

It takes some time to make him stop talking so I can ask a reasonable question. 'Can I just speak for a moment,' I say, urgently. He holds up his hand. What he has to say is as never-ending as it is imperative. 'NO, but can I just say ...' Eventually I rush out, 'So if you're an anarchist and a socialist then why are you a banker?' Disappointingly, my throat is like paper and the last words are a feeble cracked bark.

'You're not defined by your profession, rather by the impact of your actions,' he says and, turning back more generally to the coffee table symposia: 'I mean yes, it's arguably contradictory but a puritanical approach to these matters is generally an even greater impediment to progress.'

Brutal, bright, entitled and ... a right old adenoidal mess; his suit's falling off him and he has little Vs of dried foam at each corner of his mouth to match the margherita crust around his favourite, sore-looking nostril. I'd say banking ain't working out that well for him.

I need wine, I think, and make a move towards Tim's fridge full of cold Waitrose Chablis. Mmmn, wine. Just the thought of it brightens the existential gloom.

Tim and Chica's little impromptu photo shoot is over and they have turned their attention on me. I'm a bit over the talking stage. I'd like some supermarket finest plonk and to be mute. I can't think of anything interesting to say.

Chica has already told me she's a vegan, doesn't drink or do drugs and I've looked at her with the appropriate astonishment. 'Oh this. This is a special occasion. You've got to cut loose sometimes.'

'But you do drink and you do do drugs and your shorts are real leather?'

'Yes but I present as sober.'

'But you aren't sober.' I look at her jaw grinding away. 'You're fucked, in fact.'

This is a new one on me. Back in the day we wore our habits on our sleeves. It's two decades, more, since I proudly worked my Hysteric Glamour 'Junkie's Baddy Powder' T-shirt, which ripped off the famous baby powder packaging and was a staple in a certain type of young woman's wardrobe in the nineties. I also had a Betty Ford Clinic 'Clean & Serene' T-shirt, which Brits saw as a joke, while Americans rushed over waving their ten-years-sober AA keyrings. Most of my sisters in this kind of behaviour had gone on to have at least one child, aka a partyectomy. Kids gave women something the rest of us needed to pay upwards of £30,000 for. A reason to be sober. Motherhood or rehab? I'd done neither.

Tim follows me into the kitchen, telling this doe-eyed angel what old *old* friends we are and how much he loves me, about how I used to flat-sit this mansion block pad of his on Mayfair's Mount Street when I was her age. He's well-meaning, and he's been a real brick throughout my adult life – if feeding a low-level coke habit for two decades is what great pals do for one another. But he's also a raving addict, and that makes him tricky as a pal.

Chica's spotted I've gone a tad bleak and has gone into supportive – God help us – *therapy* mode. 'You're sooo cool and fun, like, I just don't understand. Were you, like, just maaassively into your career? Cuz, I, like, totally get that. I really do. Like, I don't even know if I want kids.'

The kids thing. She's latched on to the kids thing.

'It's too late,' I say with a flatness that would zip the mouth of most sensitive human beings. But Chica is off her nut. Her empathy feels real to her at the moment but what that empathy really is is just a need to talk and talk. And talk. The only thing she has in common with Sigmund Freud right now is she loves cocaine. If her Instagram career doesn't shape up she may get a job at Freud's, that PR company.

'It's totally not too late. I had a friend ...'

We've been best friends all night but now, as I go into the early stages of a comedown, she's starting to do my head in. The last remnants of fun are trickling out of the evening. There is only one option if I want it to continue. Do lots more drugs. I cannot do lots more drugs. I have to leave and I have to leave fast.

Despite me standing up and walking away, Chica is still babbling about her friend who is 200 years old or something and has just given birth to quins. I'm starting to resent her lovely legs and her eager helpful face twitching and twisting in front of me.

There's only bleak internal noise now. Non-specific dark feelings as well as more irritatingly clear ones: my legs compared to hers, will I ever wear shorts like that again, do I have enough money to remove the valley of grey in my parting. Then it starts to get big-picture and existential. Glimpses of parents, siblings, of my boyfriend, Charlie, what's the point of anything. I hate my life. And work, work, work, work … like a bird pecking at my head. I go back again and again to the moral mathematics of getting messy on a school night.

I start telling myself familiar lies: 'I can be home by six, I'll be up before midday and I can write until eight in the evening and do exactly the same work as a normal person with a job. I only have to write a thousand words for the paper tomorrow, it can be done, I can do it, I don't need to feel bad about tonight.' I'm gulping wine now like it's lemonade, from one of Tim's stemless Riedels, which, experience has taught him, are harder for wasted people to knock over.

The thought returns again and again until the existential noise is a painful screech.

Work. Work. *Work. Fuck, WORK*! My spirit claws at each rib as it sinks into the pit of my stomach. Oh God, help me; help me get out of here, help me say NO.

Somewhere in the ramped-up coke anxiety a sensible version of self is trying to get through, is soothing me. You've been here before. You can cope. Go home. Go home to your sensible boyfriend asleep in your big comfortable bed. Tomorrow is just another day.

No, tomorrow is today already. Work. Work. *Work.*

'OK in here darling?' Tim stands far too close to me where I am leaning against the kitchen counter with my shoulders scrunched up to my ears and chin on my chest. He holds his arms out like he's about to hug me and I allow myself to be embraced by him like a teenage boy rigid under the swamping arms of a moustachioed maiden aunt. 'Come here, come to Timbo, darling.'

He guides me back into the coffee-table coke-sniffing suite and gives me his beloved silver Hoover-shaped straw, a gift, like the clock, from one of his unfunny fun-loving coke buddies. 'No thanks.' I look down at the expertly razor-chopped lines arranged across the discarded wing mirror of a Peterbilt truck. No grubby credit cards and rolled-up fivers for old Timbo. There's a few freshly snipped paper straws there. Plastic ones are too harsh on the nose.

'Darling. It's so good to see you. Such a treat to have you here.'

I try to think of something to say but can't find anything.

'Fit of the miseries, Katiepooz? Just remember darling, "The road of excess leads to the palace of wisdom".'

That old chestnut. Did the great mystic William Blake have crumby vapid London nights like this? I don't think so.

'You never know what is enough until you know what is more than enough,' I say. 'And this is enough.'

Hello, I must be going.

'I'm going home.'

There are noises of persuasion. Offers of taxis. A suggestion that I wait and share an Uber back to Notting Hill with the lower-IQ hot Libore. My heart bounces around in my chest like a squash ball and my mind keeps dropping tomorrow's deadline in front of me like a manic terrier with a stick.

I should have gone home six hours ago at midnight. Midnight 20 years ago, in fact, when all the nice people stopped doing this stuff. I have to get out of here before the clock strikes Paddington Bear, though, despite my state, I am curious what sound Paddington will make. 'Gotta go.'

I leg it down the stairs. I don't wait for the cage lift in his grand old mansion block. If I run perhaps I'll run off the dread, liven up a bit. I run down Mount Street fuelled by cocaine and Chablis and desperation, willing the fresh air to perk me up. Balenciaga. Scotts. Marc Jacobs. I pass all the status shops and restaurants and flag down a black cab with an orange light on Audley Street. I crash into the seat and throw my head forward into my hands, silently screaming, 'Never again. I never want to do drugs ever again. Please God. Please help me. I have to stop doing this.'

I sit up, breathe, breathe, breathe. What goes up, must come down. I lean back and catch the driver looking at his passenger now splashed across his back seat.

'Youorroight love? Up early? Or aincha been bed yet?'

His amiable forgiving banter is briefly cheering. I roll my too-wide and staring eyes rimmed in day-old mascara and smudgy crusted eyeliner and stutter, 'Something like that.

I lean back and watch Park Lane roll by on the left. What goes up must come down. My jaw is locked, my back teeth clenched. Shoulders are sore and tight. I can smell my armpits. I try not to think of other people getting up in the morning, minty fresh and showered, listening to manic morning radio, hurrying kids off to school, queuing for the mild, socially acceptable, worker-bee buzz of coffee, all the healthy activities of the useful human. They're tired perhaps. Some might even be carrying a hangover on a Wednesday. How many idiots like me are hunched over their knees in the back of a taxi? I think about my brother Will a couple of miles north in Tufnell Park, groggily greeting his youngest child waking him up with a toy or an absurd toddler question. And of my brother Tom, learning-disabled and living in a care home by the seaside in Devon, content with a couple of beers or a nice cup of instant coffee. It hurts. It all hurts.

I feel alone in my stupidity. But I am not alone.

I'd read research that analysed wastewater in major European cities. London's urine showed by far the highest midweek cocaine usage. In 2016 nearly a gram per 1,000 people. Ballpark, there are around 10,000 others out there messing up the rest of their week. This is one of the most soothing statistical life rafts to cling on to for any person rapidly coming down in the back of a London taxi at dawn.

There aren't any upsides to this situation.

I wind down the window as the cab grumbles past Hyde Park on Bayswater Road. At this time of the morning there are a few people out, the joggers, dog walkers and jet-lagged. I envy them being on the right side of dawn. Wedging myself tightly against the window, I look out and breathe in the green-scented air blowing off the park. What goes up must come down, '... Up by two p.m.: work 'til eight ...'

Charlie likes to be in bed by nine because he has a proper job and he loves it. Early to bed, early to rise. If my calculations are correct, I will have just missed him and his sober judgement. I clank slowly up the metal steps to our first-floor flat and open the door on quiet air hanging with the smell of supper. Sausages. There are pigletty snoring sounds up above. The lazy bugger is having a lie-in. It's just after six. He has not got up for work as early as I hoped. I undress where I stand, leaving a heap of fag-scented clothes and knickers sunny side up on the kitchen floor. Using hands and feet, I climb the steep narrow stairs to our loft bedroom and lurch in a drunken sham creep across the room.

'Mmn time i'it?' His voice muffled with sleep and duvet. I say nothing. More awake now, he says, disgusted, 'Urgh, you stink.'

I want to tell him it's three a.m. There's such a difference between six a.m. and three. But there it goes. The infuriating tinkling scales of misery. All two of us know the time now: it is 6.07a.m. The time Charlie gets up, except for those days when he gets up at 5.15 to go to the gym or at 4 to catch the first flight to Frankfurt.

'Soweeee,' I say, slipping into bed.

'Loser,' he mumbles.

Assuming the recovery position, 'I know.'

Over the years Charlie got used to me crashing up the white wooden stairs at dawn. Every so often, I'd come staggering in breathing wine fumes to find him brushing down his crisp suit, polishing his Italian loafers and ramping up the rage for a day at the office.

Whatever mood he was in when he left the flat, always before seven a.m., often six, his last act was squirting himself a halo of gentleman's fragrance by an old French perfumier. He haunted every room he entered with the smell of creamy leather, lavender and Amalfi lemons. No matter how badly we were getting on the one thing I could reliably love was that smell. I'm not sure what he could reliably love about me. For a man with a serious job, he tolerated my rampages with mostly uncommon patience.

On this particular dawn sleep doesn't come easy and I have to go back downstairs and climb on the kitchen counter to get at the stash of hard booze on top of the fridge.

'The car's on a yellow line,' he calls from the sink, where he is performing his final ablution, that spritz of the £200 cologne. 'Can you manage to move it before eight thirty?' He comes out, looks at me and turns back to the mirror, shaking his head and mumbling, 'Stupid question. I suggest you put the lid back on the tequila and go to bed, Kate.'

Turning on his leather-soled Ferragamo loafers he leaves without looking back at me standing several feet above him, naked, on the kitchen counter, one elbow on top of the fridge and an eggcup of booze in my hand. 'sssmezcal acshly.'

The kitchen door slams, leaving me alone with the odour of sausages, Amalfi lemons and his moral superiority. I do feel a touch better now. I'm home.

My more extreme nocturnal habits didn't make our relationship easy. While I was frolicking in the starry gutters of London town Charlie provided a stable structure for me to hang my life around. Our relationship was an experiment in opposites that always threatened to implode but, miraculously, never *quite* did. Until him my love life was a steady cycle of relationships formed in sexual ecstasy and doomed to last no longer than the 18 months to two years until the bonding hormone oxytocin runs out, when your hormone bank is bled dry of lust and the scales fall from your eyes once blinded by love. Reality and relationships had never ever worked for me, until Charlie.

When Charlie appeared on the cusp of my forties, I was nobly thinking I was 'post-men' and wondering how to pull off this modern spinster business with aplomb. I was lying on the sofa pretending to be interested in an election debate on the television while scrolling through Twitter, where everyone was trying to make clever jokes about #election2010. I tried to focus on the telly because engaging with it, watching *Newsnight*, reading the *Financial Times* and being serious, I reasoned, would help me raise my working game above the ridiculous norm, like my most recent piece for *Esquire*: 'I Took A Walk-On Role in a Porn Movie.'

My eyes kept flitting back to the screen of my worn BlackBerry. Ping, a notification came up from someone I didn't know: 'Thought your walk-on part in a porn movie story was very funny.' We tweeted throughout the debate until I learned how close he lived to me and he suggested we meet for a drink at Julie's, a restaurant round the corner. Nah. You're all right, I said. Stalker alert!

Another week, another election debate, he pinged me again. I've admitted I'm bored of politics this time and within ten minutes I'm cycling to Julie's. If nothing else, he could stand me a couple of their overpriced gins.

As I walked in I spotted a guy sitting in the window with large blond swishy hair, he is bellowing at the lady bartender. His belly rolls over his boot-cut jeans, which last fitted him in the eighties. He is shout-talking in a posh voice – the worst shouting voice of all. Jesus. This was the guy off Twitter. At the bar, I ordered a gin for my trouble. I'd sink it and dash back home for homeopathic minutes of *Newsnight*.

'Kate?' Right there, less than a foot from me at the bar, was a tall man with short dark hair, big ridiculously clear white eyes and clean fresh skin, wearing a pair of spanking new cream Converse and dark blue raw denim Edwin jeans. Very together-looking, very much not the dickhead bellowing over there. 'Charlie.' He stuck out a hand. 'From Twitter?'

This changed things. Within a few sips of the gin, it was apparent I had myself a tall single male with no immediate evidence of: addiction issues, a flotilla of exes, a beer gut, hair loss or insolvency. There were single men around but most of the decent available ones were serial modelisers and didn't want to commit to an old crone of 40 like me. These guys were constantly on the hunt for a hot trophy girlfriend, with the emphasis on *girl*. A decent human male interested in an actual relationship with a normal 40-year-old woman who doesn't look like Elle MacPherson, that's incredibly rare. What was wrong with him?

We both laughed at the bellyaching arrogance of Lady Di hair over by the window. 'I thought he was you,' I said.

'No, sorry. Unfortunately, I am me,' he said.

I'd struck gold without suffering so much as a blow-dry. When we started spending the night together, I found it so sexy the way he woke up, neatly fucked me and then set about costuming himself for a job in the City where he did something sensible to do with deals. After he left, fragrant and sharp, I would spread myself wide across his white sheets and have another hour or three of sleep.

There were problems, there always are in relationships. The big one was that despite being six years younger than me, Charlie was a sensible grown-up and I wasn't. The messy me slugging mescal from an eggcup this morning was far cleaner and tidier than the one he'd met six years ago. Still, I struggled to keep up with his high standards, or, more to the point, I didn't want to. On Saturday mornings he got up and did stuff, immediately, even if he had a hangover. He never idled or loafed. Dilettante trust-fund kids disgusted him, whereas I thought they had the best life.

Somehow he managed to put up with an idle, permanently almost-broke, girlfriend. And somehow I managed to put up with a turbocharged, workaholic boyfriend. Occasionally we even had fun. Having motored through enough relationships to last some women several lifetimes, I knew this was as good as it got – even though it was a royal pain in the arse sometimes.

With only the 1,000 words to get up for, which I make feeble attempts to 'think about' as my spooling mind wrestles with the hangover, it is afternoon by the time I finally haul my stinking carcass from the bed. In that time I hadn't only slept, I'd made three cups of tea, and eaten one piece of toast and two bags of Quavers.

Under the duvet, in between dribbling, coma-like bouts of sleep, I sent Charlie busy texts full of lies suggesting a productive, if hungover, day. 'At market want anything', adding a green puking emoji for truthiness. I'd given up on filing the copy on time and set the alarm for 4 p.m., when I'd need to start pulling the domestic situation together if I didn't want to piss my hard-working boyfriend off.

Three or four days of half a life lie ahead, feeling emotionally low and uncomfortably numb. That's a drug hangover for you. What goes up must come down.

All I need now is strong caffeine. Time to get up and soldier on.

With porridge-coloured walls and a dark concrete floor, Coffee Plant on Portobello Road functions like a grim needle exchange for discerning caffeine addicts. In fact, that's pretty much what it is. In the mornings its loo is always busy with the motions of recently stimulated middle-aged bowels. They sell good coffee, a lot of it: if you count the 'Gershon therapeutic roast', which is a green bean used for enemas and colonics, that's 27 different types of bean behind the wooden counter.

I lock my bike to its own wheel and lean it against the wall outside. A small girl is waddling along behind her mother very slowly and I walk in front and through the heavy glass door but I do not hold it for them. The door closes on the child's face. The woman comes in after me and gets right up in my face with a righteous form of indignant maternal fury. 'You knew, you knew, you knew she was there.'

'I'm so sorry.' The emphasis on the so doesn't come out quite right. I sound a bitch. 'I just assumed you'd get the door for your own child. Is she OK?'

A squirm of shame runs through me. Had I known? Did I feel annoyed by being co-opted into plodding adoring reverence of this small child? Yes, I need coffee, but did I need to dash through the door so fast – after all one could hardly describe my day as 'busy'. The scene in the coffee shop can be fractious sometimes, over-attentive parents, kids running up and down screaming, around recovering addicts from the Salvation Army's AA and NA meetings over the road. It's an all-human-life place. I love it.

The incident stirs the dark matter I have been consciously pressing into a corner of my body for the last ten years or so of my life since my friends started breeding. I'd been at the fair a few weeks ago with a friend who was having IVF.

I was trying to persuade her to go on a scary ride but she was worried about the IVF. 'Don't worry, it'll shake the eggs up, make them more vital,' I said.

When we were on the ride with my IVF friend looking on, her eggs calm and restful, my other friend said, 'You know, Kate, that was some harsh banter. It was too harsh.'

It's like I've shut that side of myself down. I don't even know how I feel about it. What's the point of pining and grieving over a life that never lived inside you. Just get on with it. Soldier on. But there's a fractious, almost violent boredom I feel when baby chat cranks up. It comes up again as this woman berates me for not putting my hands between my knees and bending down to say, 'Can I get the door for you, you magnificent little princess?'

A shrink might say, 'Let's talk about that.'

Women disappear into motherhood; even when they're physically in the room they're more or less absent. Often friends turned mothers wouldn't register conversation or your presence or a gesture of kindness. Sometimes the mother would fold over her child as if to protect it from the entire world, including you. It's a weirdly humiliating feeling.

I'd seen a man do it as well. It was a man I had a long and crappy affair with and I'd been staying at his during an access visit from his son. His son had got up in the night and he'd cocooned the child entirely within his arms and chest and told me to leave. The sound of my feet in stupid sexy high heels as I edged out of the room and creaked across his stripped floorboards to the front door only emphasised an isolating and painful moment. Stuff like that hardens you.

Stuff like that eventually drove me away from families, and I spent more time hanging out with single friends, men especially, as most of the women were mothers now. It drove me back to Tim's so often that I could remember the six digit code for his gate. Not an excuse. I hate excuses. As someone who is constantly late with work, there is always an excuse, sometimes it's even a good one. Sometimes your grandmother really has died. The truth is all excuses are bullshit. Excuses are for babyish people.

Not having kids had left me without purpose, distraction or anything to do. Unlike for Charlie, work was not enough. Someone once said, 'Just fighting for yourself is defensive and grim.' Yes. That. It's that. I cannot escape the constant screaming question, 'Is this it?'

Very little of the Notting Hill I inhabit looks like the one in the Working Title movie. The floppy-haired posh people who sometimes drank a bit too much wine lived down the road in

Fulham and Wandsworth, and, if they had money, in Kensington. We had posh people round here, but they were party-loving flakes or flint-eyed fashionistas. We had ex-junkie gentry, and copious numbers of David Cameron's trendy Tory chums. Their public school privilege is diluted by one of the most ethnically diverse corners of this country. At last count, more than 90 different ethnic groups in North Kensington, the realest corner of the Royal Borough of Kensington and Chelsea, and the most fun. So *yah*, I sometimes waved cheery greetings to the son of a Duke or brushed past the man who wrote *Notting Hill*, pottering around his neighbourhood in an anorak.

Equally though, there were copious other strands of Britishness – the second, third and fourth generation Portuguese, Moroccans, Spanish or Colombians – the more recent arrivals from Sudan and Somalia. And underpinning it all, intensely on August Bank Holiday weekend, were the West Indian contingent who arrived with Windrush in the fifties. The magic is in the mix. I knew all sorts round here but no one remotely like Hugh Grant or his charming, bumbling, harmless pals in that movie. Hugh lives in Earl's Court on the other side of the borough. Everyone knows that, don't they?

In the coffee shop queue I see Keith, who is an elegant PR from Northern Ireland. He's so neatly pressed I don't want him to see me with my paranoid, twitchy hangover. Shrinking behind a French girl in a men's Crombie coat, I hide in the queue. Before, that is, I clock the tan and white whippet at his side. My overwhelming urge to touch it overrides any concerns about my old skanky jeans. 'Hey Keith,' I say, smiling, and bending to one side. 'Is this yours?'

'Kate!' He greets me with a warm enthusiasm that disarms me. 'Yes, this is my boy, this is Castor.' The dog stands still as I stroke him from the tip of his skull and along his back. The effect is not much different to a dose of Valium. My skin still feels crusted with the fag-drenched crud of last night and I laugh it off to Keith with some explanatory detail of my stinking hangover and dawn bedtime. His snorting laugh has a 'been there' lilt of grim empathy. 'What goes up must come down.'

'Innit!'

Keith and I sit down at a Formica table to take our cups of bastard-strong caffeine together. I soothe myself on his dog's silky ears, swirling them in my fingers, smoothing my hands over the length of his back's slithery soft fur. I am almost groaning with pleasure. 'He's lovely, Keith.' The dog is still and calm. He stands there beside me.

I could weep like a Catholic at the foot of the cross begging for forgiveness and eternal love. Instead I say, 'What are they like, whippets? Do they need a lot of exercise?'

'He's a lurcher, actually. God knows what other breeds are in there, definitely lots of whippet, maybe a bit of Labrador. I got him from a farm in Kent for £100. And no. He gets two walks a day and then he sleeps.'

'I'd love to have a dog,' I say.

We gossip about work a bit. 'I'd better get back and do some writing.'

He gives me the cynical raised eyebrow. 'Really? Come for a walk.'

'Oh, ok'.

In Keith's Audi, Castor stands in the back with his chin resting on the top of the seat behind me. I can feel his warm long snout against my neck. We talk about keeping a dog in London. 'These dogs are great. You don't need a garden. They're calm. They're clean.'

Family lore dictated dogs were unhappy in London. I'd always wanted a dog but was sent scurrying from the idea by a belief system drummed in since birth. Dogs and London don't mix. We walk at Wormwood Scrubs, a 60 acre expanse of near-deserted scrub and woodland next to the famous prison. I didn't even know it was here.

Back at home I clear all evidence of the hopeless day's recovery. I smooth the sheets and whumpf the duvet up, expelling my miserable sweaty traces. I smooth it so hard, it looks like Charlie has made it. Well, not that good. But there'll be none of his pissed-off huffing and blowing at the sight of my tangled hungover bed. In this flurry of activity and improvement, I will energy into my depleted body. What goes up, must come down; and go up again.

Tim texts me, 'Such a fun naughty night. So good to see you.' I delete it. I know Charlie's walking home, shiny shoes going clip-clip down the street, smart leather document folder tucked under his arm. He's probably taking important calls but I know, also, he'll be wondering what chaotic state the flat is in and his slovenly self-employed girlfriend too.

His footsteps ring on the metal steps up to the only door we have, windows fogged by cooking. Inside, the reassuring smell of garlic softening in butter.

I go to speak, and he holds up his hand. He is indeed on a call. I clatter about finding things to fiddle with, killing time until I can say what I so urgently need to.

'Right. Yes, sorry.'

'I saw Keith today and you know he has a dog, it's a lurcher, called Castor, anyway we took it for a walk to Wormwood Scrubs, it's huge there, I mean huge, and it's only five minutes away from here and it's great for walking dogs and I think we should get one. I think we should get a dog.'

'Good idea, Fox,' he says. Fox, the name he gave me when we were still wallowing in the oxytocin joy of first love. 'You sort it out. What's for supper?'

PART ONE
LOST WOMAN

CHAPTER ONE

A dog by Christmas, that was the plan. But the process of adopting a lurcher is far from straightforward. For two months middle-aged women in rubber-soled shoes and noisy anoraks visit us and rustle round the flat, ticking boxes and asking questions. They are like cops.

We are turned down for one-eyed Zac and for Honey. Always they mention two things. First, our lack of experience. Jesus, how hard could dog ownership be? People have kids without Maureen from Lurcher SOS approving it. I try to gain their trust, to start conversations. It is a closed shop. Forget the Carlton Club, try gaining the trust of the Lurcher SOS Forum members; it'd be easier to buy weapons-grade plutonium on the dark web.

Secondly the stairs, which they point at and gravely discuss how dangerous they would be to a lurcher with its long spindly legs. Too many stairs, sorry. No. 'But the dog will *never* go up the stairs to our bedroom because dogs don't sleep in bedrooms,' I plead. 'Dogs aren't allowed upstairs.'

That the stairs even exist is enough for them. I had not expected this. I give up with the lurcher specialists and go to a more homespun operation. It isn't a registered charity and it rescues all kinds of animals, from guinea pigs to donkeys. There we find 'Merlin, four-year-old lurcher', a scribble of roughly dog-shaped, messy biscuit-coloured fur. There is only one photograph of him on the website, and it is a black-and-white one taken of him in the boot of a car. He is sat like the Sphinx after a nasty fright. He doesn't look quite lurchery enough for me but I am desperate at this stage. I want a dog.

Again we are inspected by a woman in an anorak. This time Charlie is home too. She has issues with the deadly stairs but seems less disapproving than the previous visitors from the lurcher rescues. 'They're too steep and the fact that they have no back could be very dangerous.'

'The dog will never go upstairs. I don't let dogs upstairs,' I say, doing my best impression of a stern old battleaxe.

'And I will make backs for the stairs with glass. I will do it immediately,' adds Charlie.

'Oh,' she says. 'That could work.'

Four days later, Tuesday evening, a woman called Sara from the rescue rings and tells me 'Merlin' is mine if I want him. The glass has already been ordered, I tell her. 'Good because I'll need to see pictures as proof you've done it, I heard they were very steep.'

When Sara rings I am sitting at my heavy cherrywood desk, midway through finishing a health piece due in Monday morning just gone. It's 1,200 words about a phenomenon called 'drunkorexia'. Drunkorexia means you save all your calories up for wine. It hasn't been hard finding case studies.

My drunkorexia notes fill up with my scribbles and doggy doodles as we talk.

'He came to us because his last adopted home didn't work out. He was being bullied by the resident bitch so they put him up for adoption again.'

'What's he like?'

'Oh, he's a lovely boy. He's been with me three months now. I can't think why no one's had him. He loves his walks and he's a dream on the lead. He's best one on one. Like a lot of these dogs he'd like to be with a single woman.'

'My boyfriend's a lovely man, very gentle,' I say.

'Yes, that's fine, just concentrate on not shouting, he'll only find a corner to hide in or run away and wee himself. He's a strong boy but timid.'

I'm hearing estate agents' parlance, where every phrase has a hidden meaning. I add up 'no one wants him ... best one on one ... wees himself ... strong boy ... timid' and picture an ugly, incontinent dog that bites people and then runs away. I'm picturing a dog no one wants. 'So what are we? His third owners?'

'As far as I know, yes.'

Sara is displaying classic animal-lover conversation skills. There's a reticence to share detail that comes not from truculence or secrecy but from a simple preference not to have to speak too much to humans. My effusive gratitude receives not a mote of recognition. My curiosity feels like an inconvenience. I want to know more.

'He was originally found as a stray wandering the streets somewhere in Manchester. He wasn't chipped, he had no collar, so who knows.'

'Any idea what mix there is in there?'

'Well, he's a bit chunky, I reckon he could be a labradoodle saluki cross but I really don't know.'

Labradoodle/saluki? This wasn't the regal lurcher blend I had in mind. I liked the look of the shaggy lurchers; they were robust, like mutts, yet with a leggy, lean, royally handsome silhouette that felt all pedigree. I'd look dead cool beside one of those, I thought. This Merlin looked shaggy enough, but could a lurcher even be a lurcher if it's crossed with a labradoodle? Surely it'd just be a labrapooki or a salabrapoo. Whatever it was, it didn't sound like the skulking and skinny noble old gypsy hound I fancied.

A number of unappealing thoughts cross my mind. Not least, my consumer approach to buying a living thing. Also, now I've been accepted to adopt this Merlin I'm wondering what's wrong with the Essex rescue, and the dog. It's like when a man makes it clear he likes you, you go off him – he must be a weirdo.

'I think he'd have a lovely life with you. I can't understand why you've been turned down so much.'

This whole glass fiasco is going to take a few weeks. I'll have time to process whether I actually want the dog. So I'm taken aback when she says, 'You can pick him up Saturday.'

Too soon. I don't know if I want Merlin. Don't we get to visit him first and see how the chemistry is? Shouldn't there be more rigorous anorak and clipboard checks from these self-appointed canine social workers? I don't want a dog with Lab or poo in his genes. I want a *lurcher.*

'*This* Saturday?'

I need to tell this Sara about my misgivings.

'Yeah. I'll meet you at midday at Thurrock services in the car park. It's £160, the adoption fee, you need to bring cash and a lead.'

'See you there. Fantastic. Thanks. Great. Thanks again. Thank you *so* much.'

Looks like another of life's big decisions has been left to fate, like getting pregnant, a career path and how to survive in old age. Charlie isn't big on fate. He has five-year plans and a pension. He gets up at 5 a.m. to go to the gym.

I ring my mother. 'Mum, we've found our dog. He's—'

'Oh no, a *male* dog? Don't get a male dog. They go wandering. They wee everywhere, they—'

'Got to go. Sorry.'

I'd forgotten about my mother's prejudice against boy dogs, a latent canine misandry that I've never worked out the source of. Like most women, she loves to huff out the word 'Men!' Not all women of her generation were Gloria Steinem or New Labour MPs; the battle of the sexes for the less visible of my mother's generation was a passive-aggressive one fought not in important feminist tomes but in small victories won on the domestic front.

Rejecting the patriarchy, for her, comes in the form of never owning a male dog and moaning, constantly, about husbands. I had not cared what genitals my dog came with but now I'm delighted that it's a dog not a bitch. 46½ and I'm still childishly celebrating all the ways I'm not like mum.

*

We were both looking forward to the dog's arrival and not a day passed without us talking about what our new boy would be like. We went to walk in the places where we might take him, to reassure ourselves that we could give this beast a great life. I showed Charlie the spot under my desk where the dog could have his own 'office', a space away from humans, where it is dark and quiet and, just like me in my office, he could sit quietly undisturbed and do nothing. I liked the idea of him sleeping on my toes. Perhaps I would write more with a dog as a colleague.

In the space between deciding to get a dog and getting a dog, there was a general lift in the mood of the house. We had something to think about other than work.

In the nights before we drove to Essex to fetch him I sat upright in bed devouring Jackie Drakeford's *The House Lurcher* like an airport novel. I tried to stir Charlie into awakeness with excited readings about things like prey drive, intestinal worms and the perfect dog poo.

'Lurchers are perfectly capable of withdrawing if they do not consider you worthy of them … Lurchers may not bark a lot, but they have a huge vocabulary of noises known as "lurcher talk" … Lurchers do things with you, not for you, and are the most loyal companions, as long as you deserve them.'

'Mmmn, very interesting,' he mumbled under the duvet.

'… Raw meaty bones complete the natural diet for dogs and should be fed three or four times a week … Are you listening?'

An incoherent mumble followed by a brutal fart from under the covers suggested he was not. 'Lurchers are …' Snore. Fair enough. I'd read on for hours more while he slept beside me.

I'll be honest, we were struggling to reconcile our different lives. Charlie lived at a furious double-macchiato-and-ambition-driven pace. His downtime was sleep time. Then there was me with my siestas, missed deadlines and mess. The desire and search for the dog created a peaceful focal point that we had been struggling to find since we'd moved in together a year before.

*

On the Saturday when we went to collect 'Merlin' my left temple buzzed with a light tequila headache from a Libertines gig the night before. I'd ended up behind a rope somewhere, not because I was meant to be there, I just ambled in and saw a few people I knew. As usual, the gilded party set were chatting loudly as the artists performed. Far from delighted to have been invited, they behaved like it was their birthright. Free stuff, all the time, from everyone. These guys are invited to everything and pay for very little. Just having them there is an honour.

Natter, natter, natter. Patti Smith's supporting, you know. Oh, fantastic! Love Patti. Natter, gossip, natter, gossip. Gossip. Darling. People, places, things. Darling. Darling. People, places, things. Some of them were very successful, others were there by dint of marriage, birth, beauty, money, or all four, or simply knowing someone, probably, and being reliably good company. It was all very flamboyant, with scarves and sweeping gowns. A shoal of models floated by.

I hadn't intended to drink but I did. Patrón were sponsoring. And I love a Margarita or four. Hangovers often eat their humdrum way into momentous days like weddings, funerals, important interviews, shooting high-brow late-night culture shows you will never be invited back on to, so why not collecting your first dog too?

I'd told a couple of people at the gig I was getting this dog the following day. One said, 'So?' And the other said, 'Amazing!' Basically, no one cared. Though, given the self-interest and indifference among party people, I could have been getting an albino tiger and still roused no more than a yawn.

Charlie hadn't come with me. He rarely does – 'I'm not interested in being your plus one.'

A few moments after the alarm goes at seven he says, 'Right,' in a 'time to get organised' sort of way.

He is on crisp and efficient form. He lies in bed for a few minutes more, says, 'Right,' again and gets up. He is showered, caffeinated, shipshape, fragrant long before I've pulled my head off the pillow. He has also been and done some shopping and studied for his latest finance exam.

It's not a matter of physical suffering with this morning's light yet still very much present hangover; it's more of a mental issue. It feels like a small creature is carefully tiptoeing back and forth over my frontal lobe and this is inhibiting my executive functions, the parts of the brain that get you up and at 'em.

Added to my self-inflicted limitations is Charlie's overactive executive function. The more he does downstairs, the less I can get up. The sound of him making his smoothie assaults me from the kitchen. It's not just the noise. It's the fact that it's green and designed for him by a famous, ravishingly beautiful nutritionist. I'm thinking perhaps we can buy a bag of the M&S Salt and Black Pepper Combo Mix en route to getting the dog.

'Right. Are you getting up?' he asks up the stairs. I know what he really wants to say is, 'Get the fuck out of bed, you lazy cow.'

Yes, yes. I throw on last night's clothes and flop downstairs and try to scrabble back some good odour. I say brightly, 'Cup of tea?'

Irritated by my wanton pursuit of sybaritic elixirs like a strong Assam with whole milk, he snaps at me. 'No, Kate.' Clearly he is way beyond the tea-drinking part of the day. 'We have to go.' I feel scalded. The hangover has made me sensitive. I feel chastised just for being me.

Charlie knew what he was getting into. He claims he fell for me when he saw me eating an apple while driving in the neighbourhood with a bin bag strapped to the broken sunroof of a beaten-up Honda CR-X that cost me £400. I called it my Porsche Banana.

'Why don't you just use my car,' he'd said, when it failed its MOT. 'I hardly ever use it.'

This was the overture to a long-term relationship.

I'd looked at the £1,500 estimate for getting the Banana roadworthy, balanced it up with the rapidly shrinking freelance journalism market, and said yes, thank you, if you're sure you don't mind.

'I'd love it. I like smelling your perfume when I get in after you've used it,' he said.

What a sweet and romantic moment that was. 'I like smelling ...' Yeah, that wasn't all that happened there. It was a tipping point, small at the time but significant. I surrendered some of my independence. Charlie was starting to support me. In the brand of equality I dreamed about, I had lots of my own money. Foolishly, I had created the impression of this with the miasma of endless credit for 20 years. All those it's-not-your-money chickens were coming home to roost now – not just in my life, in the world generally – and now I lived permanently in a crowded relationship with a Visa bill, HMRC and my financially astute boyfriend.

I saw a get-out clause in the brand of equality my mother's generation taught me about. A man who supports you.

Not that Charlie is rich, not at all. We live in a sweet little flat, I pay a bit less of the mortgage than he does, he put down a lot more deposit. Given this fiscal imbalance, I feel I ought to pick his socks up and wash them. He pays for dinner more than me. Picked up my tax bill this year. You think this stuff is going to be nice but you feel like a traitor to your ideals. Ain't nothing in this life for free, baby.

Women sometimes choose relationships that are pure transaction, where each has something the other wants: his money, her sex. That isn't what I wanted.

The balance of power, it's askew when I am broke. When we argue, and it's about money, he always wins. My mum always told me, 'When money problems come in the door, love flies out the window.' Which is the definition of ironic given it was her lot that flogged us that let-the-man-support-you paradigm.

I didn't want to be like that. But it felt like we were headed that way.

'Right,' he says, again, 'I'm going to get the car.'

God, I wish he'd stop saying 'Right'. I make myself a cup of tea for the car and head outside to wait for him by our back door on Treadgold Street. I say 'back' door; it's a gate. We don't have a front door. We have this gate into a ramshackle alleyway dotted with mangy geraniums along the rear entrance to our neighbours' houses on Grenfell and Treadgold Streets. Our front door is actually a back door on the first floor up these noisy metal steps. If you want to live in London's fashionable Notting Hill, you have to forgo luxuries like front doors, unless you are rich, in which case, it's front-doors-a-go-go. And if you're mega rich, then it's all basement-swimming-pools-r-us.

Just as we are heading out of central London I admit I have forgotten to take the cash out of the bank to pay for the dog and that we are going to have to stop at a machine. Charlie's disappointment at this predictable lack of preparation vibrates from him, though no words are spoken.

After a tense five-minute silence, he says, 'How are your finances at the moment, Kate?'

Ah-ha, one of his special punishment questions. A provocative question that he knows will give him a really good excuse to be openly pissed off with me. He only ever asks it when we are in a state of barely contained animosity. My heart sinks. Now is a terrible time for a money conversation. If I admit to him that I have just enough cash in the bank to pay for the third-hand dog, the situation will descend into a conversation about credit ratings and how I am punishing our chance of a good mortgage rate with my feckless approach to money.

I have no choice. I must lie.

'They're good,' I say brightly. 'Couple of grand in the bank, another few grand owing.'

As this has not proved a fruitful outlet for his irritation with me, all his frustration is verbally channelled into traffic and other drivers; he's like a street drunk with Tourette's raging at paper bags swept up by the wind. I cringe in the passenger seat, undermined by tequila and a steadily accumulating pile of unaired grievances.

'Come on, today's a good day. I'm excited, aren't you? Aren't you? We're getting our dog.'

'Mmmn, yuh,' he says, and I wait in hope for the air to settle in the car and for warmth to return to our interactions.

'CUNT!' A Prius driver.

This is how the next 30 minutes on the M25 go by.

'Fucking CUNT!' He slams his fist on the horn as a white van man carves him up at a junction exit.

Concentrate on the dog, I think. Concentrate on the positive. Concentrate on the animal you've never met before who is about to come and live in your home.

'Sara said that we mustn't shout in front of him, you know? She said he will pee himself if you shout,' I say in my special measured and calm voice. 'Will you be able to chill before we get the dog?'

It is entirely impossible now for me to say anything without it sounding passive-aggressive.

'Yes, I am aware of that,' he says, in his own special extra-calm voice that he only uses when I put on my special extra-calm voice. He stares at the road with a face like a hammer. There's peace for a moment until the next Prius driver moves into the wrong lane.

I sigh loudly.

'Why are you sighing?'

'Because I don't know how else to release the tension in this car. Can't today be a good day?'

'Happiness is overrated,' he mumbles, but at least he isn't shouting 'cunt'. It's a truce, of sorts.

'I wonder how many poos I will pick up in the next year?'

Charlie ignores me. It wouldn't be a hard sum to do. I don't know how many times a dog defecates in a day but I am guessing it's about two, maybe a few more after greedy days like Christmas. I think about riffing on this for laughs but there's no point if the audience is only here to windmill his fists at Prius drivers.

What can I do with my excitement about the dog? Nothing. I start looking at Instagram. Pulling up Chica's page. I've become quietly obsessed by her glossy lip close-ups and dynamic leaping-off-steps-in-tiny-shorts shots. Usually she manages to leverage her gorgeous legs into everything but today she has posted an inspirational quote on a plain background: 'Every woman is your sister; treat her accordingly.'

'Word sista!' 'Truth!' 'Yes to this.' 'Love.' There must be thirty comments underneath, all accompanied by hearts and high-five emojis. It's ridiculous. It's not as if she's Emmeline Pankhurst crying, 'Freedom or death!'

I type: 'What? Every woman wants to steal your clothes and have a fist-fight about who gets the top bunk?'

My impotent silent rage at my relationship abates a bit and in its place rises a light sprinkling of Instagram-fuelled jealousy and superiority. How can this work, this Chica mixture of hot pants, lip gloss, beauty products and lame hashtag feminism? She's a spindle-legged, vapid child. How has she got nearly 50,000 followers since that night at Timbo's? Now I wanted to shout 'Cunt' at a Prius driver too.

'Am I mean or snarky?' I ask Charlie.

'You can be a bit of a bitch, yes,' he says, in a reasonable neutral tone. The traces of kindness in his voice puts an entirely different cast on the day. I cheer up. 'But I just know that however mean you are on the outside you must be feeling far worse on the inside and I try to ignore you.'

I finish my comment on Chica's post with a crying laughter emoji and an x. Hopefully that will deflate any mean or snark. Those sarky people who leave clever dick comments on people's

Instagram, they're prats really, but because I roll on the floor laughing and give you a kiss afterwards that carves me out as nicer than the average prat.

Chica is never vile on her feed, she is never sarcastic; she sometimes makes jokes about loving doughnuts, and when she is with her friends they all stick their tongues out, but— I interrupt that thought because I am starting to feel funny. The sort of funny you only feel after looking at too much Instagram. I lock the phone in the glovebox.

We cunt, I mean count, off junctions with a minimum of bickering until we find Thurrock Services. We are there well before twelve because we left in such annoyingly good time. Sara texts to say she will be late. We have an undetermined period of time to kill in this miserable humourless zombie concourse full of concrete and Vauxhall Zafiras. We buy nasty overpriced coffees, do pees and make sarcastic comments about all the people buying trays of Krispy Kreme doughnuts and Burger King. There are of course many other things you can do at service stations in an attempt to kill time – sit in the big massage chair, play fruit machines in the two amusement arcades or buy a travel pillow – but Charlie and I are middle-class, and these are *verboten* activities for urban middle-class people. I won't be having a Greggs sausage roll.

Usually, I have to buy something to eat in a service station; I get a huge thrill buying food in service stations because it was forbidden as a child. We only ever once ate in a service station in my entire childhood; neither my mum or my dad, nor my various stepfathers or my stepmother, did eating in service stations, because back then middle-class parents didn't stop at service stations for anything except the loo and even then you had to jump up and down in your seat (which was easy because kids didn't have to wear seat belts back then), crying, 'I'm desperate' for an hour.

Frazzles. I'd get some Frazzles.

My middle-class parents had found an acceptable use for service stations throughout the mid- and late seventies and that was as a place to throw suitcases and children at each other at the end of access visits.

I hesitate to argue with Tolstoy, but I think a lot of unhappy families are pretty similar. They had a textbook messy seventies divorce, Mum and Dad. You know the score: fighting over the kids, slagging each other off, hurting and hating the ex a top priority, lots of money on lawyers, resentment, screaming and meltdowns at handover, court cases, massive terminal resentments about money. All this stuff is very public; the only thing that happens in secret is the crying, which I did a lot of.

Showing the pain of missing my mum while living at my dad's was not acceptable. No one held me when I cried myself to sleep at night, my letters to her were read before they were posted, ways in which I was like my mum were ridiculed and reviled. I lived in a household that punished me for being my mother's daughter. I love my dad and my stepmum and I'm sure some of the things they said about Mum were true. I'm just not sure I wanted to hear them at seven, or nine, or 12. I don't even like hearing them now, aged 46½. She's my mum, and only me and my two brothers and my two uncles are allowed to say horrible things about her, and our granny when she was alive. Anyone else, I want to kick their heads in. I didn't attempt that though, as my stepmother was scary back then.

I don't hold any of it against anyone any more but it had left me with complex issues, the least of which is an aversion to service stations. There really is nothing good about them, except the crisps.

'I hate service stations because they remind me—'

Charlie interrupts, agreeing. 'Yeurgh. Look at that man with the giant box of Krispy Kreme doughnuts. Do you really think he's off to share it with his eleven colleagues,' he snorts. 'Who *are* these people?'

Thinking about those handovers I am starting to relive the panic and utter powerlessness of the whole situation. Even when I was with Mum on access visits, I was never able to stop counting the days, hours and minutes and then, as the final hours progressed, the seconds, until I'd have to say goodbye to her for another two months or so. I feel depressed just thinking about it.

I swallow it. That's a generation or more ago. It looks like I am trying to leverage sympathy off past misfortune. I dial it all back with a silly voice. 'This space is very triggering for me, I need to call my therapist,' I say in a whiny LA vocal fry, while dangling my fingers around like punctuating deeley-boppers.

'Don't. You sound like my ex-wife,' says Charlie, flatly.

No sympathy gained. Not even a snort of amusement. I turn back to the bag of Frazzles.

The sound of the M25 rushes and sucks at the air behind us and weak January sunlight appears between the scudding clouds. It's OK, you aren't in a car park waiting to be dragged from your mother's arms, or to drive a Prius or eat a Greggs sausage roll. We're here to get a dog.

We're getting a dog.

It's been nearly an hour now of this twitchy hovering. Sara texts again. 'In green people carrier. Parked behind lamp-post at back.'

That's helpful. The whole place is a sea of people carriers and lamp-posts. 'The back' of what exactly? I describe where we are in even more detail.

More peering between cars, more craning to look above them.

There's a corkscrew of anticipation, sad childhood longing gone and last night's hangover entirely forgotten. Where is he?

'I can see him,' I say and point at something odd slinking and rolling across the tarmac towards us. The cone of a nose sticks out of a fuzzy halo of hair the colour of an old sports sock. His back is arched, shoulders hunched like a giant grubby prawn while his head is hung low. He's kinda ugly. Half cur, half anorexic Muppet. I wave at Sara and she acknowledges us with a far less enthusiastic nod and a bare smile.

He is a stranger who in a minute or two will be joining our family. For a brief moment as I stare at him I panic and wonder if I could love him. But what a graceful bounce to that slinking step. He has a noble carriage with well-sprung suspension; it's like his joints are made of rubber. The dog manages to be simultaneously a scruffy bugger and completely regal.

He is here. Sara is sullenly making apologies that she doesn't need to make. 'There you go.' She holds out the lead. 'Sorry, he smells. The other one was sick on him.'

It's an acute, tender sensation holding either side of the dog's head gently to say hello, and feeling the small hard skull underneath thin warm skin and soft scrubbly fur. He looks at me with cautious eyes the colour of old conkers and rimmed by kohl-dark lids. Under his eyes the skin is slightly sunken and dark; it looks like he's had a few late nights. He smells like the juice at the bottom of a wheelie bin.

My heart is hurting. Some kind of valve has opened inside me. 'Hello boy. Hello. You're coming to live with us.'

Charlie takes him round the car park for a wee before we turn round and go back to west London. The dog delivers the first of the thousands of his shits we will pick up over the years. He must have been desperate.

I stay back with Sara to pay. She does not look at me as I hand over the £160 but I can feel her disapproval and disappointment. I like to think of myself as a woman of the people, but standing there in a coyote-fur gilet next to this woman who rescues squirrels and hamsters and is wearing a matted acrylic parka and worn pink wellies, I realise I am not.

Clearly, she had expected a thicker pile of notes. 'Sorry, I haven't got more to give.'

There is something unsaid, to do with her dedication to animal causes and my (second-hand) fur coat and Charlie's company car. 'Yeah, well the collar. I had to pay for the collar,' she says.

I feel like I am lying to a beggar outside a tube station. 'So sorry, I haven't got any more money.'

Truth is, I really didn't have any more money. I'd withdrawn every penny I had to pay for the dog and his things – a bed, a collar, a lead, food, all that stuff – would all have to go on the credit card.

We say our goodbyes and she softens a bit: 'I hope you enjoy him, Merlin's a lovely dog.'

'I'm going to change his name actually.'

'What!' she says, openly insulted. 'I gave him the name Merlin.'

I don't know why she called this stray pipe-cleaner dog after a mythical medieval wizard and I'm certainly not going to make myself look any worse in front of her by asking her. He's not wizard-y. He's wolf-y. He's Wolfy.

The journey home is an entirely happy one, both of us gazing with curiosity and delight at this rancid-smelling, peculiar-looking beast sitting between my knees in the passenger footwell.

All the Prius drivers have magically evaporated. There is not one cunt to shout at on the way home. Perhaps Wolfy does have wizard-y powers after all.

Halfway home we stop again and the dog gets out with me and hops back into the car and onto the back seat, where he sits looking out of the window with his jaws in what looks like a wide-open smile. I cannot stop turning round and taking photos, which I text to my family with unconfined excitement.

We stop at a pet shop in Kilburn, not far from home, to buy the dog a bed and some shampoo to wash the sick off him. I pull all the beds down from the shelf and he dutifully climbs into each one, trying them out like Goldilocks. He rests in the biggest one, coiled up like a snake. It reminds me of the china ornament sleeping puppy I had as a kid that fitted exactly inside a tiny wicker basket. Deep down, I know the bed isn't big enough, that dogs don't always sleep with their noses tucked into their behinds, but I buy it anyway. I want to buy the dog everything.

The pet shop assistant tells me that Wolfy has done a wee in the dry food aisle and I say that I am sure he hasn't. He's perfectly nice about it. 'It's OK, it happens all the time,' he says, as he mops it up. 'Don't worry.'

I'm not just sure my dog isn't the sort of incontinent ninny that does a wee in a pet shop, I *know* it. What is the point in being defensive about the fact that my dog definitely hasn't done a wee? I haven't had the dog for more than an hour. Why am I so sure? He is self-composed, sniffing round the shelves at the end of his lead, and he is eager to please, neatly arranging himself in the too small bed for my delectation. He is not secretly doing little widdles behind my back. 'Must have been another dog,' I say, with confident finality.

Back at home I strip off and shower the sick off him in our tiny bathroom off the kitchen. We don't have a bath, another compromise necessary if you want to live in Notting Hill, so this is how it must be done. I straddle his back and hold on to his collar to stop him from escaping. He hangs his head in misery as I rinse and rub with my hands. It takes a while. I hadn't considered that dog ownership would entail this. I had not considered much, in fact, other than whether there were good places to walk him.

Wet, his body looks skeletal and his eyeballs bulge from his skull like fat black marbles. I rub him down with white towels and he shakes himself off a few times before heading for the thick blue and black Turkish rug by the tiny wood-burner. He lies down and as he dries he grows bigger and more shaggy until he's plumped up, like a miniature yak. That dirty matted old-sock-coloured fur has turned a Rich Tea biscuit colour with golden highlights. It sprouts this way and that so that he has a slightly chaotic, always different look, like a fractal.

The telly is on but I just stare at him, devouring the detail. On his chest the fur is white, fine. His stomach scoops up tightly towards his hips, and there is barely any fur there covering his skin of pale piglet pink with the odd brown splotch of pigment. His long legs bend and wrap around each other like furry spaghetti.

Charlie and I sit close by each other on the sofa looking at the third member of the household. Both of us are grinning.

'Look at our dog. We've got a dog.'

He rises up off the rug, knocks out an impressive stretch that a yoga bod would recognise as an upward dog and a downward dog, pauses by my knee, where his black nose twitches and wriggles as it sniffs whatever it is the air has to tell him. He looks up at me for a heartbeat or two and hops lightly up between us on the sofa where he rests his chin flat on Charlie's thigh.

CHAPTER TWO

Wormwood Scrubs, that's where we went that first Saturday afternoon. And on the Sunday too. After a couple of walks with him on a special long lead I bent down to unclip it.

We were walking along the eastern edge of the Scrubs, by the strip of scruffy woodland next to Scrubs Lane.

When I first unleashed him he didn't register that he had freedom of movement and continued walking along beside us, but then he tentatively started to move away. Inch by inch, foot by foot, he ambled his own way, looking back constantly to check we were OK with it.

'Go on. Good boy.'

He trotted a little further on, sniffing the ground around him. Once he was several feet away he picked up his speed, really tasting freedom now, and did a little lap of glory at a zippy canter. When he came to a stop he celebrated with a couple of buckaroo kicks before trotting off to sniff a patch of scrub.

'I don't think he's been off the lead in some time,' I said. 'I wonder if Sara ever let him off.'

'Maybe those other owners never did either,' Charlie said.

I called him back. 'Come.' And he trotted over our way. 'What a good boy.' He sat politely while I fed him dog treats and stroked his back. 'What a good dog.'

Charlie goes to work as usual on Monday. Me? As soon as Wolfy arrived I'd started announcing, 'I'm on "*peternity*" leave,' to anyone who would listen. I need a few days off to bond with my hound. Wolfy and I would explore the neighbourhood on six legs.

I set off briskly for the familiar seven-minute walk to caffeine from our back gate on Treadgold Street, heading north skirting the Kensington Sports Centre, past the doctors' surgery and over Walmer Road into the rat-run that separates the 1930s red-brick social housing blocks from the 1960s ones. The rat-run is dark and narrow but Wolfy loves it. The sniffing intensifies and he pees on everything in this 30-metre stretch. I'd read that I should yank his lead up and force him onwards, but this little strip of pedestrian, dogshit-strewn tarmac gives him so much pleasure I don't have the heart to go all Barbara Woodhouse. Let him have his fun.

Tomorrow we'll drive, I decide, because with all the sniffing, the peeing, the squatting for an early-morning poo or two, by the time we reach Coffee Plant I'm starting to think not of coffee but of lunch.

The following morning, both my hair and the dog's fur sticking this way and that from sleep, we head out in my old Mini. He sits next to me on the worn leather passenger seat, alert and upright. Furry face alternately staring dead ahead and looking to the left, out the window, and right, to me; Wolfy is my wingman, like Chewbacca on the Millennium Falcon.

Newsagent, coffee, walk, in that order. I park the car in the staid white English old-money streets of Kensington, near the palace. We do a full lap of Kensington Gardens and Hyde Park.

Going back to the car afterwards I see the Kensington Wine Rooms. 50 wines by the glass. I'll just have the one with a plate of charcuterie and a green salad.

I tentatively put my nose round the door. 'You OK with dogs?'

'We *love* dogs,' says an Irish waiter polishing glasses beside the bar.

It's a rule, isn't it, not to drink alone? Drinking alone at lunchtime, that's alkie turf. Unless you have something to celebrate, that is, which I do. I have a dog. And I'm on this *peternity* leave.

Peternity leave was a stupid idea really. When you're a freelancer no one pays you any money if you don't work. In nearly thirty years of working as an adult, I've enjoyed no more than 60 days of paid leave. But this self-imposed holiday does feel pretty marvellous.

'Do you have a light red, a nice *lunchtime* wine, you know; a child's wine?'

'A Beaujolais perhaps,' says the Irish waiter, 'or,' his intonation shifts to flatter me with a suggestion that I am a distinguished middle aged lady who knows her wine, 'an Austrian Blaufränkisch?'

Efficiently flattered, of course I say, 'Blaufränkisch, but a small one, a 125?' Aren't I marvellous, asking for a small measure. I feel quite smug so reassured am I that 125ml of good red is the sort of optimum and homeopathic quantity that is nourishing and healthy.

Wolfy lies beside me, chin flush to the floorboards, his senses calmly taking in the room. He barely moves as he discreetly accepts the odd slice of *saucisson* or a ribbon of Bayonne ham I dangle beside me.

I read the papers. After a while the dog rises to sniff round the wine racks to my left. The waiting staff take turns to come and make a fuss of him.

It is the perfect arrangement; a table for one means I can eat and drink without having to talk and with Wolfy's grateful jaws beside me, no food will end up in the bin; I can drink at lunchtime because I'm not alone; and … well, I can't see a downside, other than if I have another glass then I'll have to leave the car and fetch it later.

'How was the Blaufränkisch?' says the Irish waiter, who, chatting to in my lightly lunched state, I have discovered is studying for a PhD at Imperial College.

'Loved it!'

'One more?'
'Why not!'

Most of our flat was governed by Charlie's need for tidiness.
Mess upset him, whereas tidiness did not upset me, so my
natural piggery and sluttishness was reined in. This was no bad
thing, but I needed a room of my own and not just to write in.

My office was known as many things: writing room, study,
the spare room, the west wing, the shit pit, or usually 'there' as
in 'just chuck it in there'.

I filed paper all over the floor and hung pictures crooked on
the wall. There were shelves of books stacked up and crammed in
any old way. Any gaps were filled with postcards, a broken Tiffany
keyring, hundreds of old notepads ... there were sticky notes
everywhere listing a mixture of story ideas, fitness goals and,
always, the money I owed everyone from HMRC to my mum.

If there was washing to dry and I wasn't at home, Charlie
would plonk the laundry rack square in the middle of my little
writing room. If I left clothes or shoes about the flat and he went
on a cleaning spree, they got thrown in there too. Sometimes
I returned from a weekend away to find the door to this room
of my own wedged shut by a pair of sodden men's socks that'd
been dropped on the way to the rack.

In this pit of clutter and sometimes despair was my
cherrywood desk, which looked out over the alleyway behind
the flat. Part of my preparation for Wolfy's arrival was creating
his nest under the desk. It would be a spot the dog could know
was his and his alone, a place where humans would never bother
him.

If I patted it and called to him he'd come and dutifully get
in the bed, though he rarely used it by choice. Thing is, I liked
him under there so much that to tempt him in there I'd buy
these small bags of lamb knuckles from the halal butcher on
Portobello Road for £1 and toss one in so that he'd associate

sleeping on my feet with snack heaven. When I ate at my desk, which was more usual than slipping out for bijou little lunches, I'd put the plate down for him to demolish any leftovers. Anything to keep him down there. I loved it.

Usually he'd take the swag, gnaw it and amble out to sleep somewhere with more human smells, like a pile of dirty washing on the bathroom floor or the sofa, somewhere he could straighten his long legs to their full extension, while watching from a good vantage point.

The dog bed wasn't big enough for Wolfy's rangy body. Should've trusted my gut on that one, instead of my untamed urge to spend, spend, spend. It wasn't the first time I'd bought something too small despite the certain knowledge it would not fit. Buying the dog bed was as feckless as those size 38 Gareth Pugh boots I bought online, which tortured my 39 feet, or that tight white roll neck, which had room for two bee sting tits and an upper body unencumbered by bingo wings and back fat. Good for Chica. Not for me. Same with the bed. We live in hope.

I took the bed out and instead piled Wolfy's nest with old blankets, a tired floppy pillow and a ripped Indian scarf. Over time I'd drop all sorts in there, like the odd holey sock or anything else I was too sentimental to throw away. He started to use it more and I would sit writing with my toes under his warm silky underbelly, as I'd always dreamed of doing. The nest was now Wolfy's Office, and he visited it on rotation with his other favourite spots in the house as he went about the important business of sleeping 22 hours a day. I no longer worked alone. I had a colleague. With Wolfy on staff my work life improved.

I moved the too-small bed bought in haste to the sitting room and patted it, inviting Wolfy to try it there. He dutifully got in and curled himself up so he fitted snugly in. Five minutes later he hopped onto the sofa. I gave the bed away.

The dog was not expensive to keep. I bought him blocks of frozen dog meat – tripe, beef, lamb, turkey, that kind of thing. I called them woof patties, and he had them once a day, added to a selection of leftovers from the humans. We gave him bones too. I didn't buy him anything else and he occasionally chased a ball I bought him but, for the most part, needed nothing.

I take the dog up to my friend Anabel's house in Queen's Park for a dinner party. It will be three couples and me, alone, as Charlie sees evening as time to prepare for work the next day. Wolfy will be my date. Briefly, I wonder if it is weird to turn up to a dinner party with a dog. I decide it probably is, a bit, but that since my brother Will and his wife will be there, and Anabel is a good friend, perhaps they'll all be excited to meet my new boy. It's more convenient too; instead of taking him home round the back streets of North Kensington after our Wormwood Scrubs walk, I can set straight off up Scrubs Lane on the mile or so's journey north over Harrow Road to Anabel's.

Wolfy hops up on the passenger seat next to me and sits bolt upright and alert, looking dead ahead; Chewbacca to my Han Solo again.

I sit there and just look at him for a while. He knows I'm looking at him but he stares dead ahead like a sentry outside Buckingham Palace. Once, he snaps his head quickly to the right and looks back before resuming his rigid, formal posture.

As I drive I keep looking left at him and smiling. This smile isn't just a smile, it's the sort that bursts open inside my chest. Seeing him sitting there, wow, that tickles me. I lower his window and he cautiously leans towards the wind so his fur is flat and flying away from his nose. The enjoyment this gives him is enchanting. If only I had an eye in my ear. I could watch him for hours.

It's not a long journey from the Scrubs to Anabel but the traffic's patchy. I punch on the radio. It's tuned in to Radio 4 because Radio 4 is very interesting and all that – but it is also a bit like work. Listening to Radio 4 I am productive, staying abreast of the news and improving myself. It's an arts programme. The mellifluous, confident tones of Melanie Oxbridge fill my hot, jealous ears.

Melanie Oxbridge isn't her real name. She's a journalist who is my age but far more successful and, especially since she wrote her first book of brilliant and incredibly funny feminist essays, she's always on the radio or telly commenting on something or other.

I don't like Melanie Oxbridge. We have previous. For all that she's outspoken about feminism, sisterliness, justice and, you know, righteous *stuff*, in doing this she always manages to ever so slightly trample on all those beloved 'sistas' who aren't exactly like her. There are a few Melanie Oxbridges in the media. She's actually one of the nicer ones, which, granted – I speak from experience – isn't saying much.

In the early years of this century dear Melanie and I had gone on a press trip together to the South of France and were lying next to each other poolside in a just-finished hotel on the wrong side of St Tropez bay. It was never very clear what the trip was about, but we were taken to beautiful restaurants and while we were 'working' together, i.e. lying by a pool on the wrong side of the bay drinking rosé, I thought we were also bonding. Women, bikinis, poolside … I let my guard down and as we talked about our plans for life I let slip that I'd like to be married.

'Married! Why do you want to be married?'

I knew, immediately, I had said something desperately outré and tried to coolly scrabble my way back to terra feminista. 'I would wear a white suit, yer know, like Bianca Jagger, not a stupid meringue, and I'd make a speech too. I'm not buying the fairy tale, I just …' I actually just wanted to be married because I liked the idea of it, because my mum told me I'd get married some day, because I wanted the party, because I wanted some sort of punctuation to all the sleeping around and romantic turbulence and, clearly, now I saw, because I was stupid. I was unfeminist. 'I ... I'. I stopped talking.

She ladled out the feminist critique of matrimony in a tone of withering instruction. 'Who wrote all the fairy tales? Men.' I squeaked that I knew that but she wasn't listening: 'Marriage is a patriarchal institution designed to control women. It is a fairytale curse loaded with so much bad history it's just contemptible. It's utter bullshit.'

I agreed with her; marriage had done nothing for my clever mum, trained to put the domestic ahead of her intellect. Christ, I felt humiliated. I tried to claw back some credibility.

'I just, I just ... I just want a party.'

My brittle 30-year-old's self-worth promptly collapsed like a newborn foal. I had just bought my first expensive bikini and felt so good in it and had been vamping it up and wiggling around the pool feeling like Ursula Andress. Now, that breeze pool-side was not the mistral but the air pfrrrrrting out of my bikini ego. The rest of the trip I was an anxious mess (it didn't help that, in addition to me old pal Mel, there was an ex-boyfriend there with his new girlfriend, plus a couple of vile cows in positions of significant editorial power at two glossy magazines). The whole thing sits technicolor in my memory, a horror story, one set in a just-finished hotel on the wrong side of St Tropez bay.

Of course it was for tax reasons or some worthy excuse to do with children, but the hypocritical bitch went on to get married not once but twice, while I remained a noble spinster of the parish (if that is possible, as I believe spinsters have to be virgins).

I am shouting at the radio. 'Who is the feminist now Melanie?!' I bracket the words 'twice married' in two ironic fingers while steering the car with my knee. 'Oxbridge? Eh? Eh? Tell me that.'

Clearly the answer is, still her. God it's galling listening to her now on Radio 4, wittering on, brilliantly, making the clever female presenter laugh. Still winning at feminism.

Sista? My arse!

She is just a disembodied voice on the radio but her commenting on something means I am not commenting on something. She sounds very confident and I hate her, then I hate myself for hating her, then I hate her again because she's making me hate myself.

Click. I change stations. Radio 3. I stop there. The music is big and symphonic, possibly Mahler.

For a moment I imagine myself as the sort of woman who lives in a book-lined house in north London, perhaps with a light-hearted political column that everyone loves to read for fun but which masks an actual deep understanding of the political and cultural landscape. I'd be interviewed in front of my book-stacked desk and people like me would scrutinise the shelves, thinking, Christ she's read some big books. Ah yes, I am a woman who enjoys Radio 3. No I'm not. It's aggravating and boring.

The ruler of success is well and truly out tonight. Everything, lands up there: work, body, mind, whiteness of the whites of the eyes, choice of books by the bog. Always measuring everything on there, I am.

The negative self-talk is now spiralling round my gut like an acrobatic tapeworm. It's a No to Mahler.

I switch the radio over to Radio 2. Mmmn, soothing, Radio 2. A show tune. Mmmn. Safety sounds. Urgh. Radio 2. MOR adult-oriented pop leads fairly swiftly to total irrelevance and then death. Am I so intimidated by the world I must surround myself with the aural equivalent of a Mr Kipling Bakewell Slice of unthreatening easy listening? The tapeworm cartwheels some more.

Radio 5? Gimme a break.

6 Music. Ah yes, that's me. Middle-aged, still cool, had some vinyl once. Lay in her teenage bedroom listening to the Fall, John Peel and Annie Nightingale. Only, I haven't got 6 Music in my car.

Jesus. My life is a disaster. It's all too much. I turn the volume down until *click*, the radio's off.

Next to me the dog is now sunk down and coiled like a golden furry penny on the front seat; his black button eyes peep up through his long shaggy brows. He looks at me looking down on him. Ah, there's the dog. The tapeworm dies and my heart fills up with love. He starts to lick his bum; it's heaven.

With no external noise and a third-hand dog grooming his privates at my side, I cheer right up. I stop at Borough Wines and pick up a cold bottle of Bourgogne Aligoté from the fridge. There will be wine soon, too. Plenty to be cheerful about. I've almost forgotten about Melanie. I stroke Wolfy for a couple of minutes outside the offy. Melanie's hold on me is not strong tonight. *Pouf!* Melanie's gone.

'Meet Wolfy.' Anabel opens the door and I come bouncing in, stamping my feet, while she glides around me looking serene and ravishing. 'You look gorgeous,' I say. 'Love that dress'. She is very 'this old thing' about it as I kiss her cheek and tell her she looks beautiful. I am wearing a pair of Turkish army trousers I found in Portobello Market that have been enthusiastically if amateurishly altered at the Afghan launderette at the top of Ladbroke Grove. My T-shirt is half tucked in, which as I left the flat thought looked 'very snazzy', as my mum would say.

Often the combination of Steph, my brother's wife, and Anabel can knock me a bit. They can't help it. They're impressive women. Straight outta Oxbridge! Most of my girlfriends are there on the ruler of success, markers of female achievement. Sometimes they look like rock stars in my eyes.

Steph and Anabel both always look splendid and over the years have had so much and such big news to impart. 'We are moving to Ibiza.' 'I've taken a job in New York.' 'I'm editor.' 'I'm building a modernist house in my spare time.' 'Have you heard the gossip about David Cameron?' 'So! I had dinner with Sheryl Sandberg last night.'

I felt so cool when I left the house tonight and despite these two impressive girls, for once I still feel that swagger now, largely because the dog is strolling politely in and he looks so damn cool. I (we) receive a round of verbal applause. Steph: 'Darling, he's gorgeous!' Anabel: 'Oh my God, I love him!' Steve: 'Look at this fella.' Will: 'Yay. He looks just like What-a-Mess. Remember that book?'

'He's beautiful, Kate,' says Steph. 'And so big. The kids can ride him.'

'No! They'd break his spine.'

Wolfy prowls round the edges of the rooms. Casing the joint. Anabel and Steve have the sort of aesthetic vision middle-class people often delude themselves they have, but don't. They bought a huge lumpy suburban semi in the mock-Tudor style and remodelled it. You could fit ten or more of our share of a late-Victorian terraced artisan's cottage into their whopper pad. They've not just taken out walls, they've taken out ceilings too. Unlike the half-timbered Tudorbethan neighbours' houses, they've painted the whole thing black. We call it the Death Star.

There is a cartoon-perfect crunching sound. Wolfy has followed Steve into the larder and found the cat food down on the floor. That sound is him helping himself to contraband Munchies.

Steve is not amused. ''Ere, the dog's eating Audrey's food. Go on, bugger off.' He gives Wolfy a prod with his foot. Wolfy carries on munching the Munchies. 'Kate, get your dog under control,' he shouts at me, good-natured, appalled.

Charred artichoke hearts drizzled in good olive oil are out, and petit lucques olives. Every plate, glass and dish tells a story of their effortless sophistication, a jumble of good old porcelain and quirky pieces found in a Paris flea market or on an artisan's stall in Bamako when they just happened to be in Mali a few years ago. I have to swallow the endless need to ask, 'Where did you get this?' When I grow up, I'd like to have a life like this, I think. No Kettle Chips appear with the wine.

I am absurdly proud of the dog but I know I have to contain my pride. I have not given birth, I've acquired a skulking, slightly miserable-looking, third-hand hound. The conversation moves on. What is there to say about dogs? They are a minor event. But I want to talk about the dog some more. I bite my tongue. Steph is dissecting a documentary she watched recently about big game hunting that 'presented the nuances and facets of an argument that is usually presented in simple and far too emotional binary terms'. She was so impressed by it she sat down to watch it with the elder of her children so that they could learn to think about ideas in all these different dimensions.

Anabel jumps in. 'Most of the problems in the world can be traced back to only ever presenting two sides to an argument. I took the boys to the public galleries at the Commons quite often when they were young. A decent level of debate is so important to our society but I feel it is undervalued more and more.'

Will, Steve and I are milling, dumbly absorbing their eloquence.

Feeling a bit odd? Best to drink, I find. I set about opening my wine with a corkscrew, a little too quickly than is polite. I have clocked the other bottles lined up, supermarket premium range, best of the corner shop, nothing interesting.

Get in and pour yourself the biggest glass of your own good stuff. The supermarket best will do for later when I've taken the edge off.

'Shall I open a bottle,' I say, already an inch deep into the cork.

'There's one open already, Kate,' Steve says as I pull up the waiter's friend. *Pop!*

'Oh, I didn't see that,' I say, lying. 'Would you like some?' I pour myself a large glass and take that first nourishing sip.

We sit down to eat at a marble table. The dog is well-behaved, although I have taken it on trust he will be when in fact he could quite easily have come in and immediately eaten Steve's precious pedigree cat. I didn't consider that before. I hear him drinking water noisily. Munchies must make a dog thirsty, I think. Oh that tickles me and I chuckle inside. This is one of the delights of owning a dog, the amusing sketches they present to you, hour after hour. I never knew the sound of a dog eating stolen cat food could be so precious.

He comes stalking out into the room where we're eating and does his noisy collapsing thing of folding up his gangly limbs until he hits the floor in a heap. He sleeps there for a while, then gets up and comes and sits on my lap at the table. Three foot long with awkward sticky legs, bony bum and all.

'Is that normal?' says Steph, surprised.

'I don't think so,' I say, equally surprised as I wrap him in my arms and fight the urge to lay my head on his shoulder, close my eyes and kiss his fur. His presence is the most delightful drug.

At the end of the evening I drive home, I do not consider a detour to Tim's, I do not feel short-changed or bored by life. I crave nothing. I am satisfied.

The muddle of stuff in Wolfy's Office was about creating a hiding hole of good smells and safety. His office was permanent, always there, like the sofa. It was not to be confused with the concept of the Woof Bed, which was a blanket term to denote any temporary bed. A Woof Bed was anything you could put on the floor to encourage the dog to settle and sleep in one spot while visiting or out and about. It was not limited to actual beds; I used my second-hand coyote-fur gilet turned lining down, the Burberry mac I nicked out of the bin when Charlie threw it away. I used an old sarong; occasionally, when desperate, a napkin would suffice. I could put down anything soft on the ground, clap and say in an exclaiming voice, while pointing, 'It's a Woof Bed!' and Wolfy would dutifully come and lie in it – or partially on it, in the case of a napkin.

We needed this temporary bed concept because as the dog and I rolled to an increasingly wide range of places around town together, he would always know that this was his place. Otherwise he'd get onto anything remotely sofa-like – restaurant banquettes, velvet chaises longues, other people's sofas, or, as at Anabel's dinner party, my lap.

Not long after Wolfy arrived, the singing started. I'd do a full circuit of the Scrubs repeatedly going over the first verse of 'Dear Lord and Father of Mankind'. I developed a repertoire of West End musical numbers and purposefully bad raps that were intended purely for Charlie's entertainment, which I'd sing in the dark February mornings when turning out of bed to walk Wolfy.

'*My name is Wolfy/and I'm here to say/it's time to head to the park today/I'll do some sniffs/I'll have a poo/and when I'm done/I'ma have a big snooze/Yeah.*' Waggling jazz hands down the lethal-to-dogs stairs, I'd shout down to Charlie performing his usual vigorous dawn regimen, 'Can you hear me, can you see me?'

'Fox, that's embarrassing, stop it. Have you made the bed yet?'

'I'm looking for a record deal. I'm giving up journalism. I'm stopping it now so I can really concentrate on my singing career. I think you should resign because once the deal is signed we're going to be incredibly busy.'

Was it such a mad idea? They'd made a musical about the bent businessmen at Enron, an opera about Jerry Springer, so why not a quirky West End smash. *Wolfy! The Musical*. It might even transfer to Broadway.

Charlie started joining in. Our mutual appetite for silliness was revived and turbocharged. The majority of our happy times together might have been geared around talking utter drivel and behaving like ten-year-olds, but you know what they say – the couple that can soft shoe shuffle together in their undercrackers at 6.30a.m., they stay together.

'Why are you jogging backwards?' people would ask and I'd smile at them and say, because I couldn't tell the truth, 'Oh, I'm

just being a responsible dog owner and ensuring I don't miss a
poo.'

The truth is I took pleasure from just watching him, my
saviour, my relationship's saviour. It was so absorbing to catch
him busy at his doggy doings, watching him sniff, potter and race
his way round the urban green. It felt how I imagine religious
conversion feels. 'He who follows Me shall not walk in darkness,
but have the light of life.'

I couldn't stop looking at him. Owning a dog was awesome;
literally actually awesome. My God. Or, more accurately, my
Dog!

But it also freaked me out. My reasonable mind just
couldn't fathom it all. I'd spent the last thirty years of my life
battling to get on, do OK at work, have fun, enjoy life, while
juggling the usual mass of neuroses, and now all I wanted to
do was bumble about with my Wolfy. The stuff that used to
bother me didn't any more. If I felt sad, I'd look at him lying
somewhere, and say, 'Hey you, whazzup,' and he'd lazily
thump his tail on the floor. It's a real tonic, two lazy wags of
a sleeping dog's tail. And to think, I used to need drugs to
feel joy.

In the mornings, on the streets near home, walking to
Coffee Plant, I'd see a thick-muscled and kinda bad-looking
man rolling towards Portobello Road in front of me with a
petite black Staffie bitch quick-waddling by him. His grimace,
the thick short neck combined with his dense physical heft, gave
him a whiff of menace. He was the spit of the Incredible Hulk.
His dog was always off the lead, and if she strayed too far from
him he'd growl, ''Ere,' or 'Wait' with a menace that made me
wonder if he loved his dog like I did mine, or if he went home
and kicked her and didn't care that much.

I'd wonder, why was my brain exploding, my stomach
roiling? Why, when I heard Wolfy make tiny lip-smacking sounds
as he snuggled down for a sleep next to me on the sofa, did my
heart start pulsing?

I needed to know this was normal.

Walking in the park, Wolfy would inevitably be drawn to the instructive aromas of other dogs' rear ends. Standing waiting, we owners would stare at our phones or make small talk – smell talk – as long as it took for the nose-to-anus dog communication to end.

This interaction was sometimes no more than one of those millisecond smiles or a couple of amused raised eyebrows. More usually it was brief commentary, 'Going in for a good butt sniff,' 'Speaking fluent sphincter there,' 'Sniffing his CV,' or 'Your dog obviously has a seriously delicious bum.' Occasionally, if the owner was an moron, he or she would react by yanking the dog away going, 'Don't do that, it's dirty.'

If the bum the dog was sniffing belonged to another lurcher, the areas for discussion multiplied.

If you own a lurcher you'll already know that asking about the mix is an absolute must when chatting to or stopping another owner. What's in there? Bedlington, whippet? He's deerhound-greyhound mix, got bit of collie, the combinations are copious given the many mixes that can be in a lurcher – if there's saluki in the mix it's reliable that you'll hear, 'He's a bugger for not coming back'. Salukis are Arab desert dogs that can go for a day across the dunes, stamina of a camel, speed of a racehorse, body of a supermodel. Thin. So thin. They look like combs draped in a bit of fur, with burlesque feathers for tails. Crazy-looking beasts. Magical. Bonkers. Fast.

When it came to discussing Wolfy's mix I didn't have a satisfying answer. In fact I would never give an answer at all. Dog owners become like VW Beetle drivers, very committed to their own brand. And I wasn't a labradoodle person, I had a lurcher as far as I was concerned. In shame, I kept quiet about what Sara thought she knew about him. I definitely didn't want to share that he possibly had labradoodle in him.

'How old is he?' is another question. If the answer is, 'We aren't sure' then it's a rescue dog, and you get to share your dog's more or less tragic history. 'We're his third owners.' 'Ours was rescued from a pound in Romania.' 'Mine was fished out of a lake.' 'He's got issues.'

Cue discussions about behaviour. How nervous the dog is, whether he comes back when you call him; and, if you're talking sighthound stuff, there's the big question – how's his prey drive? When a fast dog spots a moving thing, you won't be grabbing his collar for a while. Whoosh. Is that light speeding by or a sighthound after a cat? It's hard to tell the difference.

Wolfy's prey drive seems pretty feeble compared to Castor, who is a cat chasing maniac. The cats in the alley scratched Wolfy's nose a few times and he doesn't chase them anymore; squirrels only when he spots them; deer: *always*.

When people say to me that my dog is beautiful, I beam as if I had given birth to him myself.

Beauty without ego, love without conditions, regal without entitlement, packaged in fur and by my side. I'm not really a braggart or especially confident. If people pay me a compliment, I usually try to turn it into an insult. But when people told me my dog was beautiful I'd just say, 'I know.'

Wolfy often zones in on the skinny bums of dogs his shape, and there are a lot of them. West London is stuffed with lurchers. I had no idea. There are loads.

It's a grey Monday morning when we bump into Cecil up on the turf opposite the Hyde Park Barracks, home of the Household Cavalry on Kensington Gore. Wolfy spots a bum he's sniffed before and trots over, tail in ecstatically friendly 'windscreen wiper in a torrential downpour' mode. One hundred young cavalrymen and perhaps the odd woman are out practising ceremonial drills. They're wearing all the gear: scarlet tunics, champagne buckets on their head with plumes of horsehair spouting out the top; long swords bounce against strong thighs wrapped in tight white breeches and high black leather boots.

While Cecil and Wolfy have a lingering bum sniff beside us, his owner and I have our own lingering bum moment with the Life Guards trotting to and fro in front of us.

'Might as well linger a while.'

'Quite,' she says. 'Very Jilly Cooper.'

We talk a bit. Neither of us are really perving over the Cavalry's buttocks. I ask her if she has kids.

'Yes.'

'I expect it's because I don't have kids myself to spunk it all on but God, I love my dog so much. I'm worried it's a bit sad. Do you relate?'

'Oh no, no, no, you aren't sad. No!' She throws her hands up to her face and turns to look at me. 'I'm so relating to you mate. I am so in love with Cecil. I think I love him more than the children.'

'No?'

'Yes!'

'No!'

'I'm serious.'

I don't quite believe her but the opening to the conversation is so welcome I don't care, 'I'm hopelessly in love with my dog. He makes me so unbelievably happy, and look at us. Here, and this ...' I wave an arm at the jangling tack and impeccable buttocks bouncing around before us accompanied by mounted trumpeters and drummers. 'It's a whole new world of dog. I'm sure I thought I was cool once.'

'I used to take drugs with posh twats,' she says.

'I used to take drugs with them too, but if they weren't available anyone'd do. But I'm a dog addict now.'

'Yeah,' she says, burrowing her fists deep into the pockets of her parka. 'Me too.'

'Tell me, have you ever looked at a wolf fleece and thought, That looks cool?'

'No,' she says. Despite this, Sasha is my first dog-walking friend.

I have others, all lurcher owners.

One Sunday afternoon Castor, Keith, Wolfy, Charlie and I are yomping round the Scrubs and bump into Anna with her Wally, a fluffy and bonkers lurcher of extremely indeterminate mix. We walk together and by the end, high on lurchers and life, we have decided to eke out the vibes and go for celebratory pints at The Cow. The times there are so good that we all go back to our tiny flat. Will and Steph drop in with the kids; my oldest nephew, Sam, has a toy for Wolfy, his furry godfather as we call him.

At one point I look up from my seat leaning against the radiator under the window. There we all are, all sat together, while the kids watch films on my laptop in the bedroom and the dogs are curled up asleep, one to a cushion, on the sofa. I laugh, take a picture and post it to Instagram.

This is it, this is success, posting pictures to Instagram taken at an impromptu and authentically happy event. I show it to everyone: 'That's a great picture.' Yes! I mentally punch the air. I'm living the dream. I walk-run to the kitchen and crack open champagne. Woohoo, everyone yelps as I hand it round in our mismatched champagne glasses, flutes, coupes, the new ones I can't remember the name of. I feel free and bohemian. If I wanted to attach a hashtag, it'd be #livingmybestlife. This is our first dog party.

I forget about the picture until the next day, taking a shambling hungover walk round the Scrubs. Wow, lots of likes, including one from the sainted lovely-legged influencer I met at Tim's on the day I decided to get a dog. Chica. Followers now close to 60,000. Despite the fact I have only met her once she has left a kiss-strewn comment. 'He's adorbz darling. When do I meet him?'

My dog is making me popular on social media.

Pictures of the two of us together harvest way more likes than anything else, even ones with famous people. Not that I hang with a lot of famous people anyway but, truthfully, the dog is a good substitute for them.

I scroll through Chica's feed. Poolside – location, Palm Springs, a close-up on the side of her perfect lithe body in a sheer mesh and Lycra swimsuit with all sorts of flesh-exposing cut-outs and panels; she has no flab. Here's Chica again, on a step outside a white stucco townhouse in Notting Hill. She's wearing teeny shorts and ankle boots: acting dead natural. She's heading into a fashion show in Milan – so she's getting show tickets now – wearing a rock star's wife's fashion label. Her social heat is rising. I note she has dumped handsome Libore and is dating a notorious playboy posho. One who won't have terminated the activities seen round Tim's coffee table. In fact, he is someone I met, once, at that coffee table from hell. A handsome toff. A naughty one. A rich one. A devil in bed.

Am I jealous?

Am I?

I absent-mindedly scuffle the thick fur under Wolfy's throat as I think about this.

Am I?

Am I pining for a fabulous, decadent life?

I briefly remember the scruffled sheets, the cigarettes in bed, the indolence, the insolence, the frantic dash to the chemist after 72 hours, and the thrills, spills and loneliness inherent in a life that exciting.

Am I?

Nah.

It all looks like bloody hard work. 'Come on, boy. Let's go.'

It was not true that I was living some kind of quiet Christian life now, rising with the sun and living and singing among all God's creatures like west London's answer to Mary Poppins. It's the dog lover's life for me now. Praise be!

I still went out, sometimes even to what might be described as 'star-studded' and 'glittering' events. Everyone felt a bit of a spanner at these bashes. Especially the people who had to actually *pay* for their tickets. Some time previously I had realised these parties often weren't really parties; they were networking events, paid for by brands wanting to get close to the shiny people, and a chance for the shiny people to get their pictures taken.

There is one of these dos at the Victoria and Albert Museum and I've borrowed a Gareth Pugh dress that I can just about cram my body into. It is striped like a barber's pole and has a train that pools at the rear. I set about the well-trodden routine of layering on the nocturnal armour. Performing the ritual glamazoning triggers an anticipatory thrill at what might happen and who knew where I could end up. This maquillage routine can cause a soaring, if transient, ego-driven vanity, a climactic moment of self-love without which it is moot whether I'll ever get out the door.

A thick layer of dark, metallic oily shadow on my eyelids; my cheeks honed to a fantasy bone with highlighters and shade; concealer softening the perma-circles under my eyes. I dry my hair straight, then mess it up so it looks like I haven't.

Now, shoes. Since Wolfy the flats have increased and the heels dwindled. I stand up to take a look in the wardrobe and find that the dog, so used to settling and sleeping on any piece of fabric I've laid on the floor, has curled up on the dress train, which is trailing over the back of the stool. He thinks it's a Woof Bed. 'Move! Wolfy!'

Fashion isn't my natural turf, but I've hovered on its fringes for years because when you write for the style press and the lifestyle pages, at some point everything comes back to fashion. If how we dress is our armour, then fashion people could walk through a minefield unharmed.

Charlie is away, overseas and for several days too. If I do go on the rampage, there'll be no distressing scrabble to form an impression of ordered normality tomorrow. I can sink into a multi-destination night out and recover at my sluttish leisure. I've given the dog a beasting of a walk early evening. A dog that's been properly walked is a happy and settled one.

At the V&A a friendly door bitch waves me past security. The dress, the hair and the make-up had made me fizz with self-approval at home. As I pouted and fussed over the amount of shadow under my eyes in the mirror next to the passenger light in the taxi, I clock everyone else in the overlapping circles of fashion and society. My whole demeanour flags and I feel poor, lumpy and average. I am so familiar with this feeling that I no longer care. Aspiration is all about suffering the pains of inadequacy, after all.

Inside everyone is gathered round those they consider to be their peer group. Any conversations outside these groups will be mannered and briefly charming with those considered worthy, and pointedly chill for those enthusiastic climbers punching above their social weight. Haughty is an old-fashioned word, but an indispensable one when describing the monsters and supercreeps in this society sea.

The fashion editor of a women's glossy glides past, a Celine-cloaked humanoid on wheels. The last time I saw her, at a less glittering event than this, we talked for 20 minutes. 'Rebecca!' I smile and put myself in front of her, a ghastly thing to do, but the chat that last time had been profound by society standards. Not so meaningful that I can remember what it was we spoke about but sufficiently above the usual people-places-things, who, where, when, what and how much did the dress cost.

'Ewhmmnello.' Her lips barely move but her eyes look trapped. I respond, as is correct, with a similarly indifferent one-line greeting and she glides on to greener pastures than barren pointless me. The wife of a very famous homosexual fashion designer passes me. I interviewed her recently and she is extraordinary. I say hello and remind her that we've met and, obsequious and polite, I thank her for the time she gave me for the interview.

'I had such an interesting response to the piece,' I lie. I hadn't; she's far too out there and weird to speak of anything that a Middle England Sunday supplement reader can relate to. Her English isn't great, and I only really speak restaurant French, but I feel an urgent need to flatter her, more for something to do than any real interest in her feelings. With my oafish accent, I continue with the toadying in a foreign language, '*Vous êtes une inspiration pour les femmes anglaises.*' She nods with an impatient insincere twitch of a smile. I'm flogging a dead one here. We both move on, awkwardly. Brave compatriots in the shallow diaspora of fashion and lifestyle.

For all the morale-crushing failed conversations, the emotional temperature tonight is unusually warm for such an event. This is creepy and odd because society isn't generally welcoming. I feel the awkward dread of outsiderness crowd in as the adrenaline of greeting these people ebbs away. This is bad news; I am still in the early stages of a social marathon.

Oh, fuck them all. I start looking around at the second tier, the people who will be happy to see me. Their dresses are less fabulous, their photo more rarely taken but their greetings are enthused. I see someone I know and move towards them. I know this person well enough to breathe out hard through tight lips when I get close enough, the exhalation meaning, 'Am I glad to see you. Who's here? Anyone friendly?'. I don't let my intense relief register on my poker face, 'You look great, who's that dress by?'

The pop star she works for is famously tight and for all the private jets and showbiz fabulousness of her job, she survives on £30,000 a year. 'Small designer, a lend. Obviously.'

'Obviously. Same here,' I say, with a roll of the eyeballs. 'So many badly dressed people. I guess they're the ones that actually *paid* for their tickets.'

Grace has luscious shiny hair, she is pretty and her skin and eyes yet to show signs of being hardened to the environment. She is more sensitive than most people in this game. When she needs to talk it requires me to open a vein of sympathy and it turns out that tonight is no different; she has suffered a mauling in the jaws of the fashion cabal – again. I don't have much choice but to listen as I'm hardly rocking a 20-woman strong entourage here.

'On the way in the car she had her grooming team with her,' Grace says, her being the pop star boss. 'I joined in a conversation about whether she was showing too much cleavage and the other two turned on me. The stylist literally hissed, "Darling, we're fine without your input. Coffees and cars, darling, coffees and cars," the phrase that's used to put PAs in their place. It made me cry. Thank God she didn't notice.'

The tears brim again and I give her a hug. Her hair smells of coconut and almonds. 'Oh darling. They're just fashion skanks. It always amazes me the way they can use the word "darling" like a poisoned dart.'

'It's the ultimate mean girl gang, even the men, I will never get used to it.'

A tear has escaped from her brimming lower lid. I feel slightly repulsed but I pride myself on my kindness and empathy, especially when I don't have many people to hang out with. I've got a full glass of Ruinart Blanc de Blancs, which is about as good as it gets when it comes to free party champagne, and it's slipping down a treat. Grace and I circle round the edge of the throng. I shower her in reasons to buck up. 'Urgh, look at that pig of a dress ... Christ, how did *he* get in here, he hasn't worked in fashion since the nineties. How did I get in here, for that matter, I weigh more than eight stone. Shit!'

It doesn't take long to cheer her up. 'How do you feel about leaving?' she moots.

'Ace. I feel tip-top about that, girl. Let's leave these fashion cunts here and skidaddle. We don't belong here.'

I feel tangibly uplifted too, even though the after-party is at Chiltern Firehouse, to which we are NFI. NFI? It means not fucking invited. Most of the people on this planet are NFI.

Grace and I gather a posse to leave with, a shambolic crew of seven. Our friend has picked up two suits from a big fashion conglomerate and we ride into town in some guy's chauffeur-driven Merc. Wedged in on the clotted-cream-coloured leather, I give Grace a kiss on the neck. 'Vile *vile* human beings, fuck 'em all. I bet they're all sniffing crap coke in the bogs by now ... they'll all be ugly and scrawny and full of collagen by the time they're fifty. Cokehead losers. Speaking of which ...' I pause for comic effect, 'got any?'

'No, but I wouldn't say no a quick toot ...'

'I'm not an addict,' I say, 'I just love the smell of it.'

'Very moreish,' we say in unison, sniggering at this oldie but a goldie. I'm having a fun night now we've gone off-piste. It's best not knowing what is coming next.

After a few £18 G&Ts in a flashy Mayfair private members club, the sort that makes me look at Grace and say, 'I hope someone else is buying our drinks', these new corporate friends sweep us on with them to a party at a townhouse in Chelsea. In the vast, pristine and never-used kitchen, I register the light chopping sounds of cocaine being portioned out on a milky marble surface. An invisible sound system pumps out the Rolling Stones' 'Beast of Burden'. Unusual: normally the rich have tragic taste in music and their parties feature far too many House compilations made by five-star Parisian boutique hotels.

Out in the garden, a clutch of people blowing smoke into the cold air, there are lots of conversations carrying on with unusual concentration and interest. Everyone is high and 'user-friendly'. This means you can turn and talk to absolutely anyone, even the famous people, and they will be friendly back.

A thought sneaks into my giddy mind. I wonder what Wolfy is doing.

Indoors, a couple of manic cocker spaniels come skidding across the parquet towards their owner, who greets them with a mixture of alarm and gratifying joy. There are at least twenty people still bright and chatting; the mood has not darkened, the party is still full of life, but I don't just want to go home to my dog, I need to. *Au revoir.* I tuck Gareth's train into my knickers and step out into the fresh air, which seems to pass right through me, energising my steps as I lean out and flag a taxi.

When I get home Wolfy is already standing there waiting, waggling his rear end side to side and making little squeaks of happiness as he burrows into my knees. This is where a dog goes to get the best smell of you. I rock back on my haunches so I can greet him face to face, nose to nose, eye to eye.

'Mmmmn'olfy.' I kiss him all over his head, even though the dog books tell you dogs hate both kisses and being held by their heads. 'Come on! Let's go!' He dances around, sinks down into his praying, 'let's play' position, a downward dog. I pull on the first thing I find, my second-hand fur, step into muddy wellies and hitch the Gareth Pugh dress even higher up into my knicker elastic, I pick up my sunglasses and stumble out into the dawn to walk across to the Scrubs with the sun rising at my back and my dog at my side.

I should feel disgusting but, watching him gambol across the grass, shooting off, sniffing and zooming back to me at speed with his head dipping up and down, fur flying back in the wind, how can I wallow down there in my usual pit of recriminations and despair?

I run clumsily after him, tripping over my wellies and poor Gareth's dirty train, and he shoots around me in wide circles before dropping his head and belting back at top speed. He keeps suddenly making emergency stops, turning on a sixpence and heading back to some unmarked spot for an intensely focussed sniff. I pull off my old fur and, after the mandatory hypervigilance for any sensory trace of shit on the ground, I find a good spot and lay it on the grass lining-down. I put my face into his thick shaggy neck fur, sniffing in his scent of digestive biscuits and warm hay, and I make throaty happy animal sounds. He sits, panting with his mouth open wide in a canine grin. 'Mmmm, mmmmmmmm, Mmmmmmmm.' There are no words, only sounds that adquately express this kind of joy.

A bloke walks through a horde of crows pecking at the wet dawn grass. He has an Alsatian and a spaniel with him. They are the only other mammals in sight, otherwise the Scrubs looks deserted, even if it is not. I've heard that homeless people live in the depths of the woods around its edge. I've seen tents come and go. Bloke's wearing blue combats and government-issue boots – a police dog handler or a guard from the prison more probably. These are working dogs: security and drugs. He looks over at me. 'Morning!' I say, wanting to laugh, sat there in a £2,000 dress with my bum being warmed by coyote-fur underneath and an insanely shaggy lurcher in my arms. He nods, says nothing.

This walk – was it bedtime wee or first walk of the day? After a while spent loafing more than walking we go back to the flat and I chat to the dog, laughing at how stupid I am and how handsome he is, as I clatter about in the kitchen fixing a flagon of lemon water to take to my bed. I clock a large bag of black pepper Kettle Chips and add them crackling to the pile of recovery materials to take upstairs to bed. I'll be needing them tomorrow.

I sit up in bed. The sheets still have a scent of freshness and are silky smooth with age. Downstairs I can hear the dog settling himself on the sofa for the night, which is actually day. Hearing his subtle rustling and creaks I miss him already.

'Wolfy?' I call, questioning whether he wants to come, questioning whether I am really inviting him in to the realm of humans. What about my replies to the adoption anoraks, 'Dogs upstairs, never!' There is a pause, stillness and silence for about 30 seconds. 'Wolfy?' I hear the tentative skirling and clicking of his nails on the painted wood of the stairs. He stands at the top looking at me, panting with his mouth wide open. Dog smiling. I pat the bed. 'Hup Woofs?' He stops by the bedside, still dog smiling, as if he's saying, 'You sure?' before springing delightedly onto the mattress and snuggling down at the bottom of the bed. I fall asleep spread out like a starfish and with the dog's head resting on my calf. No foetal position required. This oxytocin stuff is mind-blowing.

And that is the end of Wolfy sleeping downstairs.

'Excuse me?' I put my chirruping question to the Hulk's back, the mean-looking guy with the Staffie. Wolfy and I were walking behind him on our way to Coffee Plant. It took the length of Elgin Crescent to Ladbroke Grove for me to pluck up the courage to come right out and ask, 'Is your dog the love of your life?'

'She's the only one.' His grimacing laugh rumbled like a tube train underground. A flash of gold grilles from his teeth as he smiled. Then he turned back to his walk.

This was reassuring. If loving your dog was a form of mental illness, or at least of weakness, then a wide range of decent humans were similarly afflicted. I relaxed into it. Bring it on, I say. There's a study by academics at Edinburgh University that says our oxytocin response to dogs is in our genes. This is great news. Yet another problem I could lay at the feet of my parents. It's not even my fault.

It is months since that miserable visit to Tim that had prompted my hunt for Wolfy.

He rang one evening while I was walking the dog round Wormwood Scrubs, wondering if I was around when he planned to be in Notting Hill. 'No,' I lied, 'I'm on a deadline.'

He started talking, telling me about his new girlfriend. She's young and apparently madly into anal sex. His favourite. I didn't say she's only with you for the drugs and the money. 'I don't want to know Tim, please.'

The dog was schnuffling around the edges of the little copse with the homeless guys living in it and I stared distractedly. Where was their way in through the tangle of trees and brambles? Were they OK in there? How did they live?

There was a real counterculture here that all the dog walkers took in their hearty stride. The al fresco hook-up scene cranked up with the warmer weather, and come early summer men of every age and ethnic stripe would sit along the benches at the edge of the copse on the Scrubs Lane side, looking at their mobiles and waiting for the sign to hive off into the bushes for some part-time loving. Following Wolfy, I'd once come across a naked guy in there waving a cucumber, and had screamed in shock, 'OhmyImsosorry! Wolfy, come, come, come,' I called as I blinkered my eyes with my hands.

The man was just as scared as me. 'Sorry. Sorry love.' A very apologetic English exchange, really.

All sorts went on up there on the 60 acres of the Scrubs, you just had to look for it.

I'd once thought of myself as a cool girl about town and now I am a prudish middle-aged lady in stout walking shoes screaming at cucumbers. But I still have Tim, dear old Timbo, reminding me of the past. I'm still here, half listening to him telling me about one of his portly coke pals who has kicked the bucket, suddenly but not surprisingly, at the age of 55. 'Peter died. Heart attack. Wife discovered the mistress. Children appalled. Funeral awkward.' The complexities of lives lived under the influence. The thought of it made my stomach twist.

'Oh, sorry about that. But hardly unexpected. He was an elderly coke addict.'

'We never see you darling, I miss you.'

'I've got a dog.'

'So I heard, darling, but you can still play.'

Play. *Play.* What a stupid word. Like that daft clock honking and mewling above his coffee table while unhappy grown-ups get off their tits.

'Gotta go, Timbo, let's have dinner sometime.' The universal language of, I don't want to see you.

'When, where, soon, darling?'

Over the years Tim had been the worst great friend a girl could have. Tim had lent me money and put me up when I was homeless after bad break-ups, he had boosted my confidence when it flagged. We had talked. He always listened to my every dirty secret. In fact, no secret was too dirty for him. In fact, the dirtier the better.

Reasons to have dinner with Tim: he's a mess but he's kind and he's smart, smart as hell, in fact, and if he hadn't been a just about functioning drug addict, he'd have been running the world by now. His problem was that he'd made a lot of money, once, by inventing some essential bit of code in the early nineties plus he inherited that jammy flat on Mount Street. The result, combined with an addicts gene, meant that he never really worked again.

Tim's clever. All his dirty sexscapades and late-night idiocy is underpinned by education and the personal and political insight that being a mixed-race guy at a top English public school in the seventies had woken him up to. In the years of sitting around in that grand shithole of a flat we had talked about bookish things and politics, history and religion in a way that I never got the opportunity to normally, or if I did, I'd back off, nervous that I didn't know enough. With Tim I never felt like that.

We had huge fights. Talking about the impact of the Cold War on post-colonial Africa, I'd punched his shoulder hard. He'd once walked away and left me outside a nightclub in Paris at 3 a.m. with nowhere to stay.

We were truly old friends and his addiction did not define him, not entirely, it was just something that I needed to closely manage.

There was one huge reason not to have dinner with Tim: seeing him meant drugs. I knew this with a certainty so Pavlovian I would feel high and my bowel agitated even if I just walked past his Mount Street flat at 10 a.m.

I looked down at my moist-eyed quadruped. For the last few minutes of the call he had been standing by my side under the little avenue of trees beside the Great Western Railway line. Absent-mindedly, I was soothing myself by rubbing, swirling and massaging his ears where they sprouted from their sockets.

'Wednesday?'

That's a good safe night, if such a thing exists in Tim World.

'Done! Where?'

'Locanda, they love the dog there. Did you know Lucian Freud took his whippets there for dinner. I want chestnut tagliatelle with chicken livers.'

If I met Tim for Italian food at Locanda Locatelli round the back of Selfridges on Oxford Street I could walk the dog there from my place through Hyde Park, good long walk that. We could split a bottle of Sangiovese, eat some Michelin-starred carbs and I could catch the 94 bus home. I knew I'd make better choices for my nostrils with Wolfy's wet black nose in view. Yes, I reckoned I could risk eating with Tim without getting sucked back into Groundhog Night at Mount Street.

'Did you say "the dog"? *The dog*? You *eat* with your bloody dog?!' He hooted with malicious laughter.

It was meant to be provocative. But it didn't touch the sides. 'Yeah, sometimes,' I said, with an amused 'secret smile'.

'Well, I'd better meet this fascinating canid then.'

The call ended.

I crouched down on my haunches so the dog and I were eye to eye. 'Thanks mate,' I said. He too sat back on his furry hips and I shuffled forward like a crippled frog so I could put my hands gently either side of his skull and look into his eyes.

What was he thinking as he looked back? 'Does she have any biscuits?' Or, 'She smells of toast.' Or, 'What does she want. Christ she's needy.' Or, is he in love, just like I am?

Back at home, peternity leave might have been over but the honeymoon continued. Life with Wolfy never palled. Charlie and I were experiencing a honeymoon period, buoyed on the tide of feel-good hormones the dog had brought to the flat along with the dirt he also brought in from lying by us in pubs and cafes on far-too-tiny Woof Beds. Where once we talked about work we now talked about everything in Wolfyworld.

In March I took him to dinner at Castor's house. If it hadn't been for Castor, and that conversation with Keith, his owner, in Coffee Plant that momentous hungover day I decided to get a dog, I might never have met Wolfy. My life might have remained the hollow canine-free place it was before.

Keith and I had never really been friends, more professional acquaintances, but once Wolfy became my ward, Keith and I became closer. We both loved our dogs, and discussed them like a couple of fixated new mums.

'He's been coming home from daycare a bit of a bully, I think he gets into a pack mentality there.'

'Oh, yes, I can see how that happens. Next time he's overnighting there shall I take him instead for a bit of mellow Wolfy time?'

'Would you, that'd be great. He's a great influence on Castor, he seems to calm him down.'

'It's nothing, Wolfy needs Castor too, all that nipping at his arse gets him in shape. Honestly, he's so lazy, Keith, he's like a fourteen-year-old boy, not a lurcher.'

'What are you feeding him?'

'I'm doing the barf diet, you know, meat, bone, organs.'

'My vet's very anti, I've put Castor on the kibble but it's very expensive stuff.'

'Anyway, enough dog chat. What do you think about the new collection at Dior?'

'Well, I shouldn't be telling you this, but strictly *entre nous* . . .'

Dogs were like the golf course, for me. They had gained me access. Interviewing showbiz sorts was a breeze now; the stars all have packs of rescue dogs, which they dote on and call 'my puppies' even when they are incontinent and 150 in human years. Dogs were a way in. Most people with a dog, whether they admit it or not, don't really trust non-doggy people.

Keith invited me for dinner and told me, 'Bring your boys,' Charlie and the dog. 'Let's have another one of those dog parties. I've invited Stacey and her terrier, Bo. Do you know her?'

Urgh. Her. I'd never liked that Stacey much. She was a viperous fashion person. My first encounter with her outside work functions had been at a party not long after New Year's Eve sometime in the mid early noughties. I had been wearing Uggs on my feet. I know this is nothing to be proud of, but it was well over ten years ago, when people did things like that. She'd looked at me and placed a solitary thoughtful finger on her cheek – 'Uggs. Interesting' – before mumbling to a friend, 'I thought she wrote for *Style* magazine, clue's in the name darling.'

Then she'd twirled around, showing me her skirt. 'Balenciaga. Like it?'

'Lovely,' I'd coldly smiled back, and, as I'd walked away, muttering sidewards, adding, 'You'd never know. I'd have said Primark.' Nothing particularly unusual there. My first encounter with one of the world's most famous stylists, 20 years ago, had been like that too and I have never been able to forget it. She clocked my outfit (what both she and I were wearing is fixed in my memory like physical assault). She managed to reproduce the effect of projectile vomiting in disgust, on both me and my clothes, merely by looking at me a little bit longer than necessary. People tell me she is a nice person. Even though I've heard she has a dog now, I struggle to believe it.

The sensible part of me had always known very well that all these women I marked on the ruler of success were not monsters. But these women, for some reason, seemed set up to be somehow special, different, 'better', in my mind.

The dog helped me on this front. Turning up at Keith's that night with Wolfy at my side changed everything. Stacey monster was there, and as the four canines sniffed butt, us six humans talked about dogs over a negroni. What a leveller. Not surprisingly given the host worked in fashion, there wasn't a huge amount of food and we were soon drunk. We lit a fire, the dogs settled onto the sofa, a sure sign that a dog party was under way, and we humans sat on the floor, chatting. I say the dogs settled on the sofa; Wolfy and Castor did. Fiona and Stacey both had terriers, so they ran round the walls barking.

The only person without a dog sat quietly back at Keith's dining table, watching, confused and a little or a lot bored, probably. I clocked this and thought about all those times I'd been the only woman without kids, listening mute and slightly irritated to parents – understandably sometimes, tiresomely at others – yap on about their kids. I knew how she felt not to be part of a gang and yet I didn't care. This sense of belonging and immediate camaraderie with three relative strangers was fun.

When we ran out of cigarettes, I suggested we might take the dogs out for a wee and do a little run to the corner shop. Stacey and I went together with two dogs each, two terriers pulling her arm off, two lurchers rolling along like supermodels at my side. They all took their turns to pee and crap. We should've taken them out much earlier.

Charged up with Marlboro Lights and a sneaky bag of Skips, Stacey and I sat on a wall and had a drunken chat. 'I'm so mad about my dog,' I said. 'Look, he's made us friends. Before, I thought you were a fucking monster.'

'Me?' she said. 'You're so *vile*, Spicer!'

Her BoBo, she said, was her best friend and had saved her from utter suicidal despair and loneliness when she broke up with a fiancé a few years back. Wolfy, I said, had delivered me from Timness. We gave each other a hug and I told her that the Preen dress she was wearing was 'beyond, beyond'. We went back to Keith's, where we had a disco while the lurchers placidly watched and the terriers crawled up the walls.

At the end of the night I asked Charlie if he'd enjoyed himself. 'Yes,' he said, 'Dog people are good people, aren't they.' I thought about Stacey and smiled. 'Yes. They are.'

The dog brought Charlie's and my schedules into a closer alignment. I had a reason to get out of bed in the morning.

Sometimes we were so early to Coffee Plant we had to sit patiently waiting til it opened at seven.

It was on a morning like this I'd gone round to Rococo, the newsagent on Elgin Crescent with the enormous selection of rare magazines. I was hovering round the front pages deciding which paper would be the least depressing to read. 'Jihadis burn 19 Yazidi girls to death.' Or '*Ex on the Beach* star strips off to reveal tattooed bod ...'

An Irish guy stood by the fridge opposite the till and spoke while nodding in the direction of my dog. 'Norfolk Lurcher that,' he said, matter-of-fact, quiet. 'Good for getting rabbits to a net.' He talked about how many deer there were to be caught 'out at Slough' and how the country was so overrun with deer, 'they'd be on the Scrubs soon'.

Did he have lurchers, I asked.

'Longdogs,' he says, which is a mix of two different types of sighthound. 'Got two saluki greys. Go all day they don't get tired.'

I tried to match the disengaged way he was speaking at the dog and not to me and not sound all excited and in-your-face, which is how I felt. What's he made of, I wondered?

'Greyhound, Bedlington, deerhound ...' He paused. 'Lookin' at the ears now, there's probably a bit a collie in there too. For the brains.'

The conversation ended without any kind of goodbye. He picked up his Mayfairs and was gone.

I had a deadline that day, a piece about a therapist couple who had written a book about 'mindful sex' and how having said 'mindful sex' would save the world. It seems absurd and I was struggling to give a shit about it given the 'Jihadis burn 19 Yazidi girls to death' headline, which was making me feel grossly inadequate as a journalist and as a species. The fact that my work required turning out mildly entertaining guff week after week depressed me more than the certain knowledge that I lived on a savage and arbitrarily cruel planet.

To cheer myself up I sat in the car and ate a croissant from the expensive Grocer on Elgin, or, I Saw You Coming Deli as Charlie and I called it. Flaky golden exterior for me, the white gooey, doughy centre for Wolfy. He sat next to me while I ate my bit, drooling onto the crud and dust gathered round my gearstick, with his eyes focused on what he knew he was due. Eating my part took ten minutes, he dispatched his in two seconds.

At home at my desk, the suggestion that my labralukipoo is actually an ancient and authentic proper *proper* lurcher, as identified by what I strongly suspected to be an actual gypsy (or should I say Traveller?) seemed far more important to me than saving the world through mindful sex.

I Googled Norfolk lurchers for two hours.

There were very few references but I found some deep in the forums of sites like Hunting Life where the avatars had names like 'Swirlymurphy', 'Mr Poach' and 'rabbit tourmentor' (sic).

'Norfolks is those big, fawn, rough-coated dogs, mate.' 'Yeah mate, original lurcher was always long coated as that disguised the athletick body that was capable of use when poaching.' 'They was the real poachers dogs combining the speed of a sighthound with the intelligence of a working dog.'

All the images for Norfolk lurcher were blond, shaggy and thicker-set than your average scrawny hound, a bit less regal and speedy. They looked a lot like my Wolfy. One of my dog-walking companions, a sylphlike older beauty called Sarah, was constantly accusing me of overfeeding. Her lurcher, Lettice, was tall, skeletal and – I agreed – the perfect size but Wolfy was naturally thicker-set, I'd say, like a mother excusing her tubby child with the words 'big-boned'. A lot of these gorgeous west Londoners, reformed party girls who all knew each other from NA and AA, were concerned by their dogs' size. Anna, Wally's owner, called them 'the ladies who lurch'.

I'd look forward to sharing this information with the lurcher set on the Scrubs. My Wolfy isn't overfed, he doesn't have any labradoodle in him either. He's a *Norfolk* Lurcher. My chest puffed with pride just thinking about him.

'Any sign of that sex copy?' came the email from the editor.

'Just doing a final edit,' I shot back.

By the time I'd finished my lurcher-digging it was lunchtime. As I ate, I put all my research in an excited email to Charlie. Now how to kill the rest of the afternoon without doing any work? 'Walkies!'

I considered cancelling Tim for dinner in favour of writing the piece that night. But I didn't want to be rude – and, more importantly, I didn't want to write the piece yet.

He is in nostalgic mode when we meet. 'I've missed you Katiepoo.' Before the huge bread basket has even appeared he wants to remind me of all the good times we've had: 'Remember that time you turned up wearing those patent boots with a broken heel and a red PVC mackintosh.' He's acting out a state of blissed reverie and the happiest of times remembered. 'By the time I came to the door you were on your hands and knees because you'd taken your bedtime Rohypnol before you realised you were locked out.'

Ha ha ha. It's an awful memory, I mean truly appalling, and not funny at all. He loves to tell it, proudly. Ha ha ha. I laugh along, mentally writing a list of friends I need to drop, with Tim at the top.

My good humour increases, though, as the wine in the bottle reduces.

'Let's go to the Groucho,' he says.

Oh Christ no, not the Groucho. He might as well have rolled up a fifty-pound note and said toot toot through it.

He rolls up a fifty-pound note and says toot toot through it.

'I need to go home. I've got a deadline. Already two days late ...'

He pays the bill, I feebly protest that we should go halves, then say thank you three times and we're in a cab heading off for the lie that is 'a quick nightcap'. Wolfy settles his jaw on the floor and looks up at me. 'He's very good, isn't he,' says Tim. 'I could almost be persuaded to like dogs if they were all more like this one.'

I look at Woofs. It makes me really sad to see toot toot Timbo and Wolfy in the same taxi. 'But you're not bringing him with us are you?' Tim goes on.

'Yes, I am. The dog comes with or I go home. Bernie's promised me he can sneak him in.'

Bernie is the Groucho's host, and had assured me I could bring my new dog if I wanted to. I have studiously avoided the place lately, given its associations for me, but now my resistance levels are one bottle of Sangiovese down.

At reception the pretty girl says, 'No dogs, sorry.'

'Can you fetch Bernie?' I say, confident, with a wobbly-headed touch of the 'I'm specials' about me.

Bernie will sort it. I nod in the direction of the bar. 'You go in, find us a quiet corner, I'll come and find you.'

Bernie sweeps down the back stairs from the bar and crashes open the double doors. Long leopard-print jacket and a tiger-stripe T-shirt. Quietly dressed, as usual. 'Arright daaarlin.' He comes in for a kiss but stops short and yowls, 'What the fuck is that. You're not bringin' that in here, it's massive. I thought you meant a little one. That's more like a horse. No babe! No. No dogs. Come back when you've done something with him.'

Tim is already stalking the room looking for friends. I don't bother going in after him. He'll find someone, he's a big boy. I'll send a text. Turning away, I briefly feel a bit of a berk but the dog bounces along lively as hell beside me as if to say, 'Well that's a lucky escape, I wasn't looking forward to navigating all the feet attached to greedy nostrils.'

By the time I reach the end of Dean Street I'm delighted to be going home from Soho at midnight instead of God-knows-what o'clock. I'm euphoric, in fact. I swagger down Oxford Street on nothing more than a bottle of red. I might even escape a hangover.

We reach the end of the West End's colon in that toilet bowl of an underpass: at Marble Arch. We come up for air at Speakers' Corner to take a bracing and illegal walk through the cold black grass of Hyde Park. Wolfy, let off the lead, shoots off excitedly into the deeper dark with a couple of 360-degree turns of joy. His way of saying, 'I'm happy as hell! Thanks mate.'

No, mate. Thank *you*.

CHAPTER THREE

Any memories Wolfy might have had of his past seemed to fade and his secure place in our home sank slowly deeper into his canine comprehension. The light came back to his eyes. The hunch in his back straightened out. He got his doggy mojo back.

Charlie rang me as I was heading home after a work trip.

'Erm, I've got a bit of bad news.'

'Yes?'

'It would appear that Wolfy has eaten your fur coat.'

I love to eat pork scratchings, as does the dog. We all love a hairy snack, don't we? It was only made of rabbit pelts, a little bomber jacket; it must have smelt tasty. He was a carnivore magician – he could make a whole rabbit disappear in ten minutes, leaving barely a trace but a bit of fur or a tooth in his shit a day later – so why not a fur coat? When I got home I scooped up the mauled uneaten remains and threw them into the growing nest of tattered and cosy fabrics under the desk.

Wolfy was a special dog but I laboured under no illusion that he was 'my fur baby' or me his 'mummy'. His constant quiet presence made him companionable beyond anything I could have imagined and I often called him 'mate', but I knew he was a dog and he did doggy things and had doggy urges. Chief among them the scavenger's urgent need for food.

If he was left at home for anything beyond five minutes, he'd do a lap of the flat looking for food to steal. In the early months we'd come back to find packages of food spilled, decimated or plain gone. A plastic tub containing smoked pig fat, lardo, was chewed into, the contents vanished into his stomach. Butter, cheese and bread were all popular snacks. An entire box of crispbread was torn into, half eaten and the rest trodden deep into the fabric of our furniture and rugs. Sometimes he'd steal things and shred them apart just for larks, like, say, a bag of chickpea flour. The law of Sod dictated that his preferred spot to deal with stolen food was the Turkish *tulu* rug by the fire, the plushest, tuftiest, shaggiest, most expensive and hardest to clean spot in the whole 700 square feet we three animals crammed into and called home.

Sometimes we might not notice what was gone for days, until, puzzling over some missing cheese, I'd shout through to Charlie in the sitting room, 'Can you check the rug for any signs of Cheddar.'

Under forensic examination, sure enough: 'Yup, traces of yellow cheese-like substance on the fireside edges.'

We learned to put food away.

Even when we were home, though, he still chanced it.

The way our flat is laid out is weird. It's part of the urban living compromise – like having no front door, or the bathroom being next to the kitchen as far as possible from the bed. It's a tiny labyrinth, a multi-storey burrow, and sometimes it feels like it's 90 per cent stairs. You go up 13 ringing steps to get to our back door and once inside, from the kitchen you can go down a step to the bathroom on the left or walk up three steps to the sitting room. There are more stairs there, another 13 that go up to our loft bedroom. All the stairs are steep and narrow – a death trap for skinny-legged dogs. Remember?

The whole place is on funny levels. Our main food-prep surface is next to those three little stairs in the kitchen. This means the big wooden chopping block where we prep all our food is at lurcher nose height. We called it Wolfy's Smorgasbord. If we had ever had any concerns about food hygiene, we lost them to the sight of a glistening black nose twitching over the area and a stealthy pink tongue snaffling what he could before we started the farce of trying to scold a dog while laughing.

He is on a permanent See Food diet that dog. No one's hungry like the Wolf. At first we would scold him, and use the word *No*, sharply, if he went near the chopping board. Had we kept up this discipline, I am sure that only when we left the house would he have explored the area with nose, tongue and jaw before carrying it off to Wolfy's rug, like all his other treasures.

But our discipline was patchy. We'd catch him nicking food and be tickled by these attempts at Hooded Claw-style stealth. He used the slinking approach, sidling past us, making himself flat and small and as close to invisible as he could while he snuck, nibbling up the well-done ends of the beef by shooting out a long sticky tongue with his head turned sideways and resting ear-down on the chopping board. Charlie and I would be too busy chuckling to tell him off effectively.

Yes, we loved some bad habits into him. It wasn't his fault if we condoned all sorts of naughty doggy behaviour by standing back and laughing affectionately. We created a very loveable monster by spoiling him. Otherwise, his manners remained impeccable. He peed as far away from the flat as possible, never in the alleyway behind. He pooed discreetly in the long grass and away from sight and smell-lines. He did this so efficiently that I sometimes missed where he'd dropped his crap and would be gingerly stepping through the grass, trying to avoid other people's uncollected dog faeces while scouring the ground looking for his like I was hunting for truffles not crap.

Out walking with my nieces and nephews one day, Wolfy did one of his tidy invisible jobs. 'I'd better go find that,' I said. 'It's very important to pick up dog poo.'

'Ah-ha! Now then!' said Arty, with all the certainty of a small person. 'Aunty Kate, would you like to know how you can find that poo that Wolfy just did?'

'Why yes Arts, educate me.'

'Well, what you do is you must look for the flies because the flies are really good at finding the poo.'

His theory worked. In winter you looked for steam rising. In summer, follow your nose, or, as Professor Arty proposed, the flies.

Wolfy started to make his own life, as much as a domesticated dog is able. In the alley round the back of the flat he was allowed to visit some of the neighbours. It wasn't quite like the good old days, when people would turf their dogs out on the street when they left the house and the streets were full of free-range dogs roaming around doing white poo everywhere.

The first 'friend' he made back there in the alley was Janice, who lived in one of these little two-up two-downs that had originally housed two families. One up, one down. Ours was the only little hutch that remained divided in two. Janice had lived in this house since birth and she had no central heating or washing machine, no television or, indeed, much light to speak of. It looked awful dingy in there. The top floor still had the original back door, a cheap swimming pool blue with dimpled glass panes, but was minus the outdoor stairs that led up to it as in our flat.

When I first caught him slithering in the crack in Janice's back door, I went running and calling and apologising. 'Wolfy, come, *come*, COME! HERE!'

'It's all right, he's just coming in for his biscuits,' she squawked with irritation. 'Leave him be. Woo' likes his biscuits.'

I hovered at the back door waiting for the dog to return from elevenses with Janice.

Wolfy got a very warm welcome there. He would eat any cat food left out, or run up to her bedroom to beg for the old-fashioned, cheap biccies she kept by her bed. Rich Tea, Nice, Malted Milk, Lincolns ... Sometimes if she was heading out

she'd break them up and leave them outside her back door for
Woo' to eat at his leisure.

Janice is what people like to describe as a mad cat lady. This
isn't a fair representation of her. She is an eccentric and isolated
figure, not happy, not sad, always busy and frequently fretting
about things in her tiny universe of the alley.

She enjoyed a visit from Wolfy on a daily basis. In the end
I started buying dog biscuits and leaving them in an old plastic
tub outside her back door. What amounted to eight hundred
human biscuits a day wasn't ideal. She never acknowledged this,
or thanked me. Which was fine. I'd given her an M&S Christmas
cake last year and she'd said, 'Now, you don't have to do that.'
That was as close as she would get to a thank-you.

His other daily call lived just over from Janice. Rita was
in her seventies and her husband John was a retired market
trader who loved Eric Clapton. John called Wolfy 'The
Guv'nor'.

'Rita! Guv'nor's in,' he'd shout if Wolfy came calling at
the back door when Rita was upstairs. Rita would give him
two Bonio, and both wet *and* dry cat food. 'Ahhh. He does
enjoy his cat food, doesn't he?' she'd say, looking down fondly
at him as he feverishly licked the pattern off the clattering
dishes.

Yes he did, though what Whiskas did to his breath was less
enjoyable for his human housemates.

Rita and I would marvel at how Janice loved all animals,
lived for them – when they died she went to the church and
lit candles for their souls – but never touched them. Despite
Janice's devotion to the animals, Wolfy prioritised Rita over
Janice; the edible haul was greater, plus she gave him a lot of
strokes and cuddles: big biscuits, cat food two ways *and* an
oxytocin buzz. Nice!

I was glad about this because his visits to Janice were a bit
of a problem. The sheer quantity of cats in and out of the place,
and the fact that she didn't own a vacuum cleaner nor had new

carpets since the end of the last world war, meant that above a certain temperature her place became an orgy of fleas.

Manchester Nancy, our next-door neighbour, was nearer to 90 than 80 but still loved a bracing three-fingers G&T and occasionally went out in miniskirts and with her long dyed-blond hair in bunches. Nancy didn't much like dogs. But I liked gin, so we'd pop round there occasionally and Wolfy would lie on the AstroTurf on her patio, watching while I selflessly shared a stiff gin with my elderly neighbour.

Nancy told me she'd always had her suspicions that Janice was mildly autistic: 'She doesn't drink you know; mind, neither does Rita. People are funny, aren't they.'

Janice would patrol the alleyway in men's shoes without laces, a dingy dressing gown the same colour as those cheap biscuits Wolfy enjoyed so much and a dirty baby-blue nightie. At all hours of the day and night she could be heard talking to the cats she'd adopted: Zappy, Dappy, Buster, Noggy, Felicity … All of them had originally belonged to other households off the alley, but they all ended up with Janice. 'They dint care for 'em right,' she'd say.

'Not true,' the original owners insisted. Everyone got on well enough though and that was Wolfy's world.

'Why have you put tomatoes in the fridge?' I say, whipping out three desperately underripe orange rocks. 'Never put tomatoes in the fridge.'

Charlie mutters 'For fuck's sake,' under his breath and stabs the chopping board with the knife he's using to slice himself a piece of salami.

In our tomayto/tomahtoe relationship we can agree on the pronouncing of the word; whether they should be kept in the fridge or not, less so.

My honeymoon with Wolfy was looking like it would never end, unlike the brief respite from antagonism between Charlie and me. We two had enjoyed gazing at Wolfy together for a few months after he arrived. Now that was over. We had hit a really miserable rocky patch that had me wondering if we were really meant to be.

Sometimes the only thing that kept me from walking out was the fact that we shared a mortgage, the ultimate ball and chain. If the Instagram evidence of other people's relationships was to be believed, then Charlie and I had the worst relationship on earth. In fact, I was beginning to suspect that relationships were what is technically known as a 'fucking grind'. No wonder all my others had ended after two years.

'Anything else I've got wrong here?' he says through clenched teeth.

'Well, they never ripen otherwise, and' I mutter this last, 'it's common to keep tomatoes in the fridge.'

You get the boyfriend you deserve, I think, mournful, resigned, self-pitying. A victim. And, it's true, the punishment cuts both ways – he has me too, a woman who judges people who keep tomatoes in the fridge.

There's more cross words about the tomato issue, but what savagely destroys happiness in this home isn't shouting, it's the silence. He opens his laptop. Lips in a miserable set line. We do not speak to each other for the rest of the night. It is happening too often, and it's depressing. It's not drama queen depressing, where you huff and blow and complain that it's sooo depressing because you can't get tickets to see Beyoncé at the O2. It's *actually* depressing. I feel permanently low.

I want to say something positive but I can't think of anything. When I do try to speak the intonation is inflected with coldness and disappointment, a slow drip of martyred poison. The female response to male anger is weary passive aggression.

My comeback will not emerge for another 24 hours probably, drip drip, it can last for days, little digs, sharp inhalations, overlong exhalations. For now, I say nothing but I pine for my shabby old rented flat, the real deal, the 'room of my own' where no one ever sighed because the bed wasn't made, or if I dinged the wing mirror. I had my own shit car and I could read with all the lights on until 4 a.m. if I wanted to. What have I done? Given up my every independence to be unhappy in a relationship.

The silence is cold and hateful. I attach the dog to his lead and leave the house, slamming the door so hard that a pot of pens falls off the windowsill onto the floor. As my feet ring down the metal steps there's a hollow metallic thud as, I assume, some white good takes the force of Charlie's fist or foot.

'Oh, 'ello Woo',' Janice gurgles, blocking my way out of the alley, out for a late-night cat-herd in her greige robe. 'Now. Have you seen Zappy?' she asks me, with hands planted businesslike on her hips.

'Not now Janice.'

I can't get out of there fast enough. I walk round to the green outside the leisure centre and I sit on the concrete bench down the far end by the tower block and put my head between my knees. Wolfy wanders off to pee on a favourite object, the old foundation stone dug out when they built the new school here a few years ago.

I want revenge. Revenge for what, I don't know. I want my power back. I could always get up and walk out. And go where? A women's refuge? With a dog? And the reasons for leaving? My boyfriend keeps tomatoes in the fridge? Could I afford a small flat. Could I move in with my mum? God no. I'm not far off 50. Jesus.

The dog had finished sniffing every tree trunk and street lamp outside the sports centre.

Normally this is the point at which we return to the flat.

I don't want to go back this night, though, so I carry on sitting on the concrete bench opposite a lurid pink and pointless squiggle of a municipal sculpture. I take a few deep breaths. I try to anchor myself to something strong, solid, abiding that will keep my spirits up. Wolfy comes over and crumples his gangly legs under his belly and lies on the grass in front of me, and exhales with a purposeful force that suggests he is content to park here.

Lewis Hamilton II, a beagle I'd watched over the last few months grow from a puppy into a fat overfed dog, appears to schnuffle round my dog's rear end. Lewis's owner comes over. I don't know his name, 'Lewis's owner' suffices. 'Evening Wolfy,' he says and my dog bumbles over to lean against his leg. 'I love it when they do that,' he beams at me. 'Dear old Wolfy.'

He's such an unusually cheerful guy, which tonight just makes the rot back home feel more remote. From across the way comes the transgender lady with her cloud of French bulldogs and pugs. She has a new one: 'I can't help myself. I'm addicted to them babe.' The story of the new puppy is relayed in explicit detail along with the complexities of her housing situation. Small piggy dogs aren't the only thing she's addicted to, I think, listening to the babble and looking at her heavy, sleepy eyes.

Would I like to be high now, I wonder.

Yes. No. No. Yes. I think of the repercussions. It's a terrible idea. The shortest-term and worst solution. Wolfy has come back to sit beside me and I lean down to sniff his head and kiss his ears.

The painfully posh local councillor has arrived with his dog. 'It's Wiggles the cockerpoo!' I exclaim, as the little glove puppet rushes towards Wolfy to sniff a greeting. Wolfy recognises little Wiggles and his tail starts wagging high and fast in enthusiastic welcome.

Posh chap nods at me – he is never very free with the chat – and over at Lewis's owner too. His eyes flicker at the transgender gal and back again quickly. She looks too healthy for it to be crack or white cider, too lively for smack or weed. I'm dying to know. Is it rude to ask? Perhaps I could hang out with her for a bit. She sees me staring. I wave and smile too enthusiastically. 'Babe.' She waves back in acknowledgement, coolly, lazily.

'She's a malty poo.' I notice that posh is talking to me.
'... A malty poo.'

'Oh dear. Too much Horlicks.'

'Wiggles. She's not a cockerpoo, she's a big maltipoo.'

'A Maltipoo.' What a word.

Posh is as bonkers about his dog as I am mine. He's got the doggy oxytocin gene. He's got it bad. I see the way he looks at her, adoring eyes betraying a melting heart. 'Ooh, better be off!' He chases off after the wiggly Wiggles with a poo bag over his mitt and his iPhone torch on to better find brown treasure laid deep in the bushes by Treadgold House. That's him, civic-minded to the extreme.

Mentally, I shuffle through the alternatives to going home. What I'll do is I'll go out all night and not come back and then he'll think I'm dead and that will teach him and then we can be great lovers again. I'll switch my phone off and disappear. Yeah that'll make him sorry. Where to go? My friend Elaine's. To my brother's. Too far. Timbo is only a ten-minute cab ride away. There the door is always open, once he's fought his way through the deadlocks and latches of the paranoid drug abuser. I envisage the Peterbilt wing mirror and the mountain of butts in the heavy glass ashtray, the talkative goons around the-marble-and-glass coffee table.

Posh is back, waving his hand, still covered in a poo bag. 'False alarm!' shrugging and rolling my eyes, I semaphore an amused exasperation, which neither of us feel. Our dogs can do no wrong.

No. Just, no. In the past I've walked out on men and bunked in Tim's spare bedroom, or what he calls the tantrum suite. The thought of doing that now is like inviting someone to kick me in the head.

I linger a bit longer, scrolling through Chica's Instagram. There's all her socialite chums, thin as pipe cleaners and all at the same party. I start clicking, on and on, through to the feeds tagged in her posts. More lithe-limbed girls, all gleaming and glowing and hugging on speedboats and skis. Here's me, sat outside a municipal leisure centre with a bunch of ordinary freaks like me and their dogs. Oh, why did I do that? Now, what modicum of mellow spirits I'd have scrabbled back from the company of my random doggy acquaintances has been harshed by the whipping out of the old ruler of success. Bugger.

Come on, go home, go to bed. Grind on, see what tomorrow brings. That's all I can do. My relationship might not be Insta-perfect, but we've been together for six years now, and for me that's a major achievement. Grit your teeth. Head down.

I want to go home, to *my* home. I'm not going to run away tonight.

'Come on boy, it's too late for Rita.' I steer him away from her gate as we return down the alley with the moonlight bouncing off the silver clouds and my beast friend's swaying rear end. I breathe in cool still night air. Life's not great but there's always this.

The flat still hums with the dislike we both feel for each other and I sit on the kitchen step, reluctant to join my so-called lover in bed.

Without any meaningful money of my own, I'm impotent.

Virginia Woolf famously said that a woman needs 'a room of her own'. Less famously, what she exactly said was 'a woman must have money' and then the room business. My mum, too, raising us three on her own, constantly seemed tortured by a financial want that she could not answer herself. Money is a brute. When we were kids Will and I used to fantasise about looking after Mum. When we grew up we would buy her a house and send her on great holidays and she'd never have to be hurt by a man again. If we did that, she'd be happy and free.

This was my formative experience of economic power being in the hands of men. Work, work would make women free, and I did work, I didn't follow a domestic path, still the real economic power always remained just out of my reach. My feckless spending had nothing to do with it. It was all someone else's fault.

With Wolfy beside me on the floor, I sit on the kitchen step and stew. If I had money, I could just walk out of here. I don't want to leave. I just want to know I am able to leave. I want to want my boyfriend, not need him. The risk, with need, is too high. Love is like any drug – take it, but don't be dependent.

Wolfy sits upright, looking away. The poignancy of his gentle loyal presence compared to the detached cold man upstairs brings tears stinging to my eyes. I let them go, the tears, and they fall with a slow patter on the seagrass. I hang my head, staring down at the accumulation of crud between the weave in my miserable domestic universe. I've not cried much in my adult life. I taught myself to hold it in as a kid, like real ladies do with farts. Dad said holding in farts was unhealthy. Never said anything about tears. Sniff. Sniff. Snotty nose-blow. Sniff. Sniff. Drip. Drip. It goes on and on. It feels horrible and it feels good. The dog turns and swiftly licks my cheek a couple of times before settling down on the floor beneath me.

'I wish, I wish. I …' Self-pity billows in my chest, anger simmers in ears, sadness roils in my gut. What did I wish? To leave Charlie? A few years ago my friend Britt had given me one of those indispensable maxims to live by. When she was sick of her husband and mooted divorce, her mother always said, 'Honey! No point.' It works a lot better said with gusto and an American accent. 'You're just gonna be swapping one asshole for another.' We love to chorus this to each other. At times like this, it has given me real solace.

Did I wish not to be with this specific guy who put tomatoes in the fridge and liked going to bed early? Or did I want to be free of a dependence on men entirely so that I didn't have to compromise? I let the snot and saltwater flow. Oh poor me— 'Oh! Ooh. Ah! A flea!' The little bugger is cruising through the fur on the dog's side with the entitled arrogance of a Saudi prince burning up his Lambo on the Knightsbridge streets at 3 a.m. 'You fucker.' I pincer my fingernails and go in for the kill. And another. I get off the step and down on my haunches and rummage in primate ecstasy. The comb, get the comb! I lurch to the cupboard in the bathroom where we keep the dog's grooming kit. After a protracted flea-killing spree I realise I don't want to be unhappy any more.

That miserable bastard upstairs, so flawed, so grumpy, so selfish, so ... how dare he; especially with me being so perfect and all I loathe him right now, but Charlie and I are bonded, not by kids, or marriage, but by a dog, one currently with fleas – not to mention the little matter of a cash black hole also known as a mortgage. When, on and off, the love comes back, we'll be bonded by that too.

I get into bed, thinking how reassuring it is to feel the heaviness of the hairy lump at my feet. I reach down and, through a mixture of coaxing and dragging, get his 21 kilos up the bed and lie spooning him and stroking his silky chest with my face snuggled into the warm biscuity fur at the back of his neck. He lets out a happy puff of air. 'Mmmn.'

'You OK?' I ask Charlie.

There are three possible answers to this: 'Urgh, fucking hell, I'm going to sleep downstairs,' accompanied by a thundering flounce out of the bedroom, that's one. Then there's a sharp, irritated 'Mneurgh,' two.

I get an 'Mmmmnummmnumnumb.'

That's a yes. That's good. That's animal happiness.

Training your dog is an important part of bonding, so we do the odd ten minutes. I teach him paw. Lie down. Stay.

He's iffy on stay. One morning I see a tall gentleman wearing a Barbour and elephant cords training his two gun dogs by the Round Pond in Kensington Gardens. They stay even when he turns his back and walks away a considerable distance. He can make one stay while the other fetches. He's like an air traffic controller of black Labradors. The low morning sun has just burst through the legs of *Physical Energy*, the statue of a man on a rearing horse, which Wolfy is busying himself pissing on while I watch this posh chap and his hypervigilant Labs.

Rummaging in my pocket, I find a few lint-encrusted bits of kibble, or Woof nuts as Charlie and I call them. Wolfy too, I think, thrilled with determination, will acquire this impressive skill and all the people in the park will wonder at my obedient clever animal.

'Stay!' He sits alert and still for a moment, but within a second or two he has discovered an itch. It is all-consuming. His leg is violently attacking the itch at his side and his whole body is engaged in the action. Itch scratched, he immediately bounds forward towards me, thoughts of stay long gone.

I try again.

And again.

Even without the scratching, the maximum distance I can move before he bounds towards me is about six metres. I imagine the six metres between us is a road and flinch at the thought of him plunging through traffic despite my confident 'Stay!' command.

After about eight attempts I give up and command him to go 'Down!', where I rub his tummy for a bit until his tickle leg starts cycling in reflexive response. Then we just sit. I wonder if people walk past and think, look at that gorgeous dog with that cool-looking woman. There's a patch of black on the roof of his pink panting mouth, symmetrical and abstract like a Rorschach ink blot. Wolfy, you're amazing.

We walk on, following the edge of the Long Water, which becomes the Serpentine.

He stops to drink from the water when we reach Hyde Park, at the bank opposite the Henry Moore sculpture while I crouch, waiting.

It's still early. Perhaps I'll go for a swim.

We amble on under the Serpentine Bridge, where the poet Shelley's pregnant wife, Harriet Westbrook, jumped to her death 200 years ago. Two weeks later Shelley married the daughter of Mary Wollstonecraft, the woman credited with being the first published feminist. Whenever I swim in the Serpentine, I always think of Harriet; picture her standing there in her long dress. She would have been miserable.

If only human relationships were as easy as the ones we have with animals.

At first when I brought Wolfy to the Serpentine he would howl and bark as he sat on the pontoon over the lake watching me swim two short laps. A couple of months on, we have found a little routine.

'OK Woofs, you STAY. Stay!' I say as I drop into the water. As I swim off I turn on my back and look at him and hold up my hand and say in a low voice, 'You stay!'

Thus instructed, he sits on the pontoon and watches me swim off. I look back every few minutes and he's sat there still, watching – or occasionally wandering off to find a friendly Serpentine club member to stroke him, but still staying nearby. It's not warm enough for him today, but in hot weather he'll potter off to the shallows, enter the water and keep trying to spot me. He'll wade around drinking the murky black water and watching. Sometimes, he plops his bum in to cool.

However ludicrous my attempts to ape the gun-dog chap training his black Labs in Kensington Gardens, Wolfy is trained fine enough for our purposes. We don't go shooting snipe or woodcock. I just want to go for a swim sometimes. After 15 minutes he's asking where I am in a thin, howl that travels just enough for me to hear it the water. He's not distressed, he's ready for me to come back now and I do. I swim back and when he sees me he runs excitedly to the exit ramp and paddles in up to the point where his deep ribs touch the water. He's got a spiky wet patch of fur between his ears where the swimmers leaving the water have put their hands out for a soggy-pawed scruffle of his head.

Once I've hauled myself out he springs off his four paws like a lamb, bucking his rear end in excitement. Barefoot and in my swimming costume, I run alongside him the length of the tarmac beside the lido, 100 metres of dodging huge heaps of waterfowl shite and him leaping in circles and doing loony runs up the bank onto the grass before he shoots back to jump on two kangaroo back legs until he is level with my eyes.

'Welcome back. It's so good to see you!'

'You too.'

We both sit in the sun and look out over the water. I close my eyes, breathing sunlight and morning through my pores. Wolfy lies under the bench and rests his chin on his crossed paws. This is happiness. This is it.

Today, many very rich people move among us in Notting Hill. Of them there is a breed – the rich man's wife – and they do a lot of Pilates, hire personal trainers, get regular blow-dries and in August they leave en masse for the Mediterranean for at least a month. We normals get to watch this on Instagram. I know a few of them, and I am an occasional visitor to their world. Sometimes, Wolfy comes with me.

Meet Claudia.

Clauds lives 'up on the hill' on the edge of the W11 postcode closest to Notting Hill Gate. She tells me that one of her sons is nagging her to get a dog. She says she doesn't like dogs personally – 'can't see the point of them' – but that her son is beginning to wear her down. I suggest he comes and picks up poo on a walk with me; perhaps that will put him off. I collect Alfie from the big house on the hill and we drive back down to where Charlie and I live in Notting Dale, which, as the name would suggest, is very much *not* the hill. En route to the Scrubs I point out a few famous people's houses. David Cameron and Marcus Mumford he's heard of, less so Michael Gove and Damon Albarn.

The Dale is where I live, I say, gesturing towards our back door that is also our front door, and this, I say as we drive on down Treadgold Street, is where the poor people live. Granted, it's not as if it was Victorian London, when the whole area was a fetid and disease-ridden slum, but I say 'poor' to emphasise the privilege that he clearly takes for granted.

'Have you read any Dickens?'

He mumbles something about school and the GCSE syllabus.

'Dickens wrote about London in the nineteenth century, when it was poor, like *poor*, poor. Third world poor. People lived crammed into filthy slums that simply defy understanding today unless you've been to some of the sadder places in Africa. Charles Dickens is more interesting if you read it like documentary rather than homework.'

I know why I'm using the word poor. I know a rather regal yoga teacher who lives on the Lancaster West Estate. Poor isn't really an accurate descriptor of many people living there. I'm just being a snide wanker. Alfie looks silently out of the window with curiosity. The person I am really talking to is his mother.

'Where is my house?' he asks, confused.

'It's about three streets up there.'

The streets where his parents live have no covered Muslim ladies on them, no black people. It's as homogenous up there as it is not down here in the Dale. There is no pavement traffic there aside from the odd builder or swishy-ponytailed girl walking with a yoga mat. Their street has a little car with a man and an Alsatian in it, which patrols the streets at night. It's different up on the hill.

'You know, dogs are a big responsibility Alfie. They rely on you for everything, they need to be walked, fed, training is a chore and it takes time. A lot of people think dogs are like toys but they have a soul like humans, they deserve a good life. Your parents don't really want a dog, do they?'

'No, Mum says she's too busy but that if I promise to look after it, then "maybe".'

I take my killjoy responsibilities very seriously. 'You have to pick up all their poo if you're in London. *All the poo.* That could be eight hundred poos a year if you include a busy day. When you can't be bothered to do all this stuff, or when you're at school, who would look after the dog, Alfie?'

'Mum says Ernie will care for him.' Ernie is their housekeeper Perla's boyfriend, and works as their chauffeur and handyman. 'Ernie says he loves dogs. Ernie says he is brilliant with dogs.'

An ability to delegate domestic tasks is one of the reasons the rich stay rich. They have time to ensure they remain rich and thin and pretty and socially connected. They live longer because they don't have to pick up underpants, socks or dog shit.

Man, I would love to delegate all that stuff, all the administrative gumpf, like bill-paying and permit-buying, all the blow-drying of hair, and the maintenance of fitness. I don't even like washing my own face. I'm well up for delegating all the boring stuff. But the delegation of loving and caring for a dog seems to me more like a sacrifice than a godsend. 'I don't understand why people have dogs if they don't want to spend time with them.'

Alfie isn't into walking and he drags along behind me in a teenaged torpor. After the brief flurry of chat in the car, extracting conversation is hard work and I am starting to resent the imposition of this privileged child on my precious Saturday afternoon dog walk. He does not pick up any shit because the dog extrudes his choco gifts miles off in the long grass and sometimes you gotta let these things go, though it rather negates my assertion about picking up *all the poo*.

When we get back to the big white house on the hill his baby sister greets the dog and scurries off with her little hand round his collar, scolding, petting and mauling in quick succession. 'Give me his lead, I am going to take him for a walk in the garden.' She instructs me to do her bidding in the tyrannical way of the four-year-old.

I hand her the lead. Everyone talks about how sweet it is and gets their phones out, the angelic, delicate little blond girl in the designer dress dragging my big shaggy dog along by his neck. This is what cockerpoos were bred for, this is what Wiggles was designed for, not my mellow, regal hound. The child performs for the camera, alive to the attention and ranks of iPhones pointing at her. 'Hey, don't pull hard,' I say. 'How would you like it if someone dragged you along like that round your neck?'

The little girl is shocked. She stares at me for a heartbeat and then starts wailing, the tears squirting sideways from her gorgeous saucer eyes. Mummy runs to her. 'Sorry Clauds,' I say. 'She was being a bit rough.'

Claudia concentrates on equanimity, she is polished and educated, though not so much that she threatens her husband's intellect, she is the consummate hostess. She is never rude. She is always poised, with fragrant, glossy, bouncy brown hair that seems to give off a golden iridescence under her home's subtle and flattering uplighting. She is what men dream of, I know they do, however much they protest they like tough women, weathered women, feisty women, Claudia is the perfect wife. Her protective maternal instinct is clearly at odds with me scolding her child but her charm and manners override that and she reassures her daughter who recovers and returns to Wolfy and is stroking him briskly back and forth on his fur. I try to keep a steady gentleness in my voice this time.

'Can you stroke him like this?' I ask in a 'let's play' kind of way, forcedly cheerful like a kids' TV presenter. I run my hand steadily in one direction along his back.

'Ze dog is just ze dog,' says a German man, younger than me, but with that ageing conservative dress of Euro money. He is wearing a white cashmere polo neck and a blue blazer and is standing by the wall of glass that is magnificent and functionally Claudia's back door (she also has a front door, a basement entrance and a side door; if you have a ladder, the large balcony outside the bedroom also has a wide concertina door into the house). Ze German is holding a glass of red wine and looking, very much, down upon me. 'You pay too much attention to the dog, it is not good for the dog. The dog is the servant of man, man is not the servant of the animal.

'People are far too sentimental about animals, and especially the dogs and horses. If you would eat a pig, then you should be prepared to eat a dog, they are of a similar intelligence after all.'

'Sorry, I am not clear why you are saying this to me. Clearly I have no intention of eating my dog. I love my dog.'

'We noticed,' he says. 'Very sweet.'

Claudia comes over. 'Ah, you have met Gunther,' she says, 'our in-house controversialist.' She pulls a face, but still looks exquisite. 'Is that even a word?'

He's an old friend of her husband Jim's apparently, 'from Cambridge. 'Rich List,' she mumbles through a cheeky smile, for my ears only. Oh of course you are, you patronising cunt, I think. 'Hello.' I beam a warm smile and move to shake his hand as he comes in for a two-cheek continental air-kiss. Awkward.

'Und who is this guardian of the species *canis*?' He snorts, not rudely, more flirtatiously, but still very patronising.

'Oh I'm so sorry. This is Kate and she is staying for dinner, aren't you?'

I hadn't been invited and I don't want to stay; I'm dressed for a dog walk in old sneakers and cut-off shorts. Clauds had answered the door in Altuzarra pool platforms and an Isabel Marant playsuit; the legs are worked on and smooth, her hair is salon fresh and expertly loose and undone and she smells so compelling and fragrant. I feel scruffy, hairy and heavy compared to all the honed females here.

I can feel my own snobbery setting in, driven by a complicated combination of simple envy and a compensatory British ability to feel absolute disgust at ostentatious displays of wealth.

Speaking of which, Jim rattles a bottle of white burgundy in its ice bucket. 'Corton-Charlemagne, Katie ...?' I let the Katie go, given I plan to go hard on his alcohol; he pulls out a green bottle with a yellowing label wrapped at the neck in a white napkin. 'Or there's a Côte-Rôtie, or' – he cranes his neck at another ice bucket – 'Is there some Dom open?'

The wine whore in me is desperate to stay and guzzle all the wines I can't afford, as is the nosy parker who wants to ogle their life; the rest of me wants to leave, as does the dog, now sleeping with one eye open as far under the table as possible away from small people and Gunthers. I call Charlie and see if he has plans. 'Do what you want,' he says grumpily. 'I'm going to bed.'

That settles it.

We're staying, Woofs. I send him a telepathic message. He senses this and on cue slinks from under the table and into one of the many deserted reception rooms around us on the hunt for a place to bed in for a few hours. That'll do. He hops on the grey leather centrepiece sofa. Much more comfy. He starts to go about the bum-licking, toenail-chewing rigmarole of settling himself.

Gunther moves from the correct treatment of dogs to the winnings of female tennis stars. A decibel or two above the rest of us, he polemicises, 'It's entirely correct they should be paid less. Their matches attract a smaller audience. It's simple supply and demand. What have all you feminists got to say about that?' He beams. 'Eh?'

It's an actual challenge, not just blowhard rhetoric, and I so desperately want to argue with him, but I only want to argue if I can win. I've got into spats with too many of these characters before who are clever and often have photographic memories and a drilled-in logic and skill for bullying debate, learned at the schools where they also learned Latin and to recite huge tracts of Romantic poetry.

No one rises to the challenge because among the finance tribes supply, demand and the survival of the fittest are the guiding principle. If I were to talk about the male preference for competition and battle steering the world we live in, I'd be laughed off as a Trot. To these men, feminism is a hobby for the ladies. There's not an ally in the house. All the creativity here is funded by capitalism in its rawest expression: the money markets. For these guys and girls, without money there is nothing. Nyet.

A new couple have joined us for Claudia's simple 'kitchen supper' for 12. The wife is wearing a formal A-line dress with diamanté-buckled Manolo Blahnik mid-heel pumps. She is trying not to stare at my seedy old Green Flash with the backs trodden down. I can feel her wondering if someone like me is here, then why is she? To be honest, who really knows what she's thinking? Imagining what she's thinking is a form of anthropomorphism, like when I project emotions onto Wolfy. Her face, stilled by Botox and fillers, is blank save a permanent expression of terror and hauteur. I feel an irrational dislike of her.

The wine glass is glued to my lip. I might be drinking a fine £100 wine and the welcome might be warm but I feel bloody awkward, like an animal, circling, unsure and wary. Despite the invitation being for a relaxed kitchen supper, it's a formal kind of casual in here.

This sofa Wolfy's parked on, casually licking his bum, is sculptural and oozes across the room like a car-sized piece of molten lead: a chesterfield by way of Dalí. The dog licks his willy a couple of lacklustre times and coils himself defensively tight like a Cumberland sausage, a safe shape for the business of sleep in a strange place.

Gunther is holding forth and flirting with an American woman who describes herself as an art consultant. I've met her several times. She is my age but with a freakishly incredible body, like a *Playboy* model. I assume it's the combined effect of her fitness and healthy eating regime and the efforts of a squadron of top cosmetic medics. She's something to behold, perfect in every way, I stare at her like I stare at the long-limbed girls on Instagram. Some women are so magnificent to look at, it's like they come from another planet. I almost fancy her. It's just her face – it's so surgically altered that it has lost all movement and character. In all this perfection, the face is screaming, 'I hate myself! I am vulnerable'. I have never heard her utter a hint of weakness, insecurity, fear; she doesn't moan or bitch, she is bright and positive, kind and supportive. But that face makes me want to cry.

Claudia comes through waving the heavenly white burgundy, her unusually full pouty lips pulled back over her perfect teeth. What a delightful and friendly smile. 'More?' These people have such good wine. I love it here. The caramelo pleasure of this 20-year-old nectar is palling just the merest touch.

'Thank you Clauds, but I think I might move to red.' I help myself to a glass of wine that tastes of ripe blackcurrants and pencils. God, it's so epic. I turn to Jim, smile and wave and point at the glass with a thumbs-up and my own substandard wonky smile. I must go and kiss his arse later, I think. I want to be invited back more often.

The sight of the dog on the sofa wipes the smile off Clauds's gorgeous face. 'Oh, no, he needs to get off there.'

'Of course, sorry, come on, off there. Off!' I try to drag the dog off without his claws damaging the upholstery. I shower her in frantic apologies. 'What a beautiful, er, a sofa, is it?' I say. 'Who is it by?'

I am reassured that it is from the Carpenters Workshop Gallery, which, she does not add, is like a very expensive Furniture World for people who can't bear for anything in their house not to be art. It's collectible, apparently, and (I google later) prices *start* at £100,000.

The dog slinks off, sniffing round the edge of the room, without a Woof Bed, he is trying to find his safe place.

'This is interesting.' I motion to a lump of clay glazed pink and mounted on a stick that I assume her youngest daughter, the dog-mauling cutie, has made at her elite society kindergarten. 'That's feminist,' she says and her voice drops an octave. 'It's a pretty great piece isn't it. It's her response to the history of birth control, she's drawn inspiration from the ambiguous heroism of the female back-street abortionists and of the cultural shame in women's bodies.'

'Oh. Right. Mmm.' I nod, with an affected ponderous curiosity.

The art consultant woman joins in with an even greater enthusiasm on the feminism front than Clauds. She stands next to me, I can smell the delicious chemical fragrance of her expensive blow-dry. I become hyperaware of my thick upper arms. The skin on her arms is tightly wrapped round her muscles rather than loosely draped like mine. Forget this glazed feminist knob thingumbybob, this woman is a work of art.

'... Everything she does plays with female ideas of remembered identity, the vagina and the clitoris, of course.' She laughs with delight, at saying the word clitoris and joy in the art. 'She's all about domestic utilitarian materials that she elevates to high art. A great woman.'

'Oh she really is, you'd love her Kate,' adds Clauds. I wish I'd had a leg wax, a trust fund and a blow-dry. 'She's a riot. A ball. A great girl. You must meet her next time she's over. We are great patrons of her work.'

With my head cocked to one side I act out a silent moment of enjoyable intellectual contemplation, hopefully. I'm fucking bored of the art already.

I take another big sip of the art in my glass and appreciate that, the structure, the dignity and as another dose of alcohol kicks in some more of my bitterness and envy fade. 'And this piece, is it by the same artist?' I turn towards a papier mâché puppet princess with a grotesque face, which is a naive idea of beauty with huge eyelashes and lips, slashes of dark pink on the cheeks and a tiny little button of a nose. 'It's a such a simple comment on the beauty standards imposed on young girls, yet it really works, such a direct impact.' I'm getting into the swing of it now.

'Rose made that,' – the daughter – 'sweet, isn't it.' I should have seen that one coming and now I feel a proper tit. Through the French windows I can see Wolfy perusing the herbaceous border, sniffing out the perfect spot to squirt a jet of his most precious asset, burnt gold or rather his more marker-pen-yellow urine. 'Oops, better stop that.' Too late, the rear leg's up.

'Is the dog peeing?' Claudia asks, her mild consternation only just masked by finishing-school equanimity. 'Oh Christ, no.' She leaps forward, politesse forgotten. 'If he goes there every lapdog in Knightsbridge will be pissing all over my garden on Monday. I've got a Kalita trunk show, those silky kaftan girls don't go anywhere without their yappy bloody rats.'

I apologise profusely again and ask Perla the hovering housekeeper for a jug of water. 'Sparkling or still?'

'Tap's fine.'

'Oh don't worry about it. Perla, can you wash the area down please?' Clauds says, taking my arm. 'Come back and talk to us.'

A new female has entered the fray. She is, I don't know, the wife of some other guy with loadsamoney I assume. 'It's a big plot of land, eighty acres, but the house is too big. I told him, "please, babe, let's just make this one cosy,"' she is saying, 'but he goes and gets the architect to put a nightclub in. It's just too big, and he knows it …'

The problems of the 0.001%.

'Kate's a writer,' says Clauds to the uptight woman in the Manolo pumps, who is glaring at me behind a whitened rictus smile.

'*Vogue*?' says Manolo.

'No, I did one story for them once and apparently the editor threw it out because I'm "too grubby".' I'm expecting some laughs at this but everyone makes a sad face like they feel sorry for me.

It doesn't surprise me when Manolo tells us some senior editor there is 'a dear friend'.

I'm heading out of the merry and squiffy phase of drunkenness and towards the uncensored and sloppy and make a mental note to contain myself. The guzzling of olives and breadsticks and chunks of very expensive Parmesan has not compensated for the lack so far of dinner. The 'grubby' anecdote was ill-judged, not one for this audience.

'When are you going to write a book?' says Clauds, brightly.

I start babbling about money, cringing as I do, because talking about money with this lot is a bit like talking about Christmas in Jeddah. They all love to talk about cutting back and not spending. But for them money problems mean not being able to hire a yacht for £200,000 a week; it's their husbands saying they need to stop bidding on so much stuff at charity auctions, or struggling to pay their annual £150,000 wine bill at Berry Brothers, which has functioned as a Majestic for the aristocracy since 1698 and the oligarchy since 1992.

'A lack of money has never stopped great art being made,' says the consultant.

I paw at the lace-like smashed glass of my phone. The Virginia Woolf quote. I have to find it. Here, here it is. Taking a leaf from Gunther's book, I raise the volume a touch: '"Intellectual freedom depends on material things. Poetry depends upon intellectual freedom. And women have always been poor, not for two hundred years merely, but from the beginning of time. Women have had less intellectual freedom than the sons of Athenian slaves. Women, then, have not had a dog's chance of writing poetry."'

'Using money as an excuse points to an underlying fear of not being enough.' The woman in the Manolo pumps fixes me with mean flinty eyes that burn from the mask of her face.

'That's as may be.' There's a hovering silence. I can't remember her name. I really do not like her. 'But I still think Virginia is right.'

There's a quiet as we all behave nicely like ladies should and draw a line under any controversy.

Manolo says, without moving a muscle on her face, 'Where we live in Chelsea, this dog worship thing is out of hand.' A nearly imperceptible laugh as she says, 'When will we see the first Betty Ford Treatment Center for Dog Addiction?'

Clauds ignores this crap attempt at a joke. I think she likes me more than her. I don't blame her.

'Why don't we have a little fundraiser round here one evening. You can write some of your book, and do a reading, and people can donate to you finishing it.'

'Erm, are you joking?' I mutter. She is not. 'You're very kind but I think probably there are more deserving causes than me. Another drink, anyone?'

Two of them are on neat vodka on the rocks, the slender woman's choice. Clauds is still on the Dom Perignon – 'so bloating but I just love the stuff.'

I move away in the direction of wine, and I hear Manolo say, 'Clauds dear, that came across a touch patronising.'

'I'm only trying to help,' she says. 'She's always talking about how poor she is.'

I cringe while mentally rubbing my hands in glee. Charlie will absolutely love the story of a benefit being thrown for me up on the hill. This one's gonna be a long runner. I circuit the rooms with the glass of Gevrey Chambertin stuck to my lips. No Wolfy. Where is he? I start to worry a bit and venture downstairs to the two-storey basement, where Ernie is standing in a black corridor lined with the family's sizeable collection of Tracey Emin neons. He is holding Wolfy tightly by the nose and shaking it side to side.

'What are you doing! Stop it. Stop!'

'He loves it.'

'Don't touch him.' I grab the dog's collar and take him away.

I go up to Alfie's bedroom and knock on the door. He is playing a computer game. 'Ernie is not good with dogs.' I tell him what happened and he says, without taking his eyes off the screen, 'Yes, I think he was just trying to make Mummy and Daddy happy.'

Wolfy jumps on the bed. He seems happier here. 'Can Wolfy stay here with me?' says Alfie.

'Yeah sure, I'll come and get him when I leave.'

I stand up and leave the room; 20 seconds later Wolfy is hurtling down the stairs after me.

When dinner is served none of the women eat anything, just pick at a few leaves on their plates. Clauds doesn't eat at all. Reassuringly, she is well on the way to being absolutely hammered.

After dinner Jim points to a huddle smoking Marlboros hungrily on the sofa in the garden. 'That lot are over there are doing *drugs*. Appalling. Ghastly stuff.' It's funny hearing it coming out of Jim's mouth. He's disapproving but clearly his priority is being patient with the huddle in the garden.

I wonder if the huddle is sniffing coke. Quite drunk now, I have about as much willpower as the dog with a treat on his nose. Which is to say, I walk towards the huddle and greet Gunther as if he is my dearest friend.

He put his arm around my shoulder as I looked sideways up at him. 'Got any?' I ask.

'No,' he says, 'but we want some.'

'Could you, I don't know, *sort it*?' he says, uncomfortable with the colloquial language. 'I'll pay for it. He's a big client that one'. He nods towards another in the huddle. 'I need to keep him happy. Thank God you pitched up. I knew you'd be in the loop.'

Tarik is a local drug dealer, who just happens to be Muslim. He wears a tidy beard but his moral compass is definitely not pointing towards Mecca. His main job is delivery driver. Evenings and weekends he sells a bit of gear on the side to supplement his income.

I was walking the well-trod coffee path up Blenheim Crescent one morning when I saw him cruise by in a flash motor. He normally drove a nondescript old banger. What was this silver C-Class Merc? I gave him a wave and, when he pulled over, popped my head through the passenger-side window. On the seat below me there was a Pomeranian and a chihuahua. On the seat behind, a massive beast with a square head, panting and looking out the window.

'What the fu—?' A Muslim, nunchaku-carrying wideboy with two Paris Hilton yappy rats in diamanté collars riding shotgun, and a bloody great slobbering beast in the back. 'Are these yours, Tarik?'

His wholesaler had gone down for a five stretch and now Tarik was caring for the animals because this Mr Big's girlfriend had no clue what looking after one dog required, let alone three. Turned out Tarik knew a lot about dogs. He spent so much time describing to me the special needs of the lapdog breeds: 'Their proper name's companion dog, innit, and they need to be close to people, you see, the companion breeds, all the time. You can't leave 'em too long, they'll be traumatised.' He moved on to the fighting breeds – 'They just need to know who's boss.' He reached back and scuffled the monster in the rear seat. 'You're a real softy, aren't you, Satan ... It's this one that's the dangerous dog.' He chuckled, tickling the black Pomeranian under its chin. 'Eh, Tyson, you little tosser.'

In exchange for his care and expertise, he got to use Big's car. Well, it was quite a tale and I thought I'd never get away. By the time I came up for air I had a crick in my lower back.

I punch in 'Dog Dealer' and Tarik's digits come up. I do the deal by Clauds's side door, the tradesman's entrance, by a cupboard containing row upon row of scented candles. In the house's past, I imagine it was for storing glasses.

Tarik and I hover there briefly to chat after Gunther has furnished the client with nosebag and directed him down to the depths of the wine cellar on the second basement floor, with instructions not to let the hosts or the staff see.

Tarik starts talking about dogs immediately. He's got this technique he uses for flushing his dogs' urinary tracts of any infection by getting them thirsty and then letting them gorge on a bowl of water with vitamin C powder in it. 'It's important to flush through their system every now and again.'

I'm not sure what to think about this. It's weird taking dog husbandry classes from a Muslim drug dealer.

'Tarik, you're a Muslim, you've got a beard, I thought you guys weren't allowed to touch dogs or something.'

'Nah, it's cool with dogs, it's only the nutters who think they're the devil an' that, but the thing is if you touch them when they're wet or if you touch their saliva then you know you got to wash your hands seven times after. It can get time-consuming with them three in the flat, innit' – he laughs – 'Washing me hands all day, aren't I.'

For the first time that night I laugh too, out loud.

'Thanks for the hook-up,' he says, and then mumbles, as he always does, something about needing to get out of the game.

I mumble something in return about cleaning up. He spends a few minutes talking to Wolfy, offering up lots of pats and lecturing me on Wolfy's beta personality, about how he's a real one-man dog and I need to make sure I never leave him with the wrong person. Wolfy leans into him. 'I can look after him if you like. If you ever need it. I understand dogs.'

'Sure, yes,' I say. 'Look, you couldn't give me a lift, could you, I'm too pissed to drive now.'

'Yeah no problem, mate.'

Charlie wakes up as I clatter up the stairs.

'And?'

'Bit pissed, didn't do any drugs.'

'Well done Foxy,' and he rolls over to sleep some more of his beloved sleep.

'What time are you getting up?'

I ask him this a few times more and eventually a muffled answer comes. 'Mnhix.'

Wolfy's claws come tic-tac up the steep wooden stairs a few minutes later. Up in the eaves of our little workman's cottage the room is hot and he's already panting. If he jumps on the bed tonight we will all roast. I ask him to stay in his basket by the bed and he pauses, sitting there in the dark.

'Stay Wolf. Stay.'

He collapses down in a tangle of legs and fur. I know he is looking up at me with his black marble eyes. We stare at each other in the dark for a while and then he lowers his head and closes his eyes, and so do I.

CHAPTER FOUR

If you want to be a Londoner you have to choose a point on the compass. I chose west nearly thirty years ago. I do east London, in small doses. South London? Where even is south London? And north London? Urgh. That place does my head in. 'Oh, the Heath, Highgate, Islington. Tony Blair, Jeremy Corbyn, home of liberal intelligentsia, and oh, *the schools*,' they say. Sod that.

The only good things about north London were all the friends who lived there, and of course Will, Steph and the kids. Otherwise, the air feels thin up there. You can have your great views from Parliament Hill, it's not for me. Too high, too highbrow. All those books and chin-stroking clever people, psychoanalysts, newspaper editors, and not nearly enough idiots being shallow tripping around in high heels or bragging about their trainers. I don't trust north London, it's weird.

Partly you have to choose your hood for practical reasons because London's so big it needs to be carved up into manageable chunks. Then you grow into your natural habitat.

I'm in north London tonight at a dinner for 40 people. It's Steph's birthday, and a noisy room above a well-known gastro-pub is choc-a-block with her Oxbridge chums and sundry people whose names are predicated with the unspeakably tiresome words 'multi-award-winning'. They are the sort of people who roll their eyeballs and groan, 'Sorry I'm late, darling. Had to go to another of those bloody drinks parties Number 10 are so keen on.' In fact, this is exactly what a senior staffer at the paper called

Rachel says to Steph while planting dramatic double mwahs on her cheeks. This woman, Rachel, has recently dropped me from a regular column on the paper. I'm so used to this merry-go-round I don't even hold it against her. Of course I'm not good enough. Goes without saying.

'Haw haw.' Rachel, stands back and spots me. 'It's the dog correspondent.' This one is clever, with clever parents, clever grandparents, clever kids, and clever clogs. Well connected, well educated and (need I bother to add) *of course* Oxbridge: a whale of a Melanie. The best thing about her is that she makes the other Melanie, the one I hate, look a bit thick. As I often do when confronted by women like this, I laugh nastily at myself, ha ha ha, yes, aren't I stupid, gone into retirement, going to start writing for *People's Friend*. Oh, it's closed. Well, I shall open a pet-grooming parlour, yes it's all over for me. Yes, I'm reporting live from dog poo park.

'So! Rachel! How are you?' I ask with all the whooping sincerity I can muster while pecking the air five inches away from either side of her incredibly confident cheeks.

'Very good,' she says in that urgently breezy cheerful way of people who do terribly well at everything.

She has recently been promoted and not to be friendly and interested would be a mistake. I need to appear confident and cleverish. I force an attitude of cool relaxation, although women like this make me feel like my socks are wired up to the National Grid. Women like this, more or less, run the bits of the media I regularly find myself working in.

'So good to see darling Steph.'

'Yes, so good.'

'Yes.'

'Well, must do the rounds and see the gang, got to be off soonish,' she says. 'Babysitter!' How could I forget, you've got five children as well as an amazing career and awards in your downstairs lav. 'Are you going to Melanie Oxbridge's book launch on Monday?'

'No, sadly not. I've got a deadline tomorrow – reviewing some dog food,' *ha ha ha ha ha ha*. 'I must get hold of Melanie's book though, I bet it's a cracking read.'

The birthday girl, Stephanie, my dear darling brilliant sexy sunny uber-capable sister-in-law, is another high-flying journalist and while I love her, I don't always like her. She's got a killer streak that a woman needs to succeed. I admire this in her. I envy it in her. But sometimes I wish she'd park it so that we can all be off duty, like when we're side by side sharing potato-peeling duties on Christmas Day or over a wheel of Stilton and port on New Year's Eve. She is sitting at the end of the table surrounded by a cabal of confident horrors she went to Oxford with. I make a joke of the awkward interaction with Rachel. 'Darling' – it's a 'darling' that actually translates as, 'I have little patience with this self-pitying crap' – 'Instead of constantly googling stuff about the dog why don't you look up Freud's narcissism of small differences. You may take some comfort in it. Have you considered that just maybe she was pleased to see you?'

Gaaargh! Hadn't thought of that. More wine, more wine. Is that my glass? Ah well, never mind. Glug. Ha ha. Isn't life wonderful. Aren't people so terrifying. Isn't it all such fun. Ha. Hello. Love that dress. How *are* you?

I spot a normal person, well not a normal person, a famous critic, but someone who might not make me feel inadequate just by, you know, breathing.

I flop down in the chair next to her with much melodramatic puffing and huffing. 'Looks like I've got myself a reputation.' I flail around trying to make her laugh, but she takes it all embarrassingly seriously.

'What for, Katie Coo? Have you been sleeping with horrid little men again?'

'No, no, no, still with Charlie. Dogs,' I say. 'I've just become so crazy about my dog everyone just thinks of me and thinks of dogs now.'

'Oh, how sad,' she says. 'That's not good at all. Why is everyone so obsessed by animals at the moment? There's always some cafe with owls or cats or dachshunds opening. It's infantile.'

'Because they have nowhere left to turn. Modern life, maybe just life, is too unforgiving. Dogs are loving and kind and funny, they restore your faith in love.'

'Why don't people have sex, or read books, or go out for dinner' – she sounds aghast – 'or have better friends?'

If Charlie and I managed to synchronise our schedules sufficiently to be in bed with minutes to spare and awake at the same time, then we did, occasionally, have sex. The dog barely raised a furry eyebrow. If it disturbed his rest, he'd jump down into number two bed, the Woof Bed, but most of the time he was asleep on the bed when we were at it. Like medieval people, we lived with our animals. That was us. The dog didn't care. And we certainly didn't.

'Animals make people happy.'

'What is this obsession with happiness. Where did it come from? We didn't grow up expecting to be happy. We didn't look to other people for solutions to all our problems. All one can expect from other people is common decency.'

'Dogs connect us to nature, something we have all lost, especially here in London.' She is older than me, twenty years or so. 'It's odd having to defend love so often. Why shouldn't I love my dog? You have three children, grandchildren ... Perhaps all it comes down to is humans need somewhere to channel the unconditional love usually reserved for children?'

I say this but I am thinking about Cecil's owner Sasha and the conversation in Kensington Gardens when we were watching the Life Guards' bottoms bouncing up and down in their saddles, when she'd said about her beloved 'Cessy', 'I think I love him more than the children.'

'I've heard that pugs were bred to satisfy the broody concubines in the imperial Chinese harems – you know, those big gooey eyes and cute faces were easy to pet and love. T.H.

White described his dog as a "reservoir for my love" back in the fifties when children weren't fetishised, or even seen, let alone heard, so this adoring of pets isn't just about us snowflakes today.'

She looks at me with a cynical cast. 'I understand they are loyal and trusting but …' She stops and looks frustrated. 'But they're animals, Kate. It's so wet,' she says, 'just dogs everywhere.' Her voice is warm and familiar but I know her well enough to feel the texture of disdain.

I kind of agree with her, but equally it's as though I am in a boat that is drifting away from her clever and cerebral human shore across a quiet lake to another place where people walk with dogs at their side, and the only sounds are twigs cracking underfoot, and the sniff and rustle of leaves being explored by curious wet noses. I like this place. I don't care if it's irrational.

The truth is that she is not a dog person and she isn't ever going to get it. It reminds me of the time I was in Tehran interviewing an architecture apparatchik at the Iranian Ministry of Roads and Urban Development. Foolishly I allowed the conversation to stray into religious debate and within minutes, no seconds, our fundamental and profound differences were apparent. Anything that had connected us in conversation was completely gone. It was black or white. And so it is with doggy people. You have the believers and the unbelievers.

I quietly pay my share of the bill and take a minicab back to west London. I was on the way to being sloshed anyway. As it is, the wine hand has just landed on cocaine o' clock.

As the cab hits the A40 at the bottom of Regent's Park I pull up Tim's number on my phone. I sit staring at it all the way down Marylebone Road. I want to get blitzed, really a lot. I want to switch off the boring persistence of sketchy old me and switch on some intensely nice feelings and not a lot of thinking. Nothing, really, has gone wrong tonight. I am just at that perfect pitch of indignant, insecure, bored and slightly pissed which often leads me to Timbo's front door.

The cab cruises over the Westway up above Edgware Road, blazing with midnight life and smoky with sweet-scented hookahs. I put my phone away. I don't want to get high. I think of Wolfy's golden haunches swaying and shining in the moonlight as I lead him down the alley for his bedtime wee. I think about the morning walk. It makes pushing on for the rest of the journey home that little bit more urgent and several hours (OK, ten minutes) later I'm back home in the arms of west London.

His claws descend the steep wooden lethal-to-dogs stairs with the musical, delicate skittling as I'm ascending the noisy metal ones with my oafish human steps. We meet in the middle, at the door. His tail wags wildly side to side and he breathes hotly on me from a huge wide-jawed smile. He makes little involuntary squeaks and I know how he is feeling because it is thrilling to see him too.

'Hey Woof.' I lavish scruffles and strokes around his ears until he's distracted by an urgent need to scratch an itch on the left side of his ribcage.

I pour a glass of wine. I take the box of cigarettes out of the medicine drawer directly under the kettle, where I keep all drugs, prescribed or otherwise.

We set off for the leisure centre, for a little late-night party for me plus one. The air sits around me with a reassuring familiarity helped by the sweet decay of early autumn. On a concrete bench, I set up camp and lie with my head and feet resting on the arms either end. I puff my cigarette and stare up at the tower, crooking my neck down hard to get prone sips of the wine, a slightly stale red Rully – brambly, dry, a bit of something smoky like hot compost in there. Lying under the tower, I wonder why people are still up at after midnight. Telly? Booze? A new baby? Is it Ramadan? I have no idea. Cocaine? Computer games? A deadline? Or just profligate with the electricity and didn't switch the lights off before bed? A good book, perhaps?

The cigarette makes my head spin. The blood rushes in my ears like the breaking surf. I close my eyes and smile. This is as high as I'm gonna get.

'You having a party, Wolfy's mum?' It's the fat beagle Lewis Hamilton II's owner, out too for their evening pee-poo-potter. Wolfy and Lewis do some chilled-out neighbourly bum-sniffing.

'I'm just celebrating being home,' I say. 'I had to go to a party in north London tonight.' I give a mock shudder.

He breathes in sharply as if taking an evening constitutional along the pier at Great Yarmouth. 'Nothing beats the Ladbroke Grove air.'

I'm wondering out loud as politely as I can, given the drink and the subject matter, how Lewis got so tubby when a Muslim family walk past, dad, mum, two kids clustered round a pushchair with a cool-box in it. So late, why are they still up, I tut like an old biddy to Lewis's owner, who says, brightly, 'Eid, innit?' and goes bounding over and claps the guy on his arm: 'Mate!' And raises his arm in greeting to his heavily veiled wife: 'Rania!' The wife says back loudly in a broad west London accent full of laughter, 'Orroight, Nick mate. How you doing?'

'I'm alright darlin',' he says, with ebullience. 'Oy, Lewis get away from her. My dog can't touch you can he, with you all in black.'

Aah, I think to myself, observing the culturally sensitive comment, my invisible cloak of *Guardian*-reading sensitivity rippling in smug approval.

'You're all right Nick. I'm fine with the dog. Hiya Lewis.'

'Darlin', we don't want you getting all covered in his white dog hairs, they're a nightmare to get out of black.'

They have an in-joke.

Another round of mates and darlin's and little waves from the small girls and they head off down the path towards the Lancaster West Estate. My invisible cloak of *Guardian*-reading wokeness crumbles to dust on the paving stones.

I wasn't expecting that. I feel a bit stupid.

There is a magic moment between physical waking and full consciousness when the day could bring anything. In this moment I used to enjoy a precious instant thinking I was not hungover before the remembrance of drinks past kicked in along with the accompanying full-body headache. In this moment sometimes I don't know who I am, where I am, why I am. It is fleeting freedom before reality kicks in.

Lately, the situation is reversed. I wake and assume a hangover is imminent and cringe, only to wake fully clean and serene. I have energy. I am alive. And there is Wolfy, my saviour, all 22 kilos of him now – he's put on a couple of pounds – hogging the bottom of the bed like a large furry friendly crocodile.

This morning I am woken up by Charlie singing a song: 'It's just a Wolfy furry bottom snake flying about, flying about, flying about. It's just a Wolfy furry bottom snake, so don't be afraid [hits high note, badly], it doesn't want to bite you, it just wants to play ...'

He is standing at the foot of the bed and the singing is making Wolfy's tail rear up in happiness, while the rest of his body stays slumberous and still. Charlie waves his hands from side to side. 'Come on Katie, sing along!' He continues the song, with lyrics and melody declining to a point of tuneless nonsense.

I sit up smiling and feel the laughter dancing in my chest. I add my descant to Charlie's appalling melody. 'If you're down and feeling blue, the Wolfy furry bottom snake will whistle a smelly tune for you-hoo.' I rush out the words in an attempt to make them scan.

However shit *Wolfy! The Musical* might be, it is a tonic for our relationship.

And do you have any shared hobbies, Charlie and Kate?

Well dear, we enjoy our sulking, don't we?

Yes dear, that, and singing songs about our dog Wolfy.

Charlie thinks Wolfy speaks like Ray Winstone in *Sexy Beast* and he gives voice to the dog's thoughts: 'I'm not playing this game you twat, it's my tail, you loser, it's not a fucking 'hairy bum snake" or whatever you call it, poof. It sounds like a disturbing sex game. Go on, fuck off. Go and get me some biscuits. Go away. Leave me with her. She's better than you.'

Our dog just lies there, the bottom snake coiled under his furry bottom. Charlie says in a melodramatic, fey, kids'-TV-presenter voice, 'Oh no, look, children, the Wolfy furry bottom snake has died.'

Then in a normal voice, 'Hello Woofs. You ready for a walk?'

The tail rises up off the duvet eight inches and lands back down again with a whumpf of approval. 'The furry bottom snake, it lives. It lives.' I'm laughing out loud now. Charlie goes skipping round the bedroom. 'All hail the furry bottom snake.'

So starts Sunday morning; no hangover and a song in my heart, albeit a rubbish one.

A natural drift towards doggy folk had happened almost immediately I got the dog, but by the autumn it was entrenched behaviour.

I'd started looking after Castor when Keith went away on business; instead of spending his week boarding at doggy daycare, he came to live with Charlie, Wolfy and me. Once the international fashion weeks started in mid-September, silky whippety Castor the lurcher became our long-term house guest.

When Castor wanted some emotional or comforting response from a human he also talked, like Wolfy, except Castor mostly just hooted like a timid and polite owl. He slept down-stairs on the armchair, but come morning he'd clatter up the death-to-lurchers staircase and stand waiting for some love with his long thin nose resting on the mattress beside mine, hooting softly and staring at me with one blue eye while the other roamed to the left.

In the past I'd often be away working in Paris, Milan or New York myself but life had changed; now I cared for the dog fashion week was left behind. It was interesting testing my two-dog mettle, and Keith paid me in bottles of Pauillac, the greatest of Bordeaux, which helped. Wine aside, I felt a strong and worrying sense of my old life slipping away, of my relevance waning, and sometimes when Keith came to collect his dog if he was home for a few short days, I felt self-conscious about my dog-walking clothes and frizzy, wind-ravaged hair.

At first the habit of wearing flat worker boots was confined to walking the dog, then I started wearing them all the time. I was working them into my look for meetings, or consultancy sessions. Sometimes I went out in them. Eventually I just wore them all the time. I'd open the wardrobe and look at the rows of shoes, the thick-soled white ones bought straight off the catwalk, the flash trainers, retro sneakers, the flat Greek sandals, the cowboy boots, the Argentinean polo boots, the countless black ankle boots of every height, the over-the-knee Gareth Pugh ones that never did fit, the loafers, brogues, platforms, the three pairs of Terry de Havilland wedges, the platform wedges, the strappy sandal, the 'shoe boot' – and not to forget the clutter of daft hurting stiletto heels. All were covered in dust. Every day I looked at them for a moment – shall I? Nah – and turned back to the stout brown leather Blundstone farmhand's boots. 'They look all right, don't they?' I'd shrug to Charlie on my way out the door.

'Yeah, fine,' he shrugged back.

That'd do.

To paraphrase Quentin Crisp, 'Style is knowing who you are and being it like mad,' Well, those boots pretty much confirmed who I thought I was. (And I was certainly being it like mad.)

Sometimes I'd watch Charlie walk off with Wolfy beside him on the lead, and the dog's elegant prance, his springing step and thoroughbred horse's legs looked just about the coolest thing on this planet. People in my neighbourhood, be they rich or not so rich, or not rich in the slightest, were unusually concerned with a specific sort of strong but unforced style. West London style requires insouciance. It must not look like an effort has been made. Street swagger trumped fashion to the point where actual fashionability, as in wearing the latest season-to-season fashions, was actually looked down on. Being pretty wealthy, yet wearing a lot of second-hand clothes or well-made old clothes – that was considered something of merit among the more confident rich, while being 'the sort of person who buys entire looks off the internet' is an actual insult to hurl around. I would have liked to be able to buy entire looks off the internet if I am honest. But I could not, unless I went to Top Shop, which I didn't. We choose old clothes over cheap clothes in west London, where the market had treasure beyond most people's charity shop dreams. Here on Ladbroke Grove and Portobello Road, where street swagger required owning your personal style, the dog was definitely 'a look'.

Not that my dog-walking sass was a look that travelled terribly well.

'Darling, so great to see you've updated your look at last,' said Steph when I walked in one Sunday lunchtime wearing something other than baggy jeans and Blundstone boots. Was I becoming one of those women on the makeover shows, requiring an intervention in which my family talk about how frumpy I had become?

'Aunty Kate always wears men's clothes and her hair is like a bird's nest,' my nephew would say to camera and everyone would think it was sweet and hilarious. Some naff TV personality would come and bullyingly turn me into a desperate Boden clone. 'We need to chuck out the shapeless jeans and the green jumpers and get you into something slim-fitting, you've got quite good arms' – dot dot dot, there's a parenthesis: 'for a woman your age.'

The dog isn't with me when the handsome bloke looks at me repeatedly across the bar of the Cow. I look around, dramatically, left and right behind me. He can't possibly be looking at me. I've become so used to men going for younger women that I can't quite believe these ardent stares are meant for me. He's practically winking.

'That's guy's looking at you,' says Charlie. 'He's very good-looking. Do you know him?'

I saunter over there and strike up some dazzlingly imaginative chat. 'I know you from somewhere.'

'Yes, it's Mark.' Nope, still no idea but he's got a beautiful straight nose and curled full lips like a Greek statue so we amble towards a chat general enough not to require the slightest knowledge of who the other is.

'I've never seen you in here before—' There's a crashing sound as something drops into place in my brain. It's Otto's owner, the grey whippet we walk with on Baby Scrubs, a smaller public park over the road from what was now popularly known as Big Scrubs. Now I am feeling cocky. I could rinse some kudos out of this. I turn to the guy, make good eye contact. We talk what must look like intently from across the bar. I'm leaning here, smiling and gesticulating, talking about dogs. Living the lie that this man might find me sexually interesting. Not that Charlie knows that.

Otto's owner, this Mark, is telling me, 'Lurchers, they're starter dogs really. They're easy compared to a breed like a beagle. They train easily and sleep all the time.' He starts telling me about his friend with a Hungarian vizsla. 'Starter dog?' I am crestfallen. I pretend to sparkle for a few minutes more and then go back to my boyfriend.

I love Charlie for many reasons at the moment. One of them is he never gets jealous. 'So, who was he? You seemed to be getting on very well.'

With a cocky wobble of the head, I close my eyes. 'Yeah, we were talking about …' I pause for a moment, let the belief that we were having a riveting chat abide a few seconds longer, and then admit, '… dogs actually.'

It is an inescapable fact that large tracts of my life and conversation are entirely dog led now. Notting Hill has morphed into a landscape of dogs and dog owners, of people who like dogs, and would like to talk about it. In among these folk there are some other folk but they have nothing to do with dogs so they are about as relevant as lamp posts – less so, in fact, as Wolfy won't relieve himself on a human. This canine filter is not as excluding as it seems. I guesstimate west London's dog-loving population is a majority.

En route to the Scrubs one day I spotted Tarik walking down Latimer Road with Tyson, Satan and the other little dog, Sugar.

'Wanna lift?' I stopped and shouted through the window.

'Yeah,' he said, holding up the three leads in mock despair. The three panting beasts crammed in the back with Wolfy, who moved out of the way and looked determinedly out of the window, like he could will them out of his dog bed on wheels by pretending they weren't there. Somehow the giant Satan settled in without crushing the other two.

I'd see Tarik sometimes being dragged to the coffee shop; he might as well have been waterskiing on the pavement, the monster dog dragging him along, Tarik's strong arms fully extended. When we approached him coming the other way Wolfy would swiftly steer me away from the dog, not out of fear, but out of the pure inconvenience of being 'greeted' by Satan. Any detour from the monster dog suited me so I'd follow Wolfy's lead and go for either a cheery wave or a head-down 'I haven't seen you' approach.

Tarik was getting thinner as his dog was getting bigger. One day he'd told me how much Satan ate and I immediately handed over a bag of dog food I'd just bought.

Still, it was nice to see him and we set off walking together.

'Thing with dogs, yeah, right, is you've gotta be the boss.'

The enormous Satan rampaged around Wolfy, tumbling like an elephant over my gamine bag of bones. Wolfy stayed aloof, alert and, for now, calm but there was a tension in his step that said, 'This dog is seriously doing my head in.'

I considered the dense-packed muscle around Satan's jaw. We walked with lots of Staffies, playful, roughhousing, but this dog, was something else. 'He's just massive,' I said.

'Yeah,' Tarik agreed, nonchalant, proud. 'If he wanted to kill Wolfy he could do it in a second. But that would never happen because he knows I am the boss, and he's a good boy. He's like a harmless little pup. Ahhh, look at him. He just wants to play.'

'Wolfy's not big on playing.'

'Yeah I can see that.' His drooling monster went cantering into Wolfy's ribs like a battering ram. 'You've got to not worry, mate,' he said. 'See, you're creating tension.'

Satan was now 'playfully' riding Wolfy's haunches like a prize stallion.

I tried in vain to control my anxiety. I wished I'd never gone for this walk.

Tarik clearly knew a lot about dogs but I was losing faith. This was a radical chic experiment gone horribly wrong.

Rowrarowrowrowgrrrrrrraaaaaaargh. Yelp. Scream. Yelp. Scream.

Wolfy had kicked off with the gigantic fighting dog the size of a hippo and now before my eyes they were a joined-up, indistinguishable mass of fur, foamed spit, growls, whines and barks. A dogfight.

That was it, Wolfy was dead meat. I screamed, 'Get that dog off! GET IT OFF!' A calm, constant person in me was standing back and going, 'How is screaming going to help, you berk.'

The majority of my being was engaged in uncontrolled, hysterical panic: 'Get the fucking thing off.'

Tarik strolled over and stopped the fight with a word.

'You see, you reacted wrongly there. I was always in control and the pup never hurt Wolfy. Wolfy was just teaching him a lesson and, see?' He pointed at my dog, swaggering off towards the bushes for a celebratory post-fight micturation. 'He's fine.'

I had overreacted. No doubt about it. But his dog was just so inconveniently massive. Its ability to kill was so evident that whether it would or not seemed like an irrelevance. All the times I'd sniggered at adults who threw their hands up and whimpered if a dog went near them came back to haunt me. In some ways, people were right to be scared of dogs. Like people with guns, they're able to kill.

Now I had to finish the rest of the walk with Tarik patronising me and pointing out the countless ways I had reacted badly to his 'playful boy'.

'Well, you need to not own such a ridiculous ferocious-looking dog that could "kill my dog in one second." What's the point of having this beast?'

'It's the challenge,' he said. 'Though I think I am gonna change his name to Billy. Satan gives off some bad gangsta vibes.'

I decided not to walk with Tarik ever again and returned to the ladies who lurch with their slinky biddable hounds.

CHAPTER FIVE

Living in Notting Hill with the dog feels a bit like a holiday every day. We walk those ordered streets of mustard London brick and pastel stucco to find good coffee, good wine, to test peaches for ripeness or buy exotic mushrooms from the Mushroom Guy in the market. It's the same, more or less, as I did before the furry string bean slouched everywhere beside me. Everything's changed though. The immersion is so much deeper. I notice more. For every house lavishly draped in silks with a grand piano in the window, there's another that cost a million to make it bleak and spare and another that is bleak through want, with ripped grey nets and a junkyard front garden.

Welcome to Notting Hill, where grandeur and grot live literally right next door to each other. There's Tarik's place and next door there's that nice chap who was at Eton with David Cameron.

Pootling about the place in the daytime, it still surprises me how much people salute the dog. On 'our' stretch of Portobello Road, between Elgin and Blenheim Crescents, there's cries of 'All right Wolfy,' left, right and centre some days.

As I'm caffeinating myself, there's a shrill cry of 'Wolfy,' followed by an even shriller one: 'Wolfy!' The two little girls, Betty and Audrey, arrive in Crocs and matching sundresses. 'Oh, this dog is my favourite. Can I stroke his tummy?'

'Arright Wolfy?' It's the drugs counsellor with the voice that sounds like he has a stinking cold. 'Come on then.' He coaxes him away from the children, with their mere stroking and pats, with the crunchy promises he jiggles in his biscuit-laden pockets.

'Is that a lurcher? My wife has just got one of those. Majestic-looking, isn't he,' pronounces a haughty chap in green quilted jacket. He rears up behind the children and their nanny, and the drug counsellor, all now worshipping Wolfy. The nanny is cooing at him, '*Eres un chico guapo*. Mwah mwah mwah.'

I feel like the wives of pop stars must do: superfluous, in the way, but proud.

I get up and leave slowly and wait outside the door until he notices me there and scrabbles at the smooth floor trying to quickly get to his feet. Once up he strolls out to join me. I clip the lead on, put on a pair of cheap sunglasses and swagger off.

We've not walked 20 paces before the dog gives a little tug on the lead, tug enough to pull my arm straight, as we pass Mike's Cafe, the greasy spoon on Blenheim Crescent opposite that infuriating travel bookshop where the tourists from all around the world stand in the middle of the road and take pictures while playing clips from *Notting Hill* the movie.

Danny, the son of the eponymous Mike, bellows, 'Orroit babe?' at me as we pass him leaning against his convertible Merc. He's got his roof down and the car stereo pumping out some classic late nineties UK house and garage – pronounced, of course, *garridge*.

On and off throughout my 25 years of working at home I have gone in there when the four walls at home are good only for crawling up. I'm a regular at Mike's like Joan Collins is at the Wolseley and Lucian Freud was at Clarke's. For a while I worked here almost every day – despite belonging to an expensive private members' club just round the corner – because, as the sticker on the door of Mike's says, in capital letters, 'WE WELCOME DOGS.'

Daily was too much. The problem was that I was eating too much fried food. It being a Notting Hill greasy spoon, you can get a full English, but also eggs royale or a Greek salad. But when fried bread and baked beans are available, who really orders a fruit plate?

Wolfy didn't get a sausage every time we went to Mike's. Sometimes he got two. And on the days he didn't get sausage, he got a chicken breast. He's a big fan of the place. The sausage reward system has made him strongly motivated to visit Mike's. Entirely like the feelings I had when I passed Tim's place. Our habits burned into our neural pathways created the actual physical routes we trod in life.

Danny is his usual deep chestnut brown permatanned self. He's smoking, leaning against his black C-Class and wearing a Burberry baseball cap. Danny runs the place now and Mike shuffles in quietly for breakfast every now and again, still with traces of the Greek Cypriot accent, smart in a suit, always. The caff has been there since 1963. Charlie loves an imagined dialogue between him and Danny, where he calls him Moik constantly. 'Orroight Moik? You're a proper old local incha Moik? Cor Moik. Stroike a loit. Cor blimey. It's a real pea-souper innit mate.'

The clueless and patronising new middle-class arrival to town, talking in his Dick Van Dyke East End shockney to a west London local whose name he has muddled with the name of the caff. This was a weekly stalwart in the range of skits we performed for each other at home.

I'd told Danny about the 'Orroight Moik' business and he's having a chuckle about that. Truth is you could live here a lifetime and people wouldn't think of you as a local. These errors of cross-cultural intimacy were real for the posho middle-class people who loved the multiculturalism, thrived within it, but didn't get to make jokes about white dog hairs on a black niqab. Even if you lived to 150 you couldn't please the, as they loudly called themselves, 'real locals wiv foive gen'rations on Grove, know wot am sayin'?'

Wolfy tugs towards the door and I point at him. 'Real regular inne Moik?' Danny laughs and carries on posing on his Mercedes.

As I drag Wolfy on past the caff, he squirts a jet of possessive urine on one of the plant pots outside. 'Oops, sorry,' I say.

'Nah that's all right, he's just saying, "That's mine. That's my caff, that is." I haven't got a problem with that babe.'

Wolfy is constantly steering me, manipulating me with what tools he has to do the things he is driven to do. Such is the engagement with a domesticated dog. In steering me away from my own habits, and towards his own, he has changed my life. I ain't complainin' Moik. I just had to start eating salad for breakfast because a bacon sandwich every day was out of the question.

When we near Coffee Plant, where the maximum haul on a really good day might be anything up to eight dry dog biscuits, he starts steering too, although not with the sausage-strength force that he uses round the corner by Mike's. Timing matters too: if we walk past in the morning he'll automatically veer in, such is the regularity of my caffeine habit, but in the afternoon he just bowls on past. Whenever I look after Castor he does the same whenever we pass Portobello Juice, which explains why his owner Keith is so much healthier-looking than me. Just a light pull from Castor's lead is enough to make me think about popping in for a green juice.

The biscuit-tracking instinct is strong in Wolfy. So you can imagine the problems I have keeping him out of Janice's in order to keep the fleas at bay. Were I to open the gate a crack, say if I had stinky bags of rubbish in my hands, he would somehow compress himself down to fit through the crack, and slither out down the alley and snackwards.

Early September, it's warm and it's still flea season. Wolfy has been doing his usual rounds in the back alley, yet he hasn't come back with any hoppy squatters for a few weeks.

One morning I'm walking past Janice's back gate with him unattached to his lead. I wait for his inevitable swift exit. He looks left at Janice's door, pauses and moves swiftly on as if to say, 'Yeah, you know what. You're all right mate, didn't fancy a biscuit anyway.'

He's scared. Specifically, he's scared of Felicity, a mangy-looking tabby cat that recently set up camp in her yard, looking to me tiny and terrified but to Wolfy, clearly, terrifying. Why? He could go *mano a mano (perro en perro?)* with Satan/Billy, and walk out tail up and cocksure, yet this small sad smelly cat, trembly as a squirrel, has him aquiver. At last, an effective flea treatment.

Even at the specific invitation of Janice, who is often there, kneeling on a bit of rubber in her concreted yard busy potting stalky geraniums or painting gnomes, he is not interested. 'Hello Woo', coming in for your biskit?' Nope. Wolfy trots on to Rita's.

This from a type of hound who is a thief and a murderer by nature, a stealthy poacher's best friend. Lurchers don't carefully retrieve prey the master has shot and softly drop it at your feet. Lurchers chase it and kill it. That's their job. Have the oxytocin benders he gets with me as his owner crushed his killer instinct? Or is his gentle nature the reason he was turfed out of his previous home and found wandering the streets of Manchester without a collar or a chip?

He cries sometimes when I leave the study and go and work in bed. I try to ignore his imploring 'where are you?' bleating, which is what the dog behaviourists instruct you do, but I always relent: 'I'm up here, you goon.' Click clack, he's up the killer stairs and springs onto the bed, where we both give ourselves a quick oxytocin fix as I stroke him and stick my nose in his fur. 'What do you smell of today? Mmmn, sun-toasted seaweed and hot sand.'

There's a knack to snuggling a lurcher. Get the wrong angle and it can feel like embracing a collapsible picnic table. Awkward as hell. You will find a scratchy paw, at the end of a long thin extended leg, stuck in your eye. Snuggling isn't what they're designed for.

Experience teaches a lurcher owner how to make a teddy bear of your high-speed stealth kite. Once the big cuddles start, then you get seriously addicted.

This dependency created some logistical problems. If we couldn't take him with us when we went away, where did we leave him?

The invitation is attached by a magnet to the fridge. It has loomed, silver and white, over the entire year, this wedding. We've talked about it regularly. Our social diaries operate largely independently and, if it was the wedding of a colleague of mine he had never met before, Charlie would not come; but I am going to this one. It's a big deal, for him, involving some senior staff from his company. He takes it seriously while I think it's like the set-up for an episode of a seventies sitcom. I enjoy moaning about these much-anticipated nuptials and winding him up about all the wrong things I am going to say and do. He said, 'You don't have to come if you don't want to.' I said, 'No, I'll definitely come, I'm just enjoying this excuse for a grumble.'

The wedding's not for another two months but we're already having regular fretful debates. 'What are we going to do with Woofy? I think we should take him to my mother's,' he says.

'For one night? Don't be crazy. You'll drive two hours up there and back in a day and be tired and grumpy. And who'll have to suck that up? Me. No, that's sledgehammer and nut business. Why don't we put him in doggy daycare overnight?'

'No, that's cruel.'

'There's this guy round here who moves in to your place to dog-sit, everyone raves about him.'

'I'm not having a stranger in my house.'

'I know, Tarik!'

'Are you kidding? No!'

'Why can't my brother have him? He's good with dogs, he always says he was raised by Labradors.'

'Yes, you've told me that before, a lot.'

'It's so sweet.' I go off into reveries about preschool Will, cut off from his two other siblings, tumbling around an empty house with our mum's Lab, Chloe, and riding his Raleigh

Budgie around followed by her litters of yipping and nipping black silky pups.

'Kate! Are you listening?' He repeats his concerns as if to a halfwit and points to the calendar on the fridge 'Aren't you looking after Castor then? Look. Isn't it a bit much to foist two dogs on them, they've got three small kids. Have you thought about this at all practically?'

'The kids spend a lot of time with both Castor and Wolfy when they're here. They're all great friends.'

'The dog doesn't need a friend, he just needs to be safe. I'm not happy about it.'

'For fuck's sake, it's one day. I look after the kids all the time. We don't even know if we're going to stay the night after this performance. It'll be fine. And I want him to go there. I want him to be with the family, all the familiar smells and stuff, he'll be happy there.'

He snorts his disagreement and turns to aggressively rearrange the shelf in the grill.

'It'll be fine.' I say this again in an infantilising soothing way that I know will wind him up.

The problem with living in a small space is that moods simmer, merge, mutate and inevitably grow. Over the course of this discussion an atmosphere has built and I want to escape it. Three options: I shut myself in the shit pit/Wolfy's Office and put headphones on, we stay in our common parts and cultivate the atmosphere with sharp comments and asides, or one of us gets the hell out for a while. For once, I make a wise decision.

Walking down from the top of Portobello on a sunny day on the cusp of summer and autumn is a disorientating pleasure. It's London but inflected with so much else. The dog and I weave slowly through the crowds, between the competing beats coming from houses and stalls, everything merging into one uniquely west London vibe, soul, dub, reggae, ska, the drone of the Westway A40 flyover, even the distant whistle of a goods train going up the Harlesden line by Latimer Road, the smell of doughnuts, old fruit and diesel, snatched gusts of weed or stale beer. The street sweats with a sensory funk of living. Everything is slowed down by sun; and the pulse of the place has a steady easy flow.

Not sure where we are going. Do we need a destination? The dog stops to gobble bread and sausages left discarded on the street. I go to Lucinda's vintage stall under the Westway by Portobello Green and buy an eighties Ungaro dress with a strong print, deep pockets and a pie-crust neck. It'll do for that wedding. Wolfy mooches round the stall while I try the dress on over my jeans. Lucinda's tiny black jackapoo, Bean, strains on its hind legs to get up and have a decent sniff of Wolf's bum.

Wolfy collapses down on his side for a nap while Lucinda and I gossip about the fashion label people who have been lurking round the stall, buying old clothes to copy, I mean be 'inspired by'.

There's a soothing subtle hum to Portobello life. I love it. Living here is a privilege. I'm lucky.

When Charlie and I bought our flat on Grenfell Road, the one without a front door, my friend Elaine lost her temper with me. 'No! You don't belong there. You need to move here. West London isn't interesting any more. Too much *money*. Come north.'

This is weird because Elaine's good at making money, and she only likes nice things. I'm surprised by this. 'What made you interesting back in the day was how you looked, how you behaved, how you dressed, what you did creatively, whether you were funny, or clever, or knew how to throw a great party or even just if you had drugs to give away. Now money seems to trump all these things, and what is money? Money is nothing, it's inert, it's not cool, it's not interesting, it doesn't have any good one-liners. This obsession with money is why everything's shit now.'

She's right about that but she's wrong about west London.

Next to and above Portobello Green, the metal bridge carries the Hammersmith and City Line over Portobello Road. Alongside it the Westway steadily rushes on and on. There's a manicurists called Coco under here. I know the owner, a woman called Fatima who I've known since she was a teenager. There's another way to kill time. Wolfy lies on the floor and I get into one of those lumpy electric massage chairs that pummel your back like an annoying child a row behind on an aeroplane. I put on a headset for a sneaky watch of the whiny plastic child-people of the Kardashian family.

Fati tells me her aunt is coming in and she can read coffee grounds. I always start hankering after the solutions and dubious gifts of psychics and self-appointed mystics when things are a sketchy at home.

Aunty arrives. She's got a serious-looking blow-dry and a perfectly applied coral red lip. She sets up beside me in a back-thumping chair. I drink a Turkish coffee, with its silted grounds thick at the bottom of the tiny cup, and as soon as it's finished she turns it sharp over into a saucer and then picks it up to examine the residue left on the side.

She asks me to ask a question.

'I'd like to know about my dog.'

'What do you mean, your dog?'

'My dog. Is he OK?'

'Of course he is OK,' she says, flabbergasted, looking down at him snoozing on my Woof Bed jacket. 'I see him there, asleep by your side. What other questions could you have about a dog?'

'Loads,' I say, unperturbed by her undisguised disdain for the question. 'Why do I love him so much? Do I love him too much?'

'He's just your dog, what's wrong with you. I have a dog, I love my dog, but he's just a dog. I have some advice for you. Don't think about the dog so much. What about your husband?'

'My boyfriend?'

'Or your work?'

'I don't want to ask about those things.'

'I want to tell you about your boyfriend. How are things at home?'

What a waste of a tenner.

Having Castor as well as Wolfy was a proper commitment to the cause. Much harder to stroll round town, free and easy, with two dogs than with one. So I'd often head out of London and visit my mum, who lives on the edge of Dartmoor.

Up there every solitary footstep took me further away from who I ought to be and back to who I was. Round this time of year, in the early autumn, Dartmoor's often wrapped up in a damp, grey mist. Unless you can use map and compass you're buggered navigating. But this little patch of Dartmoor between Buckland Common and Rippon Tor, I know it so well I recognise rocks and paths and tiny landmarks. I won't get lost – hopefully.

Down by a narrow strip of woodland running alongside the stream, the air was clear of mist. The world looked flat, the edge of visibility only a few feet away. I sucked on through black boggy ground. All sound was muffled by thick air, apart from a late cuckoo's fluted two-note song coming from somewhere out there in the blank beyond. I stopped to listen. I'd be very unlikely to hear a cuckoo again until next Spring.

Wolfy meandered while Castor careened around like a lunatic, nose in the undergrowth. There was a commotion in a patch of heather 20 feet away. Castor had caught something and was shaking it. I ran to look. A squirrel. I called him off but the damage was done; the poor chap was punching out with its nut-munching upper claws, while its haunches where the dog had shaken it were utterly motionless.

The squirrel's eyes were all fear and it fought with the limbs that still had life. Castor went back to sniff his catch and got a scratch on the nose. He retreated. The squirrel was paralysed, it wasn't going to get better. I needed to euthanise it.

I called Wolfy over. 'Kill it! Wolfy. Kill it!' Wolfy gave it a sniff and a worried refusal, backing off rear end first. Castor wandered off as if nothing had happened. Neither of them had any interest in finishing the job, and neither did I. Should I stove in its head with a rock? Break its neck? Could I pick it up, punching and squeaking as it was, and drown it in the stream? No, I could not.

Any ideas I had of myself as a countrywoman took an immediate pasting. Who in the country picks their way through the bog in white jeans, for a start. I pulled the neck of my jumper over my nose, a defence mechanism that I'd had since school. Mum does it too. Poof, I smelled. Not washing your face for three days or using deodorant doesn't mean a return to the earth, I reflected, it just means you're a slob.

Ending the squirrel's life was impossible. I just couldn't kill it. I couldn't kill a suffering squirrel. Perhaps a fox would come and do the job, or a hungry buzzard. My heart was thumping, my head cascading thoughts and worries and paranoia like a screen full of code streaming on the backs of my retinas. I was having something like a mild anxiety attack.

The squirrel was like a Post-it note stuck to a lump of lichen-encrusted Dartmoor granite: 'Oy! Mate! Don't forget about death.'

I always thought about death on Dartmoor. It's big, it's full of 300-million-year-old rocks, give or take the odd 50 million years. This is where I want my ashes scattered, I would think as I gazed in endorphin-induced euphoria out from whichever tor I'd just hammered up.

But old Mr Squirrel here brought death a bit nearer than melodramatic statements about ashes while enjoying a pleasant vista. Instead of wind and dust and an eternity of stars and a return to universal oneness, I saw my dead self being chomped and chewed and pecked and slimed by a series of natural predators: fat flies rubbing their shitty feet together, the common buzzard, a black slug, Mr Fox, bacteria and labradoodles out for a walk. I saw my surviving relatives getting on with their lives, no children crying or grandchildren asking if Granny is with the angels now.

This was getting silly. The questions crowded in. Mum dying, I'm not nice enough to her. I love my mummy, I want my mummy. Don't die Mum. Dad dying, oh Daddy, my darling Dad, I hear his voice and see his gentle face. I don't see him enough. Oh God, I love my parents so much it almost seems like I don't love them because they are so thickly stitched into every part of me. What if Will died before me, or Tom? Family; step-parents, faults, division, half-siblings, dogs, step-sibling, games of all-pile-on, grumpy Christmases, family in all it's fucked-up glory is everything.

I wanted to call Charlie now, tell him I loved him and that I took huge comfort in our habitual coldness, that we were perfect in our imperfection. But I had no signal. At best I'd get a 'love you too Fox', at worst he'd think I was off my head and dismiss me with the eternal words, 'can't talk, I'm in a meeting'. Real love never looks like what we are taught it is. My brain burned with the thought of all the love I had never thanked my family for, never even recognised.

It hit me: I had never suffered loss, not really. I'd been lugging around those childhood years of missing my mum like a bag of rocks my whole life, but it was over now. It had been over for nearly 35 years. Drop it. The squirrel still lay there, motionless from its hips down and punching out with its tiny arms.

What was I going to do about the squirrel?

I tried to interest Wolfy in it again: 'Come on Woofs, sort the existential elephant in the room, it's only a squirrel-sized one, and get an early supper into the bargain. Mmmn, num nums. Foooood.'

'No way mate. Not interested.' He slunk backwards and busied himself sniffing something. 'Keep me out of this mess, that's a you problem right there, not a me one.'

Castor hovered, also nervous. 'Dude, you did this. Finish it. Please?' He turned and pottered up the narrow path to find some important patch of gorse to urinate on, then from a distance he stood and watched. I squatted down. A swift karate chop to its neck like I'd seen Charlie do with rabbits? Nope. Not that, I'd be certain to balls it up. *Kill the squirrel*, the voice in my head was screaming now and I wanted to run away from it with my hands over my head, except I was the voice.

If it had been on the road I'd have run it over in the car. The lump of death metal no human was afraid of wielding. If I'd had a machine gun, I'd have peppered it with sweet release.Easy.

Maybe once my back was turned a little team of bushy-tailed rodents nurses would come out from a hidden hole down by the stream, and Squirrel's friends Water Rat, Rabbit, Toad and Vole would help him home on a cart fashioned from acorn cups and interleaved ferns. Wise old Dr Brock the badger would fix him up. Or perhaps it was a her. Damn, I felt even worse now.

What could I do to make the universe slightly less terrible? Kill the squirrel, don't kill the squirrel, take the squirrel to an animal sanctuary. I turned to the dogs one last time. They both looked away: 'You're the boss. You deal with it, big man.'

'Look, squirrel', I said, toying as a last-ditch attempt at salving my guilt with the idea of divine retribution, 'you guys have done a lot of damage to the native red population'.

Nah. It didn't work. I walked away from the squirrel, praying uselessly to a not-there God, let alone a benevolent one, and to a more certain agent, Mother Nature, to send a hungry hawk as soon as possible.

Death. It's a right big one.

Wolfy would die before me, barring tragedy. I imagined him fading away and hobbling more and needing to be carried upstairs and more poo accident episodes and then his sad face looking at me one day, as his heart beat more faintly, and he would give me his 'it's time' face that bereaved dog owners put on Facebook after they've had to make that last trip to the vet.

'Pixie has left us. She was totally deaf, with failing eyesight, and had dementia. This meant constant pacing, random weeing and pooing. But she still enjoyed her food and her walks. And she loved the cuddles. One day something very painful arose. We took her to the vet ... she left us peacefully, eating sausages.'

'Eating sausages.' What a way to go.

In France one time, interviewing a scion of a big champagne family, I had a brief but poignant conversation with a grand elderly gentleman, late seventies and, in all, pretty odious. He kept staring at my tits and telling me how unattractive women became in old age and that older men needed to have affairs with younger women. 'But it is important to still make love to your wife so she feels beautiful even if she no longer looks it.'

You met these guys sometimes. I listened wearing an insincere and emotionless rictus smile, fascinated by how much worse it could get. 'Do go on.'

Somehow, as he went on, the conversation turned to dogs, as it so often did.

He had kept dogs all his life, he told me, but no more. 'It is just too painful when they die. I cannot take it again.'

What would happen when Wolfy was gone? Had unconditional love and the routine and discipline I'd learned from an animal, from Wolfy, had it fixed something permanently in me? Or was he like a drug? Would the effects wear off?

My eyes stung with tears that didn't come. I crunched on to the Buckland Beacon and stood over the lichen-muddled biblical words on the two tablets of stone. I had never noticed that there was an eleventh commandment there below the usual ten. In all the decades I'd come up here, willingly or dragging behind a forceful parent, I'd never read this: 'A new commandment I give unto you, Love one another.'

On the way back to the car the dogs ambled behind me, seemingly subdued by the squirrel episode. Perhaps they were 'picking up on my energy', as people constantly liked to say; or – it had been a long walk – perhaps they were just tired.

PART TWO
LOST DOG

CHAPTER SIX

Wolfy is curled up at the end of the bed and before I take him over to Will's I really want a cuddle. Late October sunshine drenches the room in light and warmth. The other male animal is already up and changing the world one chore at a time. Sisyphus and the sybarite, and their dog. I'll just have a moment of hedonic bliss with the dog and then I'll get up. I pat the bed exuberantly. 'Wolfy, Wolfy, come on Woofs.'

'If he's not coming he doesn't want to be cuddled, Kate,' Charlie shouts up the stairs in between his furious bathroom ablutions. 'Wolfy, Wolfy.' Pat pat pat. Pat pat. 'Oh come on.' I quit the doggy intonation and just plead in a mockney accent, 'Gizza a little cuddle, mate.'

He half raises his body, then launches himself up the bed, close enough for me to roll him onto his back, soft underbelly exposed, where I stroke him, muttering inane nonsense, just making noises. In dogs like Wolfy with relatively small eyes, with a narrow, long, sighthound's dolichocephalic head shape, the nictitating membrane that protects the eyeball is prominent. Slowly the shining black irises roll away under the pink corpuscles of his third eyelid so he looks like a zombie. The happy teeth come out as his muzzle relaxes and drops half a centimetre to bare the tiny baby teeth at the front of his lower jaw. I close my eyes and scratch his chest, and a blissed-out and peaceful smile lights up my whole body. I'm not thinking about anything. It's taken a while to get him up here, but now he's here. It's heaven.

Soft underbelly. It's an expression that's used a lot to describe a weak spot. We use it so much we've forgotten its literal meaning. Turn over a hedgehog, an elephant, a lurcher, a woman, a shark, a sardine and there's the softest part of the body below the ribs. It's where you go in to disembowel or eviscerate an animal – or a human.

It's dangerous to show a soft spot if you're an animal, and animals like Woofs who've had unpredictable lives, who've been hurt, they don't lie with four legs in the air like a thin dead cow with their heads lolling to one side and their pink tummies fully exposed.

Don't show your vulnerability.

Castor is a different story. Raised from a puppy by Keith, he is lying exactly like this on Wolfy's bed beside me. Soft belly upward, that is how trusting Castor sleeps all the time.

'Aren't you up yet?'

There has been much talk about Will and his family having Wolfy and, since Keith is at Seoul Fashion Week, 'Castor too, if you don't mind?'

Much as I try not to anthropomorphise Wolfy, I have this idea of him as a canine cousin to my nieces and nephews.

I want them to enjoy Wolfy as if he were the human cousin I've never provided. A desire for him to be family has probably been apparent to all. I think the kids sort of love him, but probably also find him a bit boring. Only Charlie and I really give a damn about the dog, well – us two and Charlie's mum, who infinitely prefers dogs, horses, sheep, feral cats and spiders to most human beings.

Our deep bond with the dog is partly made by the amount of time we spend together. It's intimate, when you live in a small flat.

For me he will leap in the air, jump five-bar gates, do 360s – and for everyone else, not a lot: sit for a biscuit, roll over for a tummy rub perhaps. Wolfy will always go to familiar outsiders to say hello but, like a lot of dogs, his heart belongs to his owners.

Compared to Mum's gregarious Labradors and Dad's bouncy spaniels that skid across floors like manic mops, Wolfy is a bore.

Once after taking an adorable snap for Instagram of my five-year-old niece Bay cuddled up with Wolfy on an armchair, I asked her if it was a lovely thing, like being cuddled up to a giant teddy bear. 'Well, no, because teddy bears don't do the stinkiest farts.'

I peel myself off the bed. It's still impressively early, but the timekeeper is huffing and stressing. Two dogs, car, coffee. Go.

En route to Will's in Tufnell Park I walk them up on Primrose Hill. A farmer's market is setting up in the primary school at the back of the park; it doesn't open for another hour but they let me in to buy apples, raw milk and yoghurt. Raw milk. *Raw milk.*

Dog ownership has rewired my brain.

Yomping round the edge of the park at a brisk middle-class dog-walking-lady sort of a pace, I give thanks for the absence of hangover. Castor keeps hustling Wolfy to play, but my dog is grumpy and growly. After five minutes of Castor nipping and hassling, Wolfy relents and I am rewarded with the magnificent sight of two sighthounds belting round Primrose Hill together at 25 miles an hour. Strangers stop to admire them. Damn, those dogs can run when they want to.

There is a consistent worry tugging at my mind. Is it fair to leave two dogs with my brother and his wife? What if something happens to Castor? What if Castor runs away? How will I tell Keith? I shake my whole body to try to get the thought out and sit at the top of the Hill and attempt a moment of contemplative gazing over London's glorious muzzy skyline. I am going to meditate now, I think, and close my eyes. In less than a minute I'm back on my feet. I've tried to block out the anxiety but it has only risen.

Outside my brother's house I can hear Arty stomping down the hall to answer the door. It takes him some time to navigate raising his small body high enough to undo the latch and I peer through the letter box. 'Trick or treat?' He screams with excitement. Once in, I crouch down, growling like an angry bear. He chuckles in that hiccuping way kids do, the other children hovering behind, smiling and waiting for their turn to greet me. I offer Arty Castor's lead. The younger dog's exuberance to check out the new turf has the little chap pulled this way and that, which he loves. Arty trips and runs behind Castor, chortling and screeching with glee. Dropping the lead he stands back, hands on hips, and pronounces, 'Now *that* is a dog! What is this dog's name?' he demands.

'That's Castor, Arty.'

'Is Castor Wolfy's friend?'

Arty asks a good question. Are Castor and Wolfy friends? Charlie and I often wonder what Wolfy makes of the younger dog. They spend a lot of time together; and Castor is as sweet-natured and beta as our dog so there are never dominance issues. If they bump into each other on walks, cue much exuberant tail-wagging and leaping in the other's direction for these flying chest-bumping greetings that other dogs do not get from Wolfy (he has earned the nickname Aloofy).

Castor is responsible for some major shifts in Wolfy's vigour. When we brought him home from Thurrock Services he wasn't flabby, but he was unfit, and he had forgotten how to play, like some poor neglected kid who had spent too long with social services. Castor forced him out of his rescue home plod. The first time we took the two dogs for a walk, Castor pestered him to play and to chase. After a few false starts and some grumpy nips, Wolfy was running at Castor's hindquarters as if they were stitched nose to thigh. When Castor pulled away Wolfy would slow down, adjust his strategy, cut a few corners and fall back into chase. I'd watch this with delight. Regular visits from Castor had given Wolfy back his thrilling sighthound zoom. The two had fun together but when Castor left I could always sense a capacious satisfaction in the dog that he had life, sofa and us to himself again. If Wolfy had a friend, then Castor was it; most other dogs he totally ignored, after the initial bum-sniffing stage.

I give the kids some treats to feed the dogs.

'Steph?' She is in the kitchen. My brother is dashing out to take Bay to a violin lesson.

I sit briefly at the long table in their kitchen. It's all there. The big fridge dispensing ice and cold filtered water; the side return with a ceiling of glass, a mix of children's art and grown-up stuff and that optimum amount of mess that suggests you're chilled but not complete pigs. It's all there. The big family house dream.

If I didn't love them all so damn much I'd be jealous as hell. On this morning, off to a wedding at a conference centre in Surrey, and a touch anxious, I've got the ruler of success out and am measuring up the big scrubbed vintage table that seats 14 or so with our tiny butcher's block that, even with two, the plates tumble off like those shove-penny games in arcades.

Wolfy walks straight over to the sofa in the kitchen. Sofa. In the kitchen. Know what I mean? And parks himself next to my sister-in-law, collapsing his head against her chest but continuing to stare straight at me in what my anthropomorphising mind sees as defiance: 'Fine. Leave. See if I care. Go on, fuck off. I like it here actually.' We exchange a few words about food and walks. I leave a bag of raw meat, enough for both dogs, in the corner of the fridge. With a tug at my heart, which I dismiss as utterly ridiculous, I leave.

The car feels empty on the drive home.

It would be just my luck if my incredibly successful sister-in-law could not just nail a first-class degree from Oxford, roll at high levels of corporate life, write three books in her lunch hour *and* cause a massive oxytocin surge in my dog. The way he looked at me, snuggled against her, haunted me, I admit it.

Usually when I left Wolfy anywhere, even if I went to the loo at Coffee Plant and left him sitting outside, I always said,

'Wolfy stay. Stay Wolfy,' and it indicated to him that if he stayed roughly put, then I would come back. There was no 'Stay' this time; I was trying to be cool about the dog, not wanting to be fretful or fussy. And I was rushing. I had to be back in time to not to upset the punctuality fiend in west London. 'Lovely, lovely, thanks all, see you tomorrow, or maybe even tonight if we can get away,' I said. And dashed.

I ring Charlie now. 'Imagine if we get back and he's switched his loyalties to them.'

'Yeah, he's probably curled up on their giant bed already thinking to himself how he's lucked out, with a garden and a massive house and now he's got rid of those jokers with the poky flat who just sing and argue all the time.'

Ha, ha, ha.

We joke on about this as we drive to the wedding, eking the humour out of a talking dog voiced by Ray Winstone, telling my sister-in-law, 'You're much prettier than her. Oh yes, like what you've done with the garden. Mind if I urinate here on this cherry tree?'

Castor's character evolves too. He is Irish, like Keith, and talks like Dougal from *Father Ted*. 'How's that tree there, Wolfy. Sure, it's grand here. All these children with the biscuits. I hope those other people never come back.'

Now we're on the road Charlie relaxes. It'll be fun, today, and when we can't laugh with, we'll laugh at. I tell him a glossy magazine has rung and asked if Wolfy would like to feature in their Christmas Gift Guide dressed up in a *Star Wars* Death Star doggy costume. 'Any money in it?' he says.

'Don't be mad; there's no money left to pay journalists, let alone pay dogs to wear stupid outfits.'

If the costume had been for the AT-AT Walker from *Star Wars*, I'd have said yes. Wolfy reminds me of a lot of fictional characters: Falkor the flying lizard dog in *The Neverending Story*, Alf the alien, Mr Snuffleupagus, Mrs Tiggywinkle ... But more than anything, when he's shambling along in his special super-low first gear, he reminds me of those quadruped robot tanks from *Star Wars.*

'Is Wolfy doing his special AT-AT super-slow walk?' I text to Will. He does not respond. Must already be having a great time with the dog up on the Heath.

The wedding is at a seventeenth-century manor house turned conference centre. Despite the Gothic drama of the place, the fittings are pure Homebase. Hard cheap carpet, dreary veneered repro furniture, colours that don't show dirt. The sun blazes through the crimson and gold maple leaves. It is a glorious day, made for poetry and adjectives.

'We could have brought the dog,' I say, wishing he was here, imagining taking off my heels and putting on the worn-out Hunters I keep in the boot with a stash of poo bags, and taking him for a quick turn around the car park every couple of hours while I suffer the nuptials of two total strangers.

Charlie's colleagues are waiting outside the main entrance swigging on bottles of beer. I scan the assembled humans for potential banter allies. Thin pickings. An Asian guy in a shiny mohair suit tickles me a couple of times with sarcastic comments about his hangover but he has no empathy with me, a remote colleague's bird wearing a frumpy second-hand dress. I suspect what had looked cool on Portobello Road just looks like my mum's clothes here.

'Please behave yourself,' Charlie says, almost pleading.

We go inside and sit on conference chairs covered in white stretchy shiny material tied up in a fancy ruched knot behind, like supersized chair lingerie. A bloke plays a saxophone and we are invited to clap and cheer. I clap but do not cheer. The wedding ceremony passes and I register that it has not touched me, not at all. A couple of times I make comments and Charlie shushes me.

'Ladies and gentlemen! The bride and groom!' Again, I clap but do not cheer.

Now there is an interminable period before the wedding breakfast. The groom, the mutterings go, has a hangover so bad he can barely speak after drinking a bottle of whisky with the best man the night before. If his mumbled part in the wedding vows were not enough, then his mute discomfort on the receiving line has confirmed it. The humdrum of a hangover on momentous days, that thing; I feel compassion for him.

The wedding warms up a bit and as the champagne inevitably becomes prosecco the day grinds on. I think about Tim for the first time in ages. 'Throwing a bit of coke at it' would sort this wedding out.

Everyone else is gearing up for a good Irish wedding. We don't have to drive back to London to fetch the dogs. Usually it's Charlie who puts up with my friends, and his work is important to him – at no point will I act bored or impatient, I think. I dive on the nibbles like a hooligan seagull. Steph sends me a photo of Wolfy and Castor in the boot of their car surrounded by the three kids. The picture is a good one. Screensaver stuff.

When you're a stranger at a wedding, all you see is cliché. None of the love and humour touches the random plus one, not unless the best man is a professional comedian – which this one isn't. I wonder how much the whole thing cost, and whether the bride is upset her husband has a stinking clang on her big day. Charlie is seated across from me and on form. Next to me is a colleague of his, wearing a revolting shimmering green far too loosely-cut suit. On his feet are a pair of 'smart' square-toed shoes; the sort with stitching and a little too much length in the narrowing toe so that they curl slightly at the ends. He's funny in a cynical spiky sort of fashion but we are going to run out of things to say soon.

The Rugby World Cup final has just started, New Zealand versus Australia. There are some people who consider phones at the table a crime on a par with farting loudly or belching like a bullfrog. Everyone appears some degree of terrified of the bride. She has specified that her wedding breakfast will not be spoiled by anyone watching the match. Green Suit has set up his phone so he can watch; every time the bride rustles past in her meringue, he hides the screen.

The bride has also, deliberately or not, specified that the white wine be really bad because (I've learned from the speeches) she is famous for ordering the cheapest white on the list. Cheap wine doesn't cause hangovers, apparently. Jesus Christ suffered, but no one forced him to drink bottom-shelf Sauvignon Blanc. Charlie and I exchange a sequence of looks and nods.

We'll be not be staying too late here.

On the table are party favours, and a green heart for us to write a message to the bride and groom. I rack my brains to think of something and my mind goes blank and then turns puerile, the way it does when people present me with the comments section of a visitors' book. I want to write 'FUCK OFF' like I did that time when I was 20 at the Chicklade Little Chef on the A303. Instead I write, 'May your Irish eyes always be smiling.'

The wedding breakfast finally appears. First, a stack of salmon with frizzy pubic lettuce; second, a plate of lukewarm lamb cutlets. Wideboy and I are running low on chat so we take the piss out of Charlie. Mmm, don't do that, I think, don't be a bitch, be supportive.

We fall silent and I glance at my phone. My brother's name is on the muted screen. I swipe and grasp the phone to my ear. 'What's wrong,' I say, quickly, anticipating the worst but praying in that heartbeat between now and then that it is something small, nothing, an amusing anecdote, a question ...

'Kate. Your dog. He's gone. He ran away.'

Handing the phone to Charlie, I walk out of the room, my eyes fixed like rocks in my head. As if operated by remote control I walk to a six-foot-high trolley the waiting staff are clearing the plates away to. It stands at a 45-degree angle to the window, creating a corner for me to slot myself in. I press in there like a small child behind a tree. With the kitchen doors flapping open and closed as service continues behind me, I stand facing the dirty plates and the aromas of cold lamb fat and gravy. Most plates are barely touched, very few mopped clean. Despite the curveball of shock, I'm still disgusted by food waste, by the human arrogance, ignorance and decadence that cause it.

All those uneaten dead baby sheep, those carrots ripped from the earth and returning to it, untasted. It's all more evidence, as if any more were needed, that humans are spoilt egomaniacal scum. My God, the dog has left me.

My mouth is open but no sound comes out; my breathing has all but stopped, but every cell in my body screams.

'Coat.' I exhale the words.

Charlie fetches the old coyote fur and stands beside me. He is not losing it like I am but he looks scared. Scared for the dog, and scared of me, or for me. I don't know. I feel his sweetness and vulnerability beside me. I am grateful for him.

Still gulping and gasping silently, I do not cry, but my mouth is agape, wet with strings of saliva. It's now that somewhere in my mind the phrase 'He's just a dog' starts to appear like a stupid flashing sign in an ancient landscape of love and pain. 'Just a dog.' Is it an attempt to make the pain subside, a desperate relativising mantra that also succeeds in humiliating my uncontrollable terrible fear and grief? 'Just a dog.' I can hear the gravel on the drive crunching underfoot as we walk to the car. 'I didn't say goodbye,' says Charlie. They'll understand. He has his arm around me. 'Can you drive?' he asks. The bride's preference for cheap wine didn't put him off drinking it.

I kick off my wedding shoes, pushing my feet sockless into a pair of cold wellies. As I climb into the car I imagine that we'd brought him with us and his little sleeping form is coiled in the back, inside the old pink and white wool blanket, one brow cocked in greeting as we return to the car. Swift pee and poo circuit of the car park and then we can drive home. As I start the engine and drive back the way we came just a few hours earlier I start to cry, big open-jawed, slobbery, salivary bawling. Flashes of women in hijabs keening over the corpses of children murdered by dictators jab at my consciousness. 'Just a dog.' This is the most acutely terrifying thing that has ever happened to me. I drive hunched over the wheel, calling both verbally and telepathically to my hound: 'Wolfy. Wolfy. Please be OK.' Meanwhile the bitch chorus has a persistent descant refrain: losing a dog is the worst thing that ever happened to you, you're pathetic. *Pathetic.*

'Wolfy, I am coming. Wolfy ...'

Instinctively I ring my mum, I ring my dad, knowing they cannot help but desperate to dilute the pain and be soothed and calmed by a grown-up. Charlie rings his mother too. There is traffic coming into London. Cars. Trucks. Vans. Bikes. Buses ... The lump of heavy wet fat in my skull pulses out its message. Please stay away from the road, Wolf.

In the list of bad things Wolfy can do, running away has never figured. It was the same gut instinct that told me he had not cocked his leg in the pet toiletries aisle of the Kilburn pet superstore. On a certain level, I had confidence in my dog very quickly. Had it been misplaced?

By the time we hit traffic on the A3 we have already created our poster on the DogLost website:

Date lost: 31 Oct.
Registered: 31 Oct.
Name: WOLFY.
Gender & breed: Male lurcher.
Age: Adult.
Colour: Blond.
Tagged: Yes.
Microchipped: Yes.
Where lost: Finsbury Park.
Lost in region: South East.
Postal code: N4.

The picture we use for the poster is of me and Wolfy on the beach at Dungeness. I am crouched down hugging the dog like a small child, my arms wrapped around him in an adoring stranglehold. It was taken the day after the anniversary party of an ex-boyfriend, who married one of my closest friends fairly swiftly after dumping me. For a while this felt like a significant event in my life, but to take umbrage at his new-found love with my old (and now not such great) mate, would have been to heartily embrace the victim role. I didn't mind. I was glad for them. I was. I'm a big person. I really am.

It was a full-on garden party complete with marquee and a mini food court. By the evening it had turned into a carnival of middle-aged hedonism, ably helped along by a variety of psychoactive substances. Incredibly, I had remained more or less straight and I remember standing and looking at these gurning old wrinklies – pals, colleagues, enemies, frenemies, exes and old bosses – thinking these are not the behaviours I expected of 50-year-olds when I was a kid. Back then, I thought middle-age hedonism meant stiff gins and Silk Cut.

In my new spirit of avoidance, I'd turned up too late to 'get involved', as they say, plus with a dog and Charlie. My gift for them was two bottles of 1998 Pomerol, not Petrus or anything too special, but nice enough claret, a treat. This ex, flying high, had thrown it down and said, 'I don't want this shit; I only like rum.'

Some equally hammered bozo swooped in to take it, but I had the advantage of being sober. 'That, actually, is my wine. I'm afraid I'm going to have to take it from you. So *so* sorry,' I said, polite, prissy and assertive like a police officer taking keys from a drunk.

Wolfy, Charlie and I had availed ourselves heavily of the excellent and under-patronised hog roast, and even more heavily of the sheaves of crackling the others were too wasted to find interesting. Full, we headed back to our chintzy B&B and, reassuring the owner that our dog *always* slept on the floor, had gone straight to bed, with Wolfy snoozing up there with us. After sex, we drank the wine I had regifted back to myself. Simple pleasures. Bordeaux, man, dog. I'm alright. The next day we'd gone to blow away our faint gossamer hangovers with a walk on the beach. The others, poor bastards, their brains would be pain and fog. What a result. That is why I am holding him so tight and smiling so widely in that photograph on the pebbly beach.

But my God, I'm not smiling now.

I'm on the phone again to Will, who tells us where he is: on the street where Wolfy was last seen in Stroud Green, about a mile or so from his house. As we get closer to it on our way down Seven Sisters Road, we both peer into the dark, wondering if we might spot the dog in one of the dead ends, doorways or narrow streets next to the low-rent casino, the Islamic Centre, Poundland, £5 haircuts and KFC. 'He loves KFC, he'll be there, eating bones, I bet.' I slow the car and Charlie runs out to peer into the narrow alleyway beside a betting shop and a snooker hall. I can see Wolfy's fur glowing white, reflecting the street lights. 'He's there.'

'Is it him? It can't be. Is it?' Charlie can see him too.

It's all a trick of our minds. A mirage. A ghost. We are willing him to be there. It's nothing.

A realisation flushes through me as my mind's eye helicopters up high over London; I'm hit by the massiveness of the city, of the near impossibility of the task of finding a dog. The feeling of hope leaving my body is so strong, so visceral, it is dizzying. London is not a cosy village. It is huge.

There are a billion hidden places, and eight million human beings whose interest in the dog will be either non-existent or covetous, or murderous. At what speed does a car kill a dog, at what speed does it injure it? Will that injury enable Wolfy to limp off and die under a dirty buddleia by the train tracks at Finsbury Park, or will he lie in the road? There are infinite possible worlds and in only one is he curled up on the ground beside a snooker club on Seven Sisters Road, eating discarded fried chicken.

'Oh my God. Wolfy. Where are you?' The keening returns. This is hell.

We park up by the last place Wolfy has been sighted, Regina Road in Stroud Green, a terrace of bay-window-fronted three-storey Victorian houses surrounded by streets of the same – it's the sort of place a young college professor might live, or us if we were less into the idea of Notting Hill and more into the idea of having a front door.

Will is already here. We three stand on the street in the dark. He has printed off some makeshift 'Have You Seen This Dog' flyers.

'When did he run off?'

'Around two or three, I think.'

'You think? You rang me around four.'

'It's been a pretty hectic afternoon.'

'How did he get out?'

'Bay opened the door. I told the kids, "Do *not* open the door."' His voice switches from stern to loving, compassionate, defensive. 'She's only small, she was excited about Halloween.'

As we talk, herds of little kids dressed as ghosts, witches and other monsters pass by, trick or treating and herded by a responsible adult at the rear. A lone kid in a spacesuit trots by followed by mum and a small mutt dressed as a pumpkin.

I know Will. He presents, always, a calm front. The stress isn't immediately obvious, it's subcutaneous, just below the surface. Will has met several people over the last two hours who have seen the dog since he left the main road he bolted down, and we are able to patch together his movements up until 6 p.m. Florence Road, Marquis Road, Hanley Road, Hornsey Road, Regina Road … this is where we are now, this is where the trail ends. 'I've been out here and the trail's blown hot and cold. Those sightings were all sound, totally plausible ones. I was on the right track but I've got to be honest, as time's gone on the scent has grown weaker. Fewer people have seen him. I thought about bringing Castor out when I came back to search, I thought he might sniff him out.'

'Hmmn, I don't know about that.'

'I couldn't, far too terrified of losing a second dog.'

Will, Charlie and I decide to all search alone. 'Let's split up.' Despite my utter despair, I add flatly, '*Scooby Doo* style.'

As we all set off in different directions Charlie and I walk together for a block. 'Will seems to be taking it in a casual kind of stride,' he says.

'I know he feels awful.' The desire to deflect any shade from my brother is fierce. I ask, without any sarcasm, more curiosity, 'Would it be better if he was screaming and panicking?'

'OK.'

I think of the exchange in the kitchen back in the summer. All the 'It'll be fines'. Have I cocked up here or what?

At the top of Regina Road, Charlie goes left and I go right. Before long I have found a woman who tried to catch him on Hornsey Road. She describes his lurking mien, sticking close to the wall, that turned into an unpredictable dance as she got closer: 'I stopped trying in the end because I knew I would drive him into the road.'

Where was he headed?

Towards Finsbury Park.

I head straight to Hornsey Road, stop by the steps of a large house on a walk-up like the ones in Notting Hill, but menace radiates from every window. Back home, in the right frame of mind, everyone feels like a friend I haven't had a drink with yet. Here, the people feel foreign and different, even when they're friendly; it's like they're aliens. Despite the street lights and windows glowing with domestication, lamps, kitchen strip lights, big tellies, the darkness presses in on me. I might as well be in Glasgow or Frankfurt. This isn't my London.

'Have you seen a dog like this?' I say, showing a woman some photos on my phone. 'Oh. Now.' She thinks, but I'm not sure what about. You've either seen it or you haven't. 'No, no, I haven't.' I'm about to politely extract myself when she starts giving me a blow-by-blow account of this one time she lost her cat.

At what point do you just cut them off and walk away? 'I must get on, sorry.' I back away with my hands up while she is mid-flow.

The cute mini-wizards have gone home swapped for unchaperoned teenagers, more threatening doorstepping crews with fireworks and bangers in their pockets and playing shit RnB on their phone speakers.

The last woman I speak to is on Hornsey Road. Yes, she saw the dog. Strolling around, cool as a cucumber. She tried to catch him. 'I went towards him really gently but I had my own dog with me and to catch your dog, I'd have had to let go of mine. Your dog got spooked, crossed the road' – those words, *crossed the road* – 'He went down Marlborough Road.'

The kids had been so excited about Halloween, Wolfy's disappearance has majorly harshed that mellow. I feel bad that other people feel bad. And I feel bad that I feel bad ... there is just no escaping this situation. Drinking or taking drugs or having a self-pitying wail that it's someone else's fault will not fix it. Once again, my powerless sensation overwhelms me. Come on, think. Use your brain.

I pull up all those streets on a map. Almost a straight line through Stroud Green from the borders of Tufnell Park. But which came first? Is he heading back towards us or away from the area, towards Finsbury Park? Have we been chasing away from where he is? The London that is so familiar and friendly is gone. Confusions overwhelm me. Where, even, am I?

'Charlie, can we look together? I'm unravelling a bit here. Where are you?'

Charlie and I meet on what I think is the other side of Stroud Green, more towards Finsbury Park, which seems to be where the dog headed. Here the suburban Victorian streets have made way for a more urban and grubby landscape. I am still in my wedding guest dress and the coyote coat. My wellies hammer back and forth against my shins and calves.

While no one is ever really out of place anywhere in London, unless they are wearing a burqa at a titty bar or fur in Stella

McCartney, I do not feel dressed right for Finsbury Park on a Saturday night.

Here, in a scrappy residential square patches of sulphurous smoke hang in the night air: fireworks; their bangs, whizzes and whines are layered with the flirtatious kiss-chase shrieks of teenage girls, and the barks of London yoot: 'bro', 'bruv' and 'bumberclart'. I imagine the dog coming upon this and running more, deeper into an area I don't know at all, further and further from home.

With me crouched on the kerb, crying and panicking again, Charlie cannot find any words to reassure me.

We drop back into Will's on the way home. Castor comes to greet me at the door. I want to have the love he wants. I stroke him and receive him but not with the 'Cas-TOR!' he is used to. I had forgotten about Castor.

My focus is on being cheerful. Brightly, I ask, 'Has Castor been fed?'

No. Steph shudders at the sight of the portions of turkey carcass I had got both dogs for their supper as I carry it outside and feed him with his bowl on the grass. I take a few emboldening sucks at the air and go inside. We count off the dog wardens we have rung, and read the advice on the DogLost website. We have all heard from some source or another that posters are key to finding lost dogs. If I bring more posters tomorrow perhaps you can take some out and about? 'Of course, of course,' says Will. We share our experiences out hunting this afternoon. Will also had someone who wanted to tell him all about their lost cat.

I reckon I've got 30 minutes before Charlie is screaming to get out of there. He will want to be at home. This isn't his family. It's mine. We both know that his mother would never have lost the dog. But to say it would be asinine. I am thankful he doesn't.

'I need to know what happened, Will, I need more information'.

Three of us sit at the kitchen table. Steph hovers.

'Could I have a drink?' I am given a glass of white wine in a Duralex tumbler. I feel like drinking it down like water.

'The dog wasn't happy. I was aware of that. When we took them for a walk on the Heath Castor was pulling at the front while Wolfy was a nightmare, dragging along slowly like we were leading him to his death.'

Were they OK off the lead?

'Castor was dragging Sam so hard he fell in the pond. He was good though, ran around and played with the kids. There was no way we were taking Wolfy off the lead.

'When we got back from lunch Steph and I went to bed to read the papers. The kids were excited about Halloween, but they had strict instructions not to open the door because Wolfy had taken up residence there as soon as we got back.

'I hear the doorbell and in a split second the door being cracked. I'm down the stairs: "Nooooooo! Who the fuck's opened the door?" Arty is standing there looking frightened. The other two Castor and Wolfy, have gone. I run outside and find the kids holding the dogs in the middle of the road.'

The hissing sound of air escaping through gritted teeth comes from Steph, who is busying herself doing nothing around the kitchen sink. Charlie says 'Fuck' softly under his breath.

'I yell to the kids, "Get inside now!"' Will continues. 'Sam, Bay and Castor run in. Wolfy stands there. I run to get him and he moves away.

'I'm just in trackie bums. I run out onto the street where he is about 100 yards down the road. He's not doing anything, just kind of skulking, hunched up and looking in my direction. And then I make a massive mistake, I start going for the dog, heading towards him and I don't know, knowing me, I would have said "Wolfy!" in a cross way, you know, like the guy on YouTube with the Labrador chasing the deer.

'Now Wolfy starts to run, and I mean really run. He crosses the road. He's not looking left and right, no Green Cross code – that was a new level of stressful. A dog running across the road like that, it's a shocking visual. You do a weird thing, instead of running to catch them you sort of slow down in the panic, there's a strange moment where time changes. The dog could be dead in a second. Now he's bolting down the left-hand side of the road with the flow of the traffic and I'm running after him. No top, no shoes.

'A guy in a blue Transit van pulls up, he's heading east towards the dog, and he's shouting at me, "Get in the van, get in the van, I'll help you." Van starts moving before I've even shut the door.

'Wolfy's gone full greyhound now, people are shouting at him. He's a big dog in bolt mode. You're going to register that. He must have sensed other people's focus on him. He goes faster.'

Charlie asks, 'How close were you to him?'

'Listen, there was no hot pursuit. The dog's outrunning the traffic once we get to the junction with Holloway Road. We're way behind him. We had an idea he had gone left, north, towards Archway. But perhaps he'd gone right. We're shouting to the traffic on the southbound side, asking if they've seen a dog running in the road. He's obviously crossed the road as people are pointing towards the residential streets on the Finsbury Park side. There's six lanes on that road.'

Charlie and I flinch, like someone has raised their hand to us.

'The guy in the blue Transit van said, "I can't help you any more. You're better off on foot." I didn't have any shoes on but he was right. I do a semicircle crossing over the road and down some back streets. There were lots of people at that point who had seen the dog. Some are pointing me in the way of Iceland and Seven Sisters, some keep pointing me north to Archway.

'That's when I went home and called you.'

I'm confused now. My brain isn't great at logistical things at the best of times, and I start tapping the map on my cracked and battered phone. 'Riiight, so if he was here, here and here, the next place we should look is ...'

I don't know.

'I guess just go back where we were today?' says Will. It's a question.

I'm trying to formulate a plan in my head but it's numb as a rock.

Back at home the air is suffocating without a tail whipping it, without 16 claws ticking back and forth over the floorboards. The dog took up very little space in cubic centimetres, and half of that was legs. But the way he raised the energy and brought love, humour and fur into every room was vast. His absence is present, the empty spot by the wall in the hall where he comes to watch us cook, the indent on his favourite spot on the sofa, the spot on the bathroom floor with his twin bliss of cool tiles and dirty washing. There's a grey cast to everything.

Please be OK, Wolfy, go somewhere safe. I'm coming for you.

Charlie is teetering on the edge of calm, fury and defeat. These are three very different states and I am half alert to the change in his mood and half can't be bothered. I know he is as desperate as I am and we hold each other in the kitchen, knowing that only us two could imagine how devastating and frightening this is. A part of me can't believe the weight of emotion invested in one dog.

We go to bed. He sleeps. He always sleeps.

There are things you have to do when you lose a dog. Partly for your own sanity, partly because it's genuinely helpful. The first is to make an attention-grabbing poster.

I sit up in bed and work quickly on a Word document: a few colours, the words LOST DOG writ large and, aside from those essential details, both our phone numbers and a strong picture.

From among the hundreds of photos I have of the dog, which should I use?

It is a month earlier and I am in Cornwall with the dog, staying in a 1930s house my dad has taken near Constantine Bay on the north coast for a big family gathering with my stepmother and his six kids. On our first morning the dog and I rise before six, before the sun, and set out. There are snuffles from the kids' dorm, where five grandchildren are bunked up together in a room with cracked Lino, ping-pong table and two broken televisions; at the opposite end of the house there are bellowing snores from the oldies in the most comfortable rooms. My stepmother has put Post-it notes with our names on the doors. All the couples have got double rooms. The ones with kids have got the best ones.

These big family holidays infantilised me, I knew, as more and more of my siblings, all younger, married and reproduced. Charlie never came – too far, too many people, too busy, no thanks – so my learning-disabled brother Tom and I always got the bum bedrooms because us two were the least changed from our child status. Fair enough. I didn't mind being pushed further and further down the bedroom ranking, sliding ever closer to the nursery wing the older I got. There's a metaphor for old age.

This is my first time there with Wolfy and I've discovered he loves the beach – when I took him there the evening we arrived, the shambling, frankly perplexingly slow pace he assumes in the city's parks was swapped for top-speed sighthound looning. He'd hit the sand and gone at it full tilt in the scissoring double-suspension gallop of a racing greyhound. He ran around me in wide circles or chased me through the sea into the surf in an undulating motion like a needle through silk. Even in deep water he would touch the bottom and then spring up and down through the waves like a dolphin crossed with a kangaroo. It was a marvel. As his wet fur dried by the fire in the evening he smelt the very essence of sea spray.

Wolfy isn't allowed upstairs at the house at Constantine, and coming down in the morning I can hear his anticipatory whimpers as he registers the creak of my step on the back stairs. I open the kitchen door and he is right there, wagging his ecstatic welcome.

'Morning Woofs.' His cold nose touches my cheek and he gives the corner of my mouth a single brief dab with his tongue, which I think is a curious 'What does she smell like today?' and an affectionate greeting. 'Mmmmn, Wolfy.' I put my forehead on the top of his head and smell and kiss him back. 'Let's go walkies. Walkies?' Excited little squeaks and a furiously wagging tail affirm that this is a great idea and we set out through a door in the concrete wet room, which reeks of damp sour old neoprene. This house has lavish quantities of doors; we are spoilt.

Beyond the low garden wall, and it is high tide. The Atlantic Ocean shifts without breaking. Its dark breath sends a bracing tang of the sea, which mingles with the smell of cut grass and gravel.

We are happy. Acutely so. It is a moment of exquisite and simple joy. What a life. As dawn breaks the air is saturated with rose gold and that's when I take a photograph of him. He is alert, looking forward and bathed in the richest sunlight of a new day.

Breathing deep, in and out, I battle the urge to cry again and choose this picture. I attach the file and post it to Twitter. 'I've lost my beautiful dog. Last seen belting towards Finsbury Park. Please Twitter, and God if you're there, help me find him.'

CHAPTER SEVEN

At four the next morning the phone rings and wakes me with an electric start from an unexpectedly thick, heavy sleep. For a moment the dog is asleep in his bed and all is well, like those brief moments of oblivious sweetness before an evil hangover kicks in. Reality weighs back into the room and brings the grey ash of sickening misery with it. I see the mobile on the floor. Its old-fashioned telephone ringtone is savage. Next to it, nothing, a gaping hole; the dog's empty bed is at Will's house still.

'Hello.' My voice has that startled confusion of someone woken at 3 a.m. by a call from a strange number.

'Oh. Yeah. Er. Hiya. I were wonderin'. Have you lost a dog?'

'Yes. Yes! Yes I have.' Hope surges through my body and I feel daft for making such a huge fuss. He has been gone only 12 hours and now someone's got him. What a relief . . .

'I seen a dog just like yours just now, see, by the M602 . . .' My mind grinds the information like a rusty mangle. The M602? Salford? I used to go to school there. I briefly picture Wolfy on the hard shoulder. How did the dog get to Manch— 'yer, it looked dead scared,' the guy continues confidently, 'until it were hit by a . . .' As he says those last words I know it's a joke; the Greek chorus behind the caller let contained laughter through their lips with a round of raspberries and stoned hilarity.

'By a lorry.' The caller laughs too.

I can see them, rolling around, cruel nobody shitheads. And I can picture the scene they have set for me: my dog, dead, destroyed beyond all recognition to all but me, who sees the few remaining loose tufts of familiar fur not stuck and ground into his entrails. All anyone else would see is just a dog, or just roadkill, gone for ever, just hair and bone in someone's bumper.

Charlie is sitting up in bed beside me. 'What? What?'

I tell him in a neutral flat voice.

As I am slipping back to sleep, the phone rings again. I answer more cautiously this time.

'I've found your dog.'

'Where?'

'In a kebab.'

I roll over and hug my arms tight around myself and lie in bed for a few minutes, staring at the top of the rowan tree on Treadgold, visible above the slate of Janice's roof, its leaves are yellow now but a few withered berries still cling to its branches. Beyond the rooftops and chimney stacks are the maple, plane and chestnuts edging Avondale Park. That park was a huge slurry pit back when our house was built, when the area was still known for its pottery, piggeries and slums. Now it is Wolfy's favourite place for a pee and a poo before bed. It is? Or was? If he doesn't come home I will never go there again. The house still feels like it is covered in ash and the molecules in the air are as grey as I feel. Soon I'll be forced up by the bossy alarm call that is a bladder, but perhaps if I go foetal I can buy another ten minutes. I curl up and look at the middle of the bed, where the dog would leap to join us once he sensed we were waking up. He'd pad across the duvet before dramatically crashing down with his entire body stretched out, flush against Charlie's body. After a groan of happiness as he exhaled he'd cock his head sideways and back, swivel it 180 degrees like an owl and stare at me with those shiny black eyes. He'd make a small sound, the tiniest sound, like a trumpet tuning: half scratchy air, half off squeaky note.

'Hi Woofs.'

Where is he? Is he alive, is he cold, is he hungry? Has he found water? If he is alive, will he stay alive? Does someone have him or is he alone, injured and dying? Where is my dog?

I go down to make mugs of businesslike working-class tea, thick, terracotta-coloured, milky. This is not a situation that calls for weak Darjeeling with a slice of lemon in a porcelain cup. We need a proper brew. Tea and cigarettes come into their own, don't they, in grief, they acquire a whole new substance, texture and satisfaction. It must be an interaction with whatever speedy hormones the body's chemist is pumping out.

Castor moves noiselessly from where he has slept on the egg-yolk yellow woolly armchair and stands beside me in the kitchen. I try to muster feelings for him. I stroke him and give him a bowl of Woof Nuts.

I go back to bed and Charlie and I discuss our plan of action for the day while I go to check Twitter to see if anything has happened there. Castor stands beside the bed, hooting his desire to join us. He floats up almost silent, a slithery whippety lurcher with a long thin nose. He is nothing like Wolfy. 'Hey boy,' I whisper.

He stares hopefully at me, boss-eyed and looking for love. A black cylinder of pain spins in my chest. I stroke him and scroll the replies and the tweets with #findwolfy.

The one I sent last night has been retweeted by Jeremy Clarkson. It's not yet 9 a.m. and it has already been retweeted a thousand times.

'So I suppose that was some of his followers there on the phone.'

In another reality, I would have found a retweet by Jeremy Clarkson funny and amazing in a ludicrous way, but in this context, it's just a thing; a good thing because it has fuelled an insane amount of engagement, but no big thing. The spectrum of feelings I can experience has shrunk. All are subsumed by loss, panic and longing.

Wolfy's loss has been shared by DogLost.com. This charity calls on local volunteers to help ramp up local interest in finding dogs and cats. You don't realise these resources exist until you need them. When a dog disappears all you have is volunteers. It's not a police matter. There's no state resource, aside from the dog wardens, and they only get involved when a dog is found, dead or alive. They don't do the finding.

Lose a dog, and you're relying entirely on the kindness of strangers.

A lot of strangers are being kind to us on Twitter. They are full of suggestions. Some are offering credible, incredible, help. A woman called @JustEmmaPratt who appears to be an amateur lost dog hunter and a community policeman called @moonieman stand out. I know the police don't get involved with lost pets, and so the fact we have this guy on board feels like a coup.

He tweets me, 'What does he look like?'

'Small, blond, shaggy like a deerhound.'

'We're all on the lookout,' he says. A plural. We?

There are hundreds of replies, supportive mostly; and several suggestions that I try the nearest Korean restaurant. The trolling doesn't move me.

Charlie chooses to walk the streets near Will's, pinning up posters. He goes to the copy shop while I head off to the Scrubs to walk Castor. The colours are plain and flat, no more nuanced than a cheap box of children's pencils. The trees are green, the path is brown, the tarmac is grey, the air is mild. Nothing more. I limp around, then, cutting the walk short, I turn back and call Castor, only to spot him rolling gleefully. When Wolfy rolls it's to scratch his back, to express joy. When Castor rolls, all of the above, plus fox caca. Eau de Reynard. He shoots over. A broad strip of black reeking shit is dashed from his ear to the tip of his tail.

'Gargh!' I try not to sound angry. There is no point, the deed is done. 'Oh Castor.' My voice is defeated.

'Fox poo?' a cheery voice calls to me and I look across to see a woman with a pencil-thin, charcoal shaggy-haired lurcher trotting beside her.

I nod.

'Where's your other dog? What's it called?'

'Wolfy.' The lump in my throat makes my voice sound oddly strangled. 'He's lost.'

'Oh, he'll make his way home soon enough. I knew this person ...' She rattles off a story about someone else's dog running off but knowing their route home after all that leg-cocking round the streets of W11 and W10. 'Hell, of course, absolute hell and then he pops up after a night on the tiles, like nothing happened.'

She bends to one side and pats her hound, standing quietly at her side, just like Wolfy would be if he was here. I'm jealous of her, standing there with her dog. Wolfy. Wolfy. The constant internal keening ramps up. I shake my head. 'He ran away in north London, we've never walked it, he bolted, he won't have marked the route back to my brother's. He's lost. That's if he's alive.'

'Now you mustn't worry. They're hardy beasts, these lurchers, I'm sure he will return.'

'Do you think so?' I'm grasping at the hope in her breezy, almost patronising cheer.

'Of course I think so. Unless the Travellers have him.'

What?

'Terrors, they're terrors.' She has a new story now, about a lurcher stolen and thrown into the back of a van outside the post office on North Pole Road and retrieved a matter of hours later from a camp in Manchester.

I wade back through the heavy air and drive Castor home to wash off the cloying fetid musk of Mr Fox. Bent over him, scrubbing at something that I know, however long I stand in the shower, will haunt my nostrils all day. Being here, doing this with the wrong dog, takes me back to that first day

Wolfy arrived. My tears are washed down the plughole with the shitty soapy water.

Will, my youngest brother, is a handsome bugger. Out of all of us, he's got the best looks and proportions. People say he looks like Hugh Grant, but that's doing Will a disservice. He's six years younger than me and, aside from a few months with my dad and stepmother after he was born, he always lived with my mum. She came back for him and took him with her one day, and left Tom and me behind. My mum was suffering from post-natal depression and the man who went on to be her second husband convinced her we would be better off with my dad. All I knew was I came home one day and my dad said, 'Your mother has gone, again.'

So it wasn't just my mummy I missed, I also missed little Will. I remember seeing his chubby two-year-old form growing bigger through the bobbly glass in the front door of the house Dad rented near the hospital. Will would run up the path ahead of mum to collect me for an access visit, and open up the letter box: 'Katie!'

Within two years of them splitting up my dad moved up north. The weekend visits with Mum stopped and I saw even less of her and my baby brother, but I never missed them any less. As a grown-up, with all these decades between now and then, I still think of Will as something precious and golden, something rare, because back then he was in limited supply. No commodity is as valuable as a human you love and – now I understand – a dog you love too.

I bang on his front door like I have so many times before. I hear the skiffling erratic footsteps of a small person coming to the door. I do my usual thing and look through the letter box. 'Aunty Kate!'

Arty comes thumping to the door and arranges a well-rehearsed sequence of boxes and books so he can reach the lock to let me in. I sweep him up for a cuddle that turns into a dangle upside down and a walk up my legs and a kissy-monstering for ultimate giggles. The welcome ritual done, we walk into the house. Sam and Bay are playing in the sitting room and they look up at me but say nothing. 'Bay.' I put out my arms and she reluctantly lets me hold her. Any other time she would have run to the door and been there in the queue for hugs, kisses, silly voices and being picked up and turned upside down too. 'I am not cross about Wolfy. Aunty Katie loves you and it's not your fault.' She nods and mumbles and backs away with her eyes down.

I caused this, I think.

Through in the kitchen, Steph too seems subdued. 'Oh hello, Kate,' she says, a slight trace of weariness, which I am hyperalert to now.

Will is cheerful but the dynamic is unfamiliar and strained. Has he had to defend me? Is he torn? No one wants to lose their dog. But in losing mine, I'm reliving the feelings of absolute powerlessness of when I had little access to half my family. I'm in the room with them but the closeness is compromised.

I have to find Wolfy. If I don't find Wolfy how will anything ever be normal again between us?

Will hands me a big stack of posters he's printed and walks me to the front door. 'It's not your fault, Will, I should never have left him with you. I made a mistake.'

He says nothing. I suspect that he is torn between things, between me and my dog and Steph, who was being so remote. I wonder if she's angry. Angry women scare me.

I am calling his name again, walking up and down Regina Road where he was last seen. It is the first day of November and the sun is low and bright, the sky a startling cobalt. My instinct is to be uplifted by this even if my spirit is not willing. Wherever Wolfy is, if he is alive, at least he is not cold or wet. I fish about in my hot scrambled mind for hope as I walk the streets stopping people, putting posters through letter boxes and ringing doorbells. 'Have you seen my dog? He was last seen yesterday, near here.'

People are kind. 'No, sorry. Good luck. I hope you find him.'

My gut tells me to take a narrow turning over pitted broken tarmac leading to a row of garages and lock-ups. He's there, I am sure of it. He is curled up and hidden somewhere in that cul de sac, away from people. I walk slowly, calling his name. 'Woooolfy. Woooolfy.'

There's an excitement. It's the same confused adrenaline of starting a new school, of heading into the unknown with fear and curiosity. I've got this hunch. I am going to find him here in these open cinderblock garages with leaves blown into sprawling pyramids in the corners.

Behind the garages I can hear a full congregation praising the Lord in the enthusiastic Pentecostal style, loud singing and clapping that goes on for fifteen minutes or so. To this chorus of faith and hope, I creep and gently call until my voice tails off: 'Woooolfy.' Where is my God-spelt dog now? I have forensically, pointlessly explored one-billionth of London. Of course he's not there. It was just a surge of the hopeless hope.

Two dog owners called Em and Al have joined me with their cockerpoo puppy, Bua. I know their mother and she suggested they come all the way from Fulham to Finsbury Park and help me. They are hungover and as young and bouncy as the puppy they bring with them. Their little Bua wiggles and yips along beside them like an animated mop head.

I don't understand why they are helping me. 'We only just got our dog and we love her so much, we couldn't bear to lose her, we just want to help you.' I am so grateful not to be alone.

Walking the muddled grid of Stroud Green's boxy Edwardian terraces, I regularly comb Twitter. The editor of the *Independent on Sunday* tells me she lost her dog, Olive, once.

'Have you been to the police?'

How many dogs go missing every year? Thousands.

Every retweet of my original tweet generates more people telling me the dog is in kebabs, that I am a terrible dog owner, that they hope I find my dog, that they are sorry, that they are out putting up posters and looking for Wolfy and, more specifically, that a dog like him has been seen in Clissold Park, over a mile away in Stoke Newington. Charlie heads over there. I will carry on combing these streets.

I stop to drink a cup of tea in a cafe on Tollington Park. All around me couples and friends eat eggs Benedict and turn the pages of Sunday supplements. They are living the brunching dream.

It's too much, so I move outside to a table in the cold sun. An older woman, slim, bleached-blond hair with a heavy fringe and wearing 'the fashions', keeps looking over at me; she has a strong handsome face ravaged, I can tell, by countless nights on drugs in discos. I know those faces, wrinkles brined in fags and booze and cured by sunshine. Living a plain old hard life ravages a face in a different way to the high life and hedonism writ across hers.

She's not like the friendly dog walkers who have approached me throughout the morning. Maybe she heard me telling Charlie to head for Clissold Park. Maybe she clocked the stack of posters beside me. She draws on a vape and squints at me. 'Lost yer dog, babe?' Her voice belongs in a bookie's or a rough boozer, its feminine essence lost.

If I could have pretended I didn't care, and that the dog was *just a dog*, it would have been to this cool Medusa in smudged black eyeliner. I trot out the story. Brother's house, the high-speed dash from Tufnell to Finsbury, been 24 hours, rescue dog, heartbroken, hope he's alive.

'He'll come home,' she says.

I repeat that the dog's too far away from home to find his way back, that there is no scent for him to follow back. 'Where d'you live then?'

'Notting Hill, well, Dale, the not-rich bit, you know it? Down by Latimer tube. You probably don't.'

'Yeah, I know exactly where you mean.' She peers at me under the bleached fringe, jabbing at me with her vape and a glossy black nail-bar talon. 'And I know you, babe. I've seen you round Tim's.' Her gurgling, phlegmy laugh is grimly knowing. 'You still see him?'

'Not so much. Not since the dog—' Blunt needles jab at the back of my eyes. 'I've cleaned up a lot. I am a lot happier. Was a lot happier.'

'Me too. Tried AA, settled on NA – amazing who you meet in there. It's better than the Groucho. Don't go there any more, either. Even given up fags.' She waves the vape.

I ask for the bill, and she insists on paying. 'I'll be honest, I never really liked you. Not to be trusted, journalists. I always thought you were a bit of a twat. But you're a good woman. I can see that now I've discovered my inner nice person. It's taken a while.'

My dog-hunting pals return and hover like delicate creatures on the edges of her hard-boiled 1,000-year-old supermodel aura. They have to leave now. I say an enthusiastic round of thanks to them and stand up to leave. She stands up too and folds me in her creaking leather arms. She smells of men's Vetiver aftershave, Elnett hairspray and fruity vape fumes. 'Good luck finding your dog, babe.'

Charlie calls. He is walking round the perimeter of Clissold Park calling the dog's name. He says that dog walkers, out on a Sunday, come and said, 'Oh I've heard about your dog, don't worry, we'll keep an eye out, it's a great community round here.' People do care.

The people I am stopping are varying shades of middle-class, the sort who would have been tucked up guzzling tea, Malbec, Chardonnay and Kettle Chips in front of *The X Factor* while Wolfy was roaming the streets last night. I need to push on out of my comfort zone. Widen out the demographic.

The other side of Tollington Park is the Andover Estate, with flats stuffed into five-storey red-brick blocks. I walk for a few streets stopping no one, shy and awkward and weakened by one of the regular waves of hopelessness. Park that feeling, I tell myself, you have to push on.

From cheerful counter staff in crammed corner shops, to merry drinkers outside pubs, people are consistently warm and interested. I stop a police van full of hatchet-faced coppers. 'I've lost my dog, can I show you a picture of him? I'm going out of my mind.'

'How long's it been now?'

'Over a day.'

'Give us a poster, we'll put it up in the station'. As the light fades, I end up on a low-rise street with the sort of tall but narrow hutches the state rents to large families. I approach three men shouting at each other in a concreted front yard. 'Excuse me ...'

This is not London in my own image.

One guy steps to the side and leans over his creaking gate to look at my lost dog flyer. It's not easy to understand what he is saying but he is determined and so am I. I listen, intent, to his thick accent. It reminds me of the times when I can't understand my brother Tom's speech. He tries again and again, and again. At first he asks me simple questions: 'Where you lose?' Tufnell Park. 'How old he?' About five.

Then in this fractured English he starts to tell me his story. It is impossible to track and he knows it, so he repeats it over and over while I try to tune in. I nod along, clueless, my earnest sympathetic nodding the epitome of middle-class politesse. 'I have dog. Stolen, stolen. Very bad man, he lie. He take dog.' I nod, thank him. Dark brown skin, Caucasian features, straight thick black hair, short, agile. Despite the month, he wears Nike pool slides with a suit jacket and tracksuit bottoms. Where is he from? Albania? No, this isn't a European language. Iraq, Iran, Algeria ... is he a Kurd? I don't know. 'I loved my dog like my children.' In his thick broken English, this I understand.

'You understand,' he says.

'I understand,' I say.

'Very stressful time for you.'

'Yes, it's stressful.'

He walks me to the end of his street, talking to me still. I shake his hand and punch my number into his phone. On Hornsey Road we say goodbye.

I'd read something recently about all the dogs euthanised on the orders of the British government at the start of the Blitz in 1939, nearly a million of them, some completely pointlessly. In his memoir *Sleeping with Dogs*, the art critic Brian Sewell writes about his father taking his first childhood dog down to the beach and shooting it in the head as the Second World War began.

I've never known real suffering.

What I feel is what I feel. It's not going to change because I've rationalised it and deemed it insignificant in the grander scheme of human suffering.

This guy, what has he left behind? Why is he here?

I try to breathe hope into my body, which is fizzing with sadness. I ring Charlie to tell him I am coming home. I'll walk back through Finsbury, Holloway, up Tufnell Park Road, tracking back near the main arteries that brought Wolfy here. I set out and pass a dumped fake-leather sofa by a row of industrial wheelie bins in a scrappy dead end behind a row of shops. I imagine Wolfy asleep on it.

I perch there, crying with frustration, tiredness and just the utter insignificance of all these human lives piled on top of each other, whether it's behind £5,000 curtains or greying broken glass. Stupid fleas in our ugly concrete universe. I cry until I remember my bladder, which has been distended and aching for hours now. I piss rivers behind one of the bins, hidden away from the orange street lights, and wonder if Wolfy can smell it.

Reversing back along the route that I know Wolfy ran, I run my hand along the walls hoping to leave a scent and willing the traffic in his favour should he follow it. A cold wind blows down Seven Sisters Road, and I can hear fireworks popping randomly. Guy Fawkes and Diwali are a few days away. The fireworks will get worse.

I mistakenly drift back towards Stroud Green. The streets are empty, their unfamiliarity disorientates me and the architecture flattens under the street lights; all I can see is light and dark, lots and lots of malevolent darkness, like the whole experience rendered into a negative. After a light rain shower, the wet leaves glisten on the pavement like broken glass. More of the people I stop now are rambling and unwell.

I stand on the steps of a large Victorian house converted to flats and a woman with her hair piled up under a head scarf is initially curious and concerned, but quickly her conversation moves to complaint and the problems she's having with the 'drug addicts' who live upstairs. She needs to get it off her chest. I sympathise and put my number in her phone. She is still talking as I back away saying, 'If you see the dog, please call me. I'm desperate.'

On the corner of Hanley Road and Hornsey Lane, I stop a man. 'Excuse me, have you seen this dog?' I raise my phone, holding up the picture of Wolfy in Cornwall.

'It's me. Remember? Marwan? You spoke me already.' It's the man who had explained with such persistence how he had lost his own dog. 'You still looking?'

CHAPTER EIGHT

It's 6 a.m. and Charlie's alarm is thrashing our waking synapses. They start to spit and crackle and that second of blissful ignorance is overwhelmed once more by the reality Wolfy: gone. It comes rushing in with an electric jolt of worry and grief. Newsflash. Everything's shit today! Kapow. I am wide awake.

Castor does not come upstairs to hoot his usual morning greeting. Downstairs and he is curled up tight in the yellow armchair. He opens an eye and looks up at me. Am I projecting sadness and caution on him or is he feeling the immense downer here?

'Come on little chap.' I drive him straight to the Scrubs and as on every other day he rolls in the pitch-black, sticky pointy-ended caca of fox – smellmageddon. Once again I am in the shower reliving the moment when Wolfy first came home, when I realised the intimacy of dog ownership was about way more than Bonio and throwing sticks. Owning a dog was profound, a physical and emotional investment. With love, always, comes the promise of pain.

Where are you Wolfy?

I've been sitting at my desk for a couple of hours, writing a bit, combing Twitter a bit more. I respond to every tweet, eager to cultivate the attention of strangers. Charlie works from home, sitting on the sofa, making booming phone calls of fake confidence to his clients. Oblivious to the situation.

My phone rings.

'Is Marwan. I talk you yesterday. My daughter, she thinks she saw your dog in the bus station.'

'Hello.' His daughter comes on the line, north London accent through and through, innit. 'Yeah, I think I seen your dog in the bus station. It was just kind of wandering about. Looked a bit lost but calm.'

Is this for real? When? 'About nine, a bit later maybe, on Saturday night. Near the stop for the number 19.'

A dog wandering around a busy bus station doesn't sound quite right but the location makes sense. I decide to talk about the reward. If they sound greedy or eager then my caution will rise.

'We would never, never take money.'

Charlie is looking at me, mouthing, 'What?'

I come off the phone. 'Someone says they saw the dog at the bus station in Finsbury Park on Saturday night. Would he go to such a busy place? Could he have got on a bus? He can't have got on a bus.'

I visualise him getting on a bus.

The lady in the information office stares at me, blank and bored. She takes on the information of a bus-riding dog that looks like a skinny yak with the same indifference as a query about the next bus to Oxford Street. Hence, I am surprised and touched that when I ask her to put a poster on the glass in her booth she says in a West African accent, 'Of course, I hope you find him.'

As she places it I motion for her to put it somewhere more prominent, which she does. Every time someone does something unexpectedly nice for me, a worm of hope wriggles through my core.

Finsbury Park was very Irish back in the day. Now it is, like a lot of London, very everything, but the pubs retain an Oirish flavour. It's not even lunchtime, yet a few wiry stalwarts are supping pints of lager and Guinness in a high-ceilinged, ugly, proper drinkers' pub called the Twelve Pins, calmly committed to the alcohol, stolid, quiet, elbow up, elbow down. No eggs Benedict here.

Finsbury Park is an armpit. I haven't been to a pub here since I was a student, when I used to go to gigs at the George Robey, a live music pub on what was known in gigging parlance as the 'toilet circuit'.

I stand at the bar by the door delaying the moment when I will lurch into the personal space of complete strangers and deliver the lost dog spiel.

'Excuse me …' The guy barely registers my presence. I leave a flyer and move on. 'Excuse me …' My next approach is to a tiny man in a flat cap, no more than five foot or so. I show him one of the flyers.

'Ah, that's a fine-looking lurcher there, what is he, a fen, looks like one of Mik Douglas's, under twenty-three is he, got a bit of weight on him' – He starts wheezing out a little chuckle and his shoulders shake – 'that'll soon go if he's gone walkies on his own.' More wheezy chuckles.

His speech is as rapid as his accent is thick and I have to keep stopping him to repeat what he's saying. 'Used to know a dog like this back in Ireland, Lord Conan Finnegan he was called, champion he was, oh I won a few on that dog on the track at Powerstown, mind his legs are a bit short, you know the old story, "I think my dog is a Norfolk lurcher, every time I slip him on a hare he has got norfolking chance of catching it".'

This last elicits choking and delighted wheezes. 'You want to visit the Traveller folk, there's nothing those fellas don't know about the running dogs, he may have found his way there, always a home for a lurcher with a Traveller if he can run.'

He returns to face his pint, smiling. 'Can I buy you a drink?' I ask.

'Why not just a half, I won't say no, you can for sure. Ah, what a dog, ten euro I put on 'im, went home that night with three hundred in me pocket, I hope you find your boy, they're a strong fecker, the lurcher, he'll be doing OK out there with the foxes, don't you worry.'

I buy the guy a pint and move on to the next man, who grunts and ignores me.

On the way home I drop in at Will's. He is working from home and on the table in front of him is a jam jar full of cat munchies that he has been cycling around with, shaking them and calling Wolfy. The dog has always liked eating his cat Norfolk's Munchies – could the sound of them rattling in a jar bring him home? We debrief on the Wolfy hunt.

'Did you see Ronnie Wood tweeted your poster?' says Will. 'And Clarkson.'

'He started it,' I say. 'It's why we have all these retweets.'

'Nuts,' says Will.

'The power of celebrity.'

One of the pressing reasons I have for going back to my desk is to set up this week's story about a new Asian restaurant in Mayfair, London's most mind-bogglingly expensive neighbourhood: three-bed flat, six million quid. It's called Sexy Fish and is huge, flashy and owned, like so many things are now, by an intensively coiffed and tanned billionaire. This one is called Richard Caring.

Come Thursday, I'll be sat in Sexy Fish watching the social mob in a feeding frenzy. Half of them, no, most of them, won't be paying for their dinner, but the people who follow them in will, and through the nose at that. Be it a lost dog or a fancy restaurant, a celebrity endorsement is worth its weight in normal punters.

Kay Burley, Ricky Gervais, Amanda Holden, Jane Fallon … the celebrity retweets are piling up but Jeremy's fans are the easiest to spot. A certain type of male tweeter ensures they copy him in on their supportive tweets or their tweets about seeing Wolfy being put in a kebab. Some of them make jokes about Argentinans. They're so desperate to impress their hero. He's lording it up in Barbados on a mate's yacht and Grant from

Swindon's desperately jumping up and down hoping he spots his stupid pub humour on Twitter.

I pull up the screen and read, '@jeremyclarkson @spicerlife Think I've found that dog, just been to that new Korean restaurant. I especially enjoyed the meatballs, they're the dog's bollocks.'

I tweet back to the guy, 'Thanks so much for your support. My dog's neutered so it can't have been him.'

'Why do you answer?' Will is disappointed in me. The basic rule of social media is don't feed the trolls. 'It's a waste of energy.'

'I try to answer all the tweets.'

'Oh dear,' says Will.

'I can't help myself. This guy. "You can bet his new owners keep him on a lead, why didn't you?" I told him the dog was inside and he goes, "Lost your sense of humour as well as your dog, you silly woman." "The two are intrinsically linked you sad, fat, bald, bad sunglasses-wearing c**t."'

'Did you say that?'

'Yes. It gives me a thrill.'

'I sent a tweet to Jeremy Corbyn,' says Will. 'He's the MP round here.'

'Me too, and David Cameron. I wonder if they will help the Twitter hunt to #findwolfy? I feel like one of those starfucker parents that pretends their child has a terminal illness just so they can meet their favourite member of Girls Aloud.'

'Yes, that *Little Britain* sketch had crossed my mind,' says Will.

I tell him about my visit to the Twelve Pins. He says, 'I went in all those Irish pubs on Sunday saying "have you seen a lurcher" and of course, ask a silly question. They all had.'

'Will, I think that's racist.'

'No it's not, it's a matter of fact. Irish people love a lurcher.'

'I had an interesting chat with one of the guys I approached this morning, he said to talk to the Travellers.'

This entire exchange is full of subjects that would usually prompt a round of piss-taking and silly voices – Jeremy Clarkson, *Little Britain*, Irish pubs, sending tweets to politicians, it's all ridiculous really – but the whole thing passes without a single laugh. I say sorry to Will again and he says, 'Don't say that. It's OK, I understand, we have to find him. Wolfy is family.'

I spend the afternoon flicking between Twitter and wardens and neighbourhood groups and carry on setting up that week's dumb story (which was my idea) about the new restaurant with a silly name.

Charlie asks me what Will's been doing. 'What'd he have to say then?' His lip-curling and sarcastic tone shocks me. 'Did he bother to even look for the dog yesterday?'

There have been dark clouds around Will's name for the last two days, but now Charlie's anger is no longer just a threat; the clouds have opened and his fury is out in the open.

'Yes, he's been out but he has three kids, work, of course he has to do other things.'

'They've made no effort at all.'

'That's absolutely not the truth and anyway it's my fault the dog ran away. It's straight up my stupid fault.'

He falls silent, loudly reserving his opinion on the matter. I shut myself in the shit pit and wonder what will happen to us if Wolfy isn't found, or if he turns up dead. What will happen to my relationship with Will, and Steph, and the kids?

I put the phone down on mum this evening. She rang to console me but with little in the way of dog lost conversation starters I'd lost my patience when she had offered the conciliatory and sage advice that, 'You'd better get a female dog next time . . .'

'Next time?' I'd growled in response, furious that a next time was even being mooted at this stage. Surely we were still hunting for Wolfy? 'Mum, your phobia of male dogs, of all males in fact, is not what I need right now. I'm planning on finding my dog.'

I have hurt her now. Damn, why do I always do that? She's just trying to maternally soothe me from a long distance. And whatever do you say to someone who has lost their dog? Why am I such a punishing brute to my mum, why do I make her suffer? Why do we torture the people who love us the most and dance around kissing the arses of the mean ones? Why? I hate myself now; I'm miserable *and* I hate myself. I have a good idea, in fact. I'm beginning to accrue a long list of what people say. By now I have stopped enough people, received enough phone calls and read enough Tweets to know.

Someone's got him, taken him in out of kindness, an old person probably ... Have you thought of having a barbecue in the middle of the park, that'll bring him out ... The gypsies will have him. No, the Travellers have ... Check all the animal rescues. They put them to sleep after seven days ... Battersea Dogs Home have him and haven't bothered to call you, go down there before he's adopted ... What are you doing working – you should be out there looking for your dog ... Have you tried all the vets in London? ... Your dog has been eaten by Africans ... He'll come back ... Is he chipped? ... The immigrants have eaten him ... He's in a kebab: a bit stringy, but generally quite delicious ... Korean restaurants. Korean restaurants. Korean restaurants. ... Don't worry, he'll follow his scent home ... Your dog is dead, get over it ...

That last advice is sent, so thoughtfully, with a local newspaper story about a dog hanged from an M5 flyover.

When I wake up on Tuesday morning the theory I am most attached to is that someone has him. How could there have been so many sightings, and then none? If he was dead he would be starting to smell now. A corpse would have been found and its chip read. That means someone has him.

The alarm on Charlie's side of the bed is beeping more and more furiously. I sit on the edge of the bed and send a tweet, 'Got a neighbour with a new dog? Is it like Wolfy? To have not seen him for three days suggests the worst. Or, does someone have him?'

My relationship with Twitter, like most people's, is ambivalent. Social media is the ultimate ruler of success: followers, retweets, likes, they're all solid data by which to measure yourself.

I could waste whole mornings on social media but I justify this by thinking of it as 'work' – I am surfing the zeitgeist, or some other self-deluding bollocks. Occasionally I'd actually use it for work; with leading questions I could coax out case studies for stories. In that respect, I used it to my advantage; in other respects, social media was messing with my mind, rewiring my brain to go back constantly, for stimulation and self-validation.

Like me, need me, am I good enough, where do I sit on the scale of popularity, let me look at my phone again and again and again.

Looking for my dog has the same push and pull. My need was feeding other people's desire to be entertained and participate in a collective activity. The dog has been endorsed by famous people, I am drip-feeding social media with information about Wolfy, about me, about the hunt for him. People have engaged. I have an audience the size of which, in the past, only a national newspaper, telly or radio could have brought me.

This @JustEmmaPratt lady, we've started sending each other direct messages. She's constantly encouraging when I surrender to bleakness and wailing. She reassures me, 'I am so sure Wolfy is alive. I am sure.'

The community support officer, 'Moonieman'. He is unbelievably good news. I imagine him walking the streets in his heavy copper's boots and hi-vis tabard, flicking through Twitter, keeping his eyes peeled. We are all so rude about the police but when we need them, damn it's reassuring to know they are there.

His most recent tweet: 'I will be calling on all 200 community wardens tomorrow in the hunt for Wolfy, from Manor House up to Holloway. Wish us luck.'

'You are like an angel,' I say. 'I can't believe how lucky I am to have you there in the north while I am over here useless and west.'

This @moonieman, he doesn't feel like 'an angel' if I'm honest; this is just the kind of desperate, mealy-mouthed, eager-to-please language I have been using while sat at my desk, feet resting in an empty Wolfy nest and impotent. My pleading and excessive gratitude has the same one pathetic dimension as a beggar who only needs to impress upon one part of you, and that's the compassionate bit. It's like I have chopped a limb off, like Eddie Murphy on his trolley pretending he has no legs at the start of *Trading Places.*

I have gone from a life lived in three fleshy west London dimensions in Notting Hill to one lived in my head, through avatars on Twitter and in the alien landscape of north London.

Moonieman feels how all of these disembodied helpers feel to me. Like a character from *Trumpton*, a children's stop-motion animation from my early childhood. Moonieman is the friendly local bobby, PC McGarry. 'Have faith,' goes his next tweet. 'Boys in blue were in Newington Green today. It's only a matter of time.'

My day is punctuated by strangers who claim to have seen the dog, or who want to advise us. Charlie and I have put our phone numbers on all the posters. Anyone can call. We have no choice but to trust the majority are decent and want to help; patently cruel people crop up sometimes, but far less than I'd expected.

Twitter gives me hope. Twitter is my lifeline. What Twitter gives me is company and validation. And empathy.

Charlie and I don't speak to each other about how we feel. We both know the other is suffering. To discuss it is pointless. I watch him vacillate between three moods. There's a controlled numb pragmatism: 'It's not worth looking, he's either dead or he's alive. All this running around won't get him back.' There's despair, which manifests itself as him sat staring at the wall like a blind man. And then there is anger, which he directs mostly at the wall and other inanimate objects, but sometimes at Will and Steph, via me.

For my article, I am on the phone to the designer who did the interior of Sexy Fish, which with every unfolding detail seems more and more like a Silly Fish. He is talking to me in intricate detail about the Iranian onyx and the backlit marble he used in the lavatories.

While he talks I post a picture to Instagram of the dog sleeping on a train, typing, 'Where are you Woofy, I miss you.'

The designer has moved on; to the importance of commissioning Damian Hirst to create a mural for the wall and statues of mermaids for the bar. There is work by the great architect Frank Gehry too, a friend of Richard's apparently. I dully ask what all the art is worth and am fobbed off: 'no comment'.

'My cat ran away last year but he came back.'

'How long was he gone?'

'Three weeks. I know what you are going through. Stay strong.'

I call the auctioneer Simon de Pury – perhaps he knows how much the art at Sexy Stupid Fish cost – and ask gauche questions. He is not unkind, but I can hear an appalled note of hauteur creeping into his voice as my ignorance about the art market becomes apparent. 'I suspect at auction these pieces may make five or six million perhaps. It's rare for restaurants or hotels to have great art,' he says, which makes Sexy Fish 'formidable ... timeless ... cherished'. After he finishes speaking, there's a pause as he waits for my sycophantic response, but I am distracted answering a dog tweet.

'I live in Finsbury Park. Out shaking the Bonio box for you.'

'That's so good to hear. Thank you.'

Heart emojis, puppy emojis, praying hands. My eyes are locked on the screen, fingers responding as I offer a paltry 'Mmmn', 'very interesting' and 'I see' to de Pury's sage art-world commentary.

My breath is so shallow, sometimes it stops altogether as I push on through threads of #findwolfy tweets and on into other people's feeds.

I have the maître d's of Sexy Fish on conference call now, telling me who is in, who is out. Apparently the dining room will be open to all, as long as they look the part: 'If a lady has a great hat or hair, who cares who she is, she dresses the room,' says one.

Will the reality TV types be welcome, I wonder.

The other chips in, 'Of course we'll let some of the reality stars in, who doesn't love a bit of tragic TV?'

I respond to a tweet from a lady called Anna Marie: 'My dog is my most significant relationship! I can't bear the thought of him being lost and scared. I'd be frantic. I'm in Highgate hunting for you.'

That's what I should be doing but I have *more* questions, can you believe it. 'And ... will the suits and out-of-towners up to take in a West End show or the Christmas lights, those sorts, will they be allowed in?'

I've lived in London for nearly 30 years now. I'd put my last penny (Lord knows I'm often down to it) on Sexy Fish being a suits and a bridge 'n' tunneller's paradise by the end of the year. But I can't say that, explicitly, because all this hype, it's a game. Famous people, rich and beautiful people, will come down, they'll be invited, they'll want to look at each other. It's opened just as the winter party season is hotting up and this place too, for a brief season, will be hot. Then not. So they let a grubby but tame journalist sort like me in to gawp at high society, mock them a bit perhaps, but not too much, and open the door to the plain folk, the wannabes and the rubberneckers. Though everyone's a rubbernecker in my experience; no one can resist 'seeing who's in', as Jeffrey Bernard used to say.

I make approving noises as a maître d' says, 'I love going out of my way to make people from out of town feel like superstars.' It's said with the largesse of a man who has just moved a few families of Syrian refugees into his spare bedroom. 'But,' he adds gravely, 'you can't have a restaurant full of them, maybe just one or two tables.'

'Oh no, can't have too many of them. Ghastly!' I agree with hammy vociferousness.

The aquarium specialist who designed the huge tropical fish tanks in Sexy Fish's basement private dining room is deflecting my questions about how much they cost. I keep on and, by a process of elimination and reduction, we settle on it probably being somewhere between £100,000 and a quarter of a million quid.

Some bastard tweets that he found my dog in Manchester. I ask him if he was the tosser that rang me at 3 a.m. to say the dog was on the motorway and I have to grovel respectfully when he tweets back, 'No. I saw this.'

Turns out he's not a bastard. He's just trying to help. It's the Facebook page for North Yorkshire Police, with pictures of about 19 dogs that have been recovered from a smallholding in Selby. That's some distance from Manchester but nonetheless, one of the dogs does look like Wolfy. It's a shagbag of bones and fur. A Norfolk lurcher just like mine.

It's not Wolfy. And I know it. But I want it to be him. I think back to the woman who had her lurcher stolen from outside the post office by the Scrubs. The words 'Traveller types ... Found in Manchester two hours later' echo round my head.

I call to Charlie, who comes in from the sitting room and stands over my shoulder looking at the picture. 'It could be him, is it him?'

He too is willing the dog in Selby to be our dog. The magical thinking is taking over even his logical mind.

Someone else sends a dog they saw on the street in Alexandra Palace. 'Too skinny and gingery, but thanks.'

The phone rings. It's a man, English-speaking, excited. 'I saw your dog.'

Oh God. 'Oh God.' I'm breathless, where, where? 'Where!?'

'I just saw your poster. He ran into Upper Holloway station around six o'clock on Saturday night.'

Oh. Saturday. The disappointment is brief. It is overtaken by anxiety. A train station.

I immediately share the information with Twitter and ring Network Rail and British Transport Police to see if any animal corpses have been found on the line. I find train drivers on Twitter, ask them to share the poster, keep an eye out.

I can work no longer. I have to head back to Finsbury Park.

After I've crossed Holloway Road at the bottom of Will's street, I walk up the steps to the station. I backtrack and traverse residential streets until I am lost. I'm on a busy road but I don't know which one it is. I don't bother to try reorienting myself. This is how the dog experienced his escape. He has no Google Maps. He can't stop and ask someone the way.

Drifting, I tap posters to telegraph poles and lamp-posts. They're covered in plastic pockets; I turn them upside down and push the pins down tight so the poster won't fall out, and the damp and the wind can't get in. How long will they last? Is there even any point doing this? How many posters like this have I walked past in my life? If I even notice them, it's with barely a glance if it's a cat, barely a second glance if it's a dog.

I walk round residential streets that all look the same in the dark. 'Woolfy. Wooooolfeeee.' My voice is thin. My heart's not in it any more. On I plod. I'm back on a main road now. Which one it is, I don't know.

There's traffic, buses rumble by, but the pavement is oddly quiet even though most of the shops are still open. Turkish supermarket, a banqueting centre on a first floor with bright white tiles and unforgiving neon strip lights in its raised basement, a barber; there are slivers of cheap real estate, little wider than a car, which house minicab offices and phone shops. Somali food, Afghan Grill; outside the Blue Nile cafe a few people smoke hookahs, there's a supermarket that is also a 'business centre'.

Despite the familiar grey and brown chill of a London autumn, the smell of the traffic, this stretch of road feels exotic. There's a patch of Uxbridge Road near home that is full of Syrian shops. I like going there to buy buckets of yoghurt, value packs of za'atar and gigantic watermelons.

Here, away from familiar turf, grindingly miserable, wrung out on adrenaline as I am, the difference, this exoticism, more familiar from travelling than from any London I inhabit, makes me feel insecure.

A sign advertises a 'Mall'. I live near Westfield, the 50-acre mega-mall of consumer dreams, where teenagers and shopping fiends roam around like zombies with their mouths half open; gone to 'look at the shops'.

This 'mall' is a normal-sized shop, a large newsagent's or a corner shop sort of size, divided into tiny units selling dates, tea, brass teapots, North African shampoos with packaging that looks like the seventies, there's tins of baby formula and malty Milo powder, knick knacks in cheap gilt. Inside the door on the right is a stall selling a few religious books and pieces of modest Islamic dress. Two women stand there talking to each other, one in brown, the other in a dreary sludgy blue. Their clean faces are tightly framed into a diamond shape by their hijab. These are not the heavily made-up Gulf Arab women in twinkling abayas you see on Edgware Road.

There are men at the back of the shop. My instinct is to speak to them first. I notice this, stop myself, turn to the women and say, 'I've lost my dog and I wondered if I could put a poster in the window?'

What are they. 20, 30? I have no idea. They stare. I don't even know if they understood me. Then, 'Ask him,' says one, pointing to a man sitting working on a calculator.

Looking at how little people here have, the cheapness of the materials, the sad cost of things, I feel wretched.

A few doors down from the mall in a cab office a fleshy, jowly guy in a brown cardigan sitting behind the window says

'No, I cannot put a poster in the window, it is not possible.' He does not look up or make eye contact.

I have to go out onto the street and stand with my eyes closed and take several deep slow breaths.

Smile at people. Move on.

Next I step into the white stairwell up to the eye-scorchingly bright banqueting suite and speak to a man in a simple shalwar kameez. 'Hello, good evening, I'm so sorry to disturb you, I've lost my dog round here, he's been gone a few days. I'm so worried about him. Could I put a poster in your window?'

'Yes, yes, we are about to close, do you have something to stick it, put it here, everyone will see it here. And next door, go to the cab office.' I tell him they said no. 'I will tell him yes, he is my friend.' We fix up the poster and walk next door. A couple of drivers are outside now. They ask me about the dog. I tell them I can't stop crying, that the dog is my friend, that I love him. One of the drivers is sitting out on the street on a tatty, once-grand conference centre-type chair, gold bent metal and wine-coloured plush. His English is simple but he wants to make it clear to me that 'I know British people love their dogs, that they are like family.' He nods in the direction of the office. 'We put a poster here' – he points to the window – 'and I take one for my car too.' He walks me to the booth where the guy had told me no. The guy takes a poster silently and grudgingly tapes it up to his window.

I've been out for three hours now. I feel like I should stay out longer but my spirits are super-low.

I head home via Will's.

The easy patter I always had with the older children is stuck still. The big kids' greetings are muted and remote. Arty stays the same and runs me through a jumble of childish interests, 'Katie. Norfolk the cat's friend is naughty and he stole Norfy's food Katie.'

'No! What a naughty cat. He should go to cat prison.'

'Cats don't go to prison, don't be silly Katie.'

'Yes I am silly.' I go in for a hug and he hangs on to me like a little monkey for a while. I take the affection greedily, like a vampire.

I sling him round on my hip and carry him through the house towards the kitchen. He looks serious and says, 'Woofy he go "Aoooo, aoooo, aoooo."'

I stop. Say that again Arty?

The small person imitates a howling dog. It's a quiet howl, a little thin one. His baby lips pucker as he goes aaaaahooooh.

I know it, exactly, that howl. He's got it spot on. The smallest member of the household has just added a detail the others had failed to. 'Thanks Arty, clever boy.' I kiss his soft cheeks, mmnwahmmnwahmmmwha. 'It's helpful for Aunty Kate to know that. Thank you. You're a clever boy.'

'IsssOKKatie.' He wraps his little arms around me very briefly and for a second rests his head on my shoulder, before wriggling away and stomping off to find Lego Batman.

That howl is an enquiry. Where are you? I miss you. I'm here. Where are you? Can you hear me? Where are you? It's pining and plaintive.

Have I created this howling needy monster by treating Wolfy like a companion animal and taking him everywhere?

When I was a kid I had a comfort blanket called Cluggy. My stepmother took it and threw it away when I was seven because it was time for me to grow up and not be a baby. Depending on your parenting style, you will either think that throwing Cluggy in the bin was unnecessarily cruel or that it was a necessary lesson in life.

The question 40 years later was, had I turned Wolfy into a giant living breathing Cluggy? Had I, in my own dependency, created a dependency in Wolfy that made him run away?

Wolfy and I were tightly bonded. We'd opened the sluice gates in each other's bodies and, like a Tetley teabag, let t'oxytocin flood out. We were joined at the hip, fairly literally given his ear fitted very neatly under the top of my femur. I knew people were saying things about my attachment to him. I liked life so much more that I didn't give a toss if there were snide comments here and there and Charlie didn't mind. All was well with him.

Both parents on both sides were muttering about my attachment to Wolfy, I knew that. When Mum spoke to her friends about me and the dog she called him, patronisingly, Dear Wolfy. My stepmother had acquiesced after one too many visits where the dog howled and cried in the kitchen and now tolerated the intolerable: *dogs upstairs.* She liked to remind me that other people may be less understanding. I once overheard my stepfather talking to some fellow baby boomer who was choking in horror as Wolfy hopped up on Mum's sofa. First came the explanatory and, again, patronising, 'Ah, meet Wolfy. Very precious.' Then loudly to the dog, patting him: 'We're a special case, aren't we Wolfy.' Then, *sotto voce*, with a nod and a wink in my direction, he said, 'First child, you see.'

I shouted from the next room, 'I can hear you, by the way.' I did not give birth to a dog.

One of my favourites, that. I used to do it when I was a teenager. Dad was living in South Africa and Tom and I were back living with my mum, who, freshly out of a crap second marriage, had moved in with my grandmother.

We lived miles from any of my school friends, up on a hill on the edge of Dartmoor. We lived there together, one house, three women, three generations, one Dalmatian, one Labrador, two hamsters.

If I caught Mum and Granny talking about me, I'd listen, breath suspended, still, and wait until the perfect moment to announce they had an audience.

'I don't like that hippy boy she seems very impressed by. He came the other day and didn't even say hello. And the reek of patchouli is unbearable.'

'Oh that's what it is. Is she smoking, or is that the boy? I don't think she smokes, no, but I see she's had another little go at dying her hair.'

'I can hear you, you know.'

I'd leg it then, laughing – I loved the way they stopped and went deadly silent, as if by being silent I'd unhear their gossiping.

There were some fights in that house. I remember going into Granny's sitting room after a particularly furious scrap with Mum – it had ended with her chasing me shrieking, 'You little madam.' This led to more hilarity on my part but eventually it turned to tears. Tears are the real full stop to any conflict.

Granny was doing the *Times* crossword, and I leapt on the sofa beside her, hoping to get the key third party on my side and hence win a majority. Granny listened. 'We are three women. Three difficult women. It's not going to be easy living together. You need to be grown up about it.'

My response was shock. I had never considered I would grow up to be a woman. I wasn't sure I fancied that. Couldn't I just stay a girl?

'I don't want to be a woman.'

Steph passes me, coming home from work, as I go out on my way back to Notting Hill. 'Oh, hi Kate,' she says, in a strange distracted way that I can't read but which makes me feel uncomfortable. She goes on, wearily, 'Any news?'

Anxiety strikes! Is she angry with me? It could be anything; she has a serious job, she deals with office politics and board-level braggarts and egos, she's successful in a way I am not. Probably she's had a hard day, is worried about one of her kids … there might be many reasons for her voice to come out that way, but my instinct, always, is to assume some sort of blame and isolate myself mentally. It's just you. Rely on no one. Hide your feelings. That's how I felt when my mum wasn't around, and that's how I feel now.

I lock away my anxiety about what Steph is thinking, I lock away what I feel for dear little Bay, who looks at me with new frightened and remote eyes; and for Sam, whose eyes flicker nervously away when I come into the house. I lock away what I feel for Wolfy, who is gone.

I say brightly, 'So sorry about all this, it must really be a pain but we'll find him, he'll come back. We will be laughing about this by Christmas.'

She responds, kindly, but still that tone of weariness. What is it?

I shrink further.

As I shut the front door in Tufnell Park I look at the bowl of water left out for the dog on Will's front doorstep in the hopeless hope that he might return there. It has bits of black crud in it, and a small brown leaf, floating. I've put a dirty T-shirt of mine there too, in the equally hopeless hope that I am the Bisto and Wolfy is the kid. In his Buddhist realm of smells perhaps his nose will find his way back here.

I get the bus back to Notting Hill from my brother's because I don't want to be anywhere. Something about the glacial speed at which London buses travel through the city mirrors the treacle pace of every minute that Wolfy is gone. These last four days have felt like weeks.

A dog can survive nine days without food, three without water. There have been no real confirmed sightings since Saturday evening and we've had barely any rain for weeks. Where is Wolfy finding water? Even after a shortish walk, forty minutes, even in the winter, he'd head in the direction of the nearest brown puddle for a long delicious noisy lap. Once, dying for a poo, I'd broken into the Linford Christie Stadium at 7 a.m. and wildly run this way and that trying to find a loo. Finally sat, in mighty relief, I'd called out to Woof to ensure he'd not lost me. The answer came in a series of echoey enthusiastic schlurps as he made free with the facilities too; for him this was not just a posh Portaloo, it was a large, deliciously smelly porcelain dog bowl. That had made me laugh out loud. I feel a squeeze of remembered joy in my heart.

Staring out the bus window as it rumbles past Camden Market I consider how life will be if Wolfy doesn't return. There will be a period of real grief that no one will really understand or care about because he is just a dog. The joy will drain out of life. And work. How will I work? My bank account is nearly empty. I look at my phone, aimlessly checking my emails for the first time in hours. A press release from some new app which is giving away 888 limited-edition pink custard buns to celebrate their launch. Am I really reading this shit?

I want my dog back.

At home I relay the howling business that Arty did for me to Charlie. Before I've finished speaking I can see where his mood is headed. He starts to rail against my brother again. I beg, 'Stop it, that's my brother you're talking about. Stop. Stop! I can't listen.' The silence vibrates with anger.

'Well one thing's for certain,' he says, 'If the dog doesn't come back I won't be going there for Christmas, I can tell you.'

CHAPTER NINE

Wednesday, and I trudge round the Scrubs with Castor, swiping between every form of social media as I go. Of course he rolls in fox shit.

When I walked Wolfy I'd often chuck my phone under some empty crisp packets in the car and let our time together be unadulterated by external distractions. I don't do that now. What if someone calls?

Last night I created a dedicated Find Wolfy Facebook page and paid to boost its first post, which means it will pop up on the side of several hundred thousand Londoners' Facebook pages. It costs me about £30 for a day.

'This is Wolfy. He is six years old. If you see him, dead or alive, or know someone who has him, please contact me here. There is a substantial reward for his return. No questions asked. I just want my canine brother back.'

I've posted it on Dragon Driving too, a sort of eBay for gypsy and Traveller communities: horses, traps, gigs, tack, caravans, dogs, donkeys – and lurchers. One of my new allies on Twitter suggested it. The woman who took down my ad could not have been more helpful and understanding, suggesting the wording that would cause the least offence and invite the most interest. 'Good luck love,' she says. 'I know how much the dogs mean to us all. I hope you find him.'

Talk of gypsies, Travellers and 'pikeys' wasn't going away. The tone of these varied. From a respectable consideration: 'Might have found his way to a Traveller site, they love their lurchers' to something far darker: 'He'll be with the gypsies now if he's any cop, swinging from a bridge if he's not.'

I responded to a guy ranting on about pikeys killing dogs and was told I was a 'virtue-signalling PC wet' and 'a fucking bunny hugger' who needed to 'open your eyes'. In his bio, a quote from Enoch Powell.

One of my #findwolfy ladies on Facebook calls me this morning. It's been five days now. She tells me what she has been doing: 'We've postered all around Queen's Wood and Highgate now. Have you been up there?' I say I haven't. 'Now Parkland Walk, that's going to be very attractive to a dog, have you been up there?' No, I say, but Charlie has it on his places to visit. 'We've got to make him too hot to handle.' She's urgent, like a policewoman in a TV show. I want to say, 'Yes Sarge.'

I mention that people keep talking about gypsies and Travellers and I don't know how seriously to take all this talk. 'Well,' she says, conspiratorial, knowing, 'you've got to consider that. The way they treat their animals, it's shocking. And they do steal dogs. They're terrible.'

'But Wolfy's not a hunter or a killer. He doesn't have his balls. What's he useful for?'

I've got the woman on headphones and am walking round the flat, picking things up, pairing socks, Wolfy's bed is back by our bed, minus its blanket, which is among the items piled outside Will's for their smell. Castor slept on it last night. I think of the sound Wolf makes as he's shifting in his bed, the contented puffs and exhalations of breath as he settles in for the night.

'Oh *they* don't care,' the emphasis of immense difference on 'they'. 'They find a use for them, or they use them as bait.'

I am lugging the Hoover back into the crawl space under the eaves where it lives. 'Bait?'

'With the dogfighting. Oh it's terrible, ahh they're terrors, terrible people, they don't care about their animals, keep them in terrible conditions. Terrible.'

My victim side is willing a suitably terrible image of my savaged dog's corpse into my mind's eye. Another side of me is battling that urge, and feels thrillingly certain of something. I've never spoken to this woman before in my life and she seems very kind and pleasant but what she's saying is waking me up.

I back out of the crawl space. It's impossible to pull yourself metaphorically up to full height when you aren't able to physically stand up. Unusually, carefully calm, hyperaware that she is an ally in the #findwolfy hunt, I contradict her. 'I don't think that they are inherently evil. These are marginalised people who operate outside mainstream society, of course it's a more grey economy.' I'm quite impressed by my use of words like 'marginalised' and 'grey economy'. Where has this come from? 'I really don't agree with what you are saying.'

This isn't a forced form of righteousness. If I thought it'd get my dog back I'd say or do pretty much anything short of murder (and even that would be up for discussion). What's happening here? Am I a virtue-signalling wet? A gullible bunny hugger? A Blairite liberal multicultural capitalist with a bad dose of underdogism? Or am I just right?

She's immediately rowing back, going, 'I'm sure you're right, yes, they aren't all bad. Perhaps it's a few bad apples.'

A few bad apples. Jesus. She ought to meet some of the bad apples in the aristocracy or the abattoir business, or politics or the priesthood. I don't want to listen to this crap. Next thing you know she'll be telling me all gay people have AIDs and never to touch one.

There seemed to be a whole community among the #findwolfy tribe determined that the dog had fallen into gypsy hands, Traveller hands, 'pikey' hands and was being used as bait for dogfights. Facebook provided me with a photograph of a dog that looked remarkably like my boy, stitched back together with the vet's needle into a patchwork approximation of the lurcher it had once been. Bait. He'll be used as bait in dogfights.

Like someone just diagnosed with cancer, I turned to the
internet with these ideas and was sucked into forums explicitly
detailing horrors I didn't need to imagine. I was unable to tear
my eyes away from the savage imagery.

Gypos, Travellers, pikeys, the words came up again and
again. 'My friend's very friendly lurcher ran over to play with
their dog and was bundled into the van and gone. She got him
back about two weeks later, he was on a Traveller site.'

'Same happened to me. We never seen her again. More than
anything I just hope she hasn't met a bad ending, she is such a
wonderful trusting dog and I love her to bits. I can't tell you the
worst of my fears. I'm completely heartbroken.'

'Just last week a 16yo terrier got out of its garden in Newport,
he nipped under a chain-link fence into some industrial units
where the usual suspects collect scrap there. He was later found
dead in a ditch with all his feet taped together.'

'Bait animals are used to test a dog's fighting instinct and
are mauled or killed in the process. A dog used as bait will have
his snout taped shut.'

I needed to get offline.

I have a friend called Rob whose dad was 'born in a caravan'
to a mother from an old Romany family and a father who was
a 'showman' and described himself as a Traveller. I ring him.
'Rob, I've lost my lurcher. Can I talk to your dad?'

'Yeah, hard not to notice that, your ad pops up on my
Facebook. How's my dad gonna help?'

'A lot of people are saying the gypsies have got him, or the
Travellers or the pikeys. I don't know what to do. Where to
turn. I just want a dose of reality.'

'Yeah, I can see why you'd not want to walk straight into
a camp asking that. It's not going to look good. You can ask
him anything but don't use the word pikey, it's as bad as the
N-word.'

Rob's dad is happy to talk: 'In my mum's day they'd put
canvas round the bottom of the old high wagons and in the

summer all the kids would sleep down there with the dogs. Gypsies love their dogs, they're well fed, well looked after. My grandfather used to trade in horses and lurchers, greyhound/ collie they were.'

I say I'm thinking of going to visit some Travellers' sites and he doesn't think going to a camp will do any harm. 'If a gypsy purloined your dog they'd want it for hunting. I think the Travellers treat their dogs well too, though I don't like the coursing they do, ripping the hare to pieces. I used to go walking across the fields for hours with my grandfather and his dog, they train the dogs to make a clean kill, hunt for the pot.'

'What about all this talk of animals becoming bait?' I ask.

'What do you mean, "bait"?' he says.

'That they're using him as bait to test a fighting dog's aggression.'

'There's no reason to use a dog for bait. They just tease and tease the fighting dogs until they're bad-tempered. I've spent a lot of my life not telling people I'm from travelling people. Before I say anything I always weigh it up and see how prejudiced people are first. There's a percentage of bad in any community. Is that a reason to judge them all? Are you a reporter? Rob tells me that you are.'

I think of the Sexy Fish story. 'Kind of.'

'To brand a whole section of the community by the actions of its worst, it's just wrong. Like what some of your kind did at Hillsborough.'

With no recent sightings of Wolfy, and in this information vacuum, the magical thinking is strong. I am convinced the dog is with the Travellers.

If he is curled up and confused in a yard somewhere, having been found and kept – the ambiguous theft by finding – then I will simply go and ask for him back.

Immediately, fired up by certainty, I get up and walk down to the Travellers' site under the Westway about half a mile away.

It's where the underbelly of several roads intersect and enclose the land like a vaulted concrete cathedral.

I like the certainty of knowing where I am going, and why. I've been there before, to parties, to get my car fixed and to stand and stare at the dissonant sight of a heavily graffitied riding school right under the A40. But I have never been deep inside, to the land the Travellers rent from the Royal Borough of Kensington and Chelsea.

The camp is down a rutted, age-bleached road. I walk past the scrappy shipping container workshops where men black with oil and dirt tinker with mechanical parts.

There's a man not far from the first of the caravans on a site with about ten. I approach him. 'I've lost my dog, I need some advice.'

'Pat, you need to talk to Pat, come back later, after seven. He will be back then.'

Charlie comes home from work early and stares at me with weary eyes. There's no point asking if there's any news because we both know there isn't any. He scours DogLost and calls the wardens every day. I scavenge on social media.

'I've had an idea,' I say. 'I'm not going to put posters up tonight, I'm going to go down to the Travellers' site under the Westway and ask their advice. Everyone says, where there's gypsies or Travellers there's lurchers. Dogs often turn up on Traveller sites.'

'Kate, is that a good idea? Is that safe? I don't want you to go at night.'

'I have to go then.'

'Well I can't stop you, though I think you're mad.'

I turn back to the crutch, back to social media. Some of the #findwolfy people from the internet, the majority of them female dog walkers from the north London parks, text me directly. I like this. It makes me feel less alone, like there is a plan in place and vast numbers are acting on it. The most prominent disembodied help comes from @JustEmmaPratt. But she is by no means the only one.

@BeautifulMumsie has taken my original tweet and poster and retweeted it to loads of famous people. I can see that she sends these tweets morning, noon and night to newsreaders, comedians, novelists, TV presenters, actors, politicians. Where could this energy and compassion come from but her own suffering. Her bio says, 'Beautiful daughter Laura 31 died of colorectal cancer' and the month, year and day of her death. Because of BeautifulMumsie the picture of Wolfy at Constantine must have been seen by thousands more people now. My eyes flick back to her bio again and again. I think of my pain and times it by a thousand. It's not possible for me to imagine it but from that unimaginable pain comes kindness.

The Find Wolfy Facebook page soon has hundreds of followers. Dawn, Natalie, Rebecca, Siobhan, Emma, Tan Tan, Vicky, Alexandra, Carrie, Charlotte, Ruthie, Felicity, Lulu, Sue, Deborah, Debra, Debs, Debbie, Rhea, Tina, Sammy, Tash, Verity, Jody, Jenni, Jane, Jani, Joanna, Nicky, Hilary, Anne-Marie, Sarah, Katie ...

At any point in the day when I am not trudging the pavements of Finsbury Park, my neck is hooked over the screen, my chest is hunched over my hips. Every so often I hear the squeaky floorboard at the door to the study. That's Wolfy coming in, I wonder if he will get on the sofa or head for his nest. I hope he comes to his nest. I ready my toes for the wriggle under his smooth pink belly ... Breathing deep and pulling the tears back inside me, I let the ghost of my dog leave the room.

A babysitter from my childhood, now a professor of nursing, gets in touch: 'Dear Kate. You are doing all you can. My cat went missing, I was distraught. He just sauntered back.'

It isn't lost on me that they are all women.

It's November, and dark by half four. Tomorrow, on Thursday, it will be Bonfire Night, the annual excuse for pyromaniacs to come out of their hidey holes and start throwing explosives around in the name of a foiled seventeenth-century Catholic fundamentalist terrorist plot to blow up the Houses of Parliament. Tonight, it's random whizz-pops and bangs, but tomorrow and through to Sunday, it will crank up.

I imagine being my dog. I am cowering beside a big blue wheelie bin while fireworks skid across the street and explode nearby. I don't know where I am. There are no familiar smells. The smoke confuses me even more. I am trembling, petrified, confused and hyper-anxious. Where is the big pink animal that gives me oxytocin and biscuits?

A singer in Chippewa Falls, Wisconsin says, 'I see him coming back to you soon, healthy and safe.'

Half of me reads that and thinks, 'How the hell would you know, goon?', and the other half writes, 'Why. Please tell me why?'

'I'm psychic,' she says.

I make my way back down to the Travellers' site by a strange route, avoiding the way Wolfy and I would always go when we walked to the Scrubs. I edge the narrow sandy rat-run down the side of the riding school and into the camp. There's a kid wheeling about on his bike and I ask him if Pat is here. The kid throws down his bike and runs to two nearby vans separated by a courtyard decorated with painted plaster horses' heads and a few bright flower boxes. I follow him. Two tiny lapdogs, a grubby white poodle and a toffee-coloured Pomeranian, shrilly announce just how big and scary they are as I hover by the gate.

A woman comes out. 'Can I help you?' She has an Irish accent, but it's not strong. She's dressed smart, with a gigantic baby under her arm, which she puts down. The child, who can't be more than one, looks up at me, waving a cloth doll.

'I wondered if I could see Pat. I wanted to ask him something, about my dog.'

She looks at me for a long moment. 'A dog?'

'Yes, I've lost my lurcher. I wanted to ... to ask his advice.'

She calls inside the larger of the two vans, while barely taking her eyes off me, before turning into the doorway to have a muttered conversation.

'He's eating his dinner but you can go in.'

I go through the gate. The child squawks in amiable greeting and the scruffy designer dogs yap on without menace. Inside, Pat is sitting at a small table between the living area and the kitchen, watching a telly on the wall. He's about 50, with the ruddy cheeks of someone who works outside.

He's got a plate of chicken nuggets, beans and chips in front of him. I've interrupted his tea. What am I doing here? Hunting down the exotic and the out-of-bounds? Proving I'm not scared? Or am I undoing the magical thinking and the fantasies that have grown up around the lost dog? Whatever, it's suddenly apparent to me that what I'm doing is pretty rude, really. I'm coming down to accuse 'his kind' of having, nay, nicking, my dog, lost on the other side of a city of eight million people. After a quick muddled think about some plausible white lies to make what I am about to say look better, I settle on telling the truth.

'I've lost my lurcher, he's been gone five days. I heard that these kinds of dogs often turn up with your people and I wondered if you had any advice.'

The patience in his response is excruciating.

'Where did you lose him?'

'North London. Finsbury Park.'

'I can't help you. Not my patch.'

'Do you have any advice? Do you know anyone in Finsbury Park? Do you think I should go and visit them? Where would you go if you had lost a lurcher?'

'Was he chipped, tagged? Have you been on that DogLost website?' His advice is no different from that of the nice ladies up on the Heath. 'If what you're saying is have I got your dog, no I haven't. I've got twenty-two dogs down there in the kennel. I can show you them now if you want to check if I've got your dog.'

Yup, he thinks I'm accusing him of stealing my dog. 'Of course you don't have my dog. I suppose I wanted advice.'

'I lost one not long ago. Started running on the Scrubs and never stopped. Never did find out what happened to him. They do go, you know?'

I walk home in the dark, the adrenalised hope of the visit long gone and the brief spike of hopeless hope exhausted. Wolfy being co-opted into a large Traveller kennel of hunting dogs was pretty unlikely; he is a soft bumbling middle-aged dog, so pampered by love that he'd once let a couple of aggro magpies peck his bum with barely a glance backwards. If he was wanted for hunting, he'd very soon be unwanted and a stray again ... or bait. Oh, for fuck's sake stop thinking this drivel. I sit on a low wall opposite a bank of graffiti on a wooden hoarding around the Travellers' camp. I smack my temples with my fists.

Sat here underneath the Westway, I look at my phone. The keener #findwolfy ladies on Twitter have been very active. The Sky News presenter Kay Burley has tweeted 'Let's get this lad home.' The whole thing is surreal.

Emma Pratt has sent me a text telling me to keep my spirits up, that her and her son have been combing and flyering Hampstead Heath that afternoon after school. Attached is a picture of a dog on Gumtree. It's an online classified ad for an adult lurcher for sale. 'This couldn't be him, could it?'

No amount of willing it to be so can make it my hound.

Emma's dedicated search for the dog is more total than mine even – she has her kids out hunting with her after school. I don't even know what this woman looks like.

I ask her if I can call her.

I walk down Bramley Road, past the red-brick thirties houses and the old Victorian arches under Latimer Road station. Here, normally, I turn to the left, past the western edge of the Lancaster West Estate, down a paved pedestrian access to the grassy area between the tower and the leisure centre. This is the little locals rat-run where, night after night after night,

Wolfy and I have dawdled until he's voided bowel and bladder and is ready for bed.

I walk on and take the main roads back to the flat. I can't even look at the places where we used to be together.

Charlie is on his way back from flyering and putting up more posters around N4 and N7.

His voice is weary when he calls me on the way back. 'Is there anything to eat?'

I cook some sausages, which we eat with Presbyterian simple joyless accompaniments, boiled potatoes and peas, the sort of food people cook when they no longer have a lust for life.

In bed, his warm body is reassuring and for once I curve around his back instead of rolling into my side of the hump in the mattress. 'I can't stop thinking about him, it's so painful,' I say in a whisper.

'I know. It's uncomfortable. We can't crack up though. No point in that, is there? How were they down on the Travellers' site? Any help?'

'Singularly unsatisfying. This guy Pat tolerated it, politely, but I got nothing out of it other than I still had no idea where the dog was. I'm still going to try some of the north London sites though. I suppose the one good thing I got out of it was it proved they aren't anything to be frightened of.'

'Were they ever?'

'The stuff I've been reading on social media, on the internet, on some of these dog forums, it's insane, Charlie.'

'Well I don't need to tell you what the answer is to that.'

'Yeah, farkin' get off t' 'internet.'

'Precisely. Where's it getting us? Our numbers are everywhere. If people have information they'll get us the old-school way. Right, I have to sleep.'

He's gone in 60 seconds. Man could outsleep a hibernating Grizzly.

I lie on my back listening to the Wolfy-less silence. Castor breathes softly in Wolfy's bed beside us.

Rolling onto my side, I curl up in a foetal ball. Don't cry. Don't cry.

Two hours later I sit bolt upright, already crying and choking on my breath as if I am suffocating. Now I am fully awake the tears turn to out-of-control bawling. 'Charlie, Charlie. Help.'

'Get a grip, Kate. Get your shit together, for fuck's sake.'

I hadn't expected him to be so cold and angry. It surprises me to silence but the tears keep coming, in torrents and convulsions from my gut. I get up and mechanically put on my grandmother's old ragged Chinese dressing gown. Snot still running down my face, I tiptoe downstairs to the dog's nest under my desk and climb inside, covering myself in his blankets, holey old socks, chewed fur and ratty sheepskins. There, I howl until I am exhausted.

Wrung out, finished, I pull down my laptop, check Twitter, check Instagram where dear flawless Chica has posted a picture of Wolfy's poster. 'Help gorgeous @Spicerlife find her dog'. That's sweet; it sits, ugly, between a lovely shot of her feet in a pair of Nicholas Kirkwood shoes and a cute tongue-out shot of her standing legs akimbo in a jumpsuit beside a vending machine in Tokyo. She is utterly gorgeous and doing well. For once I feel no shiver of envy.

Check Facebook. Check my new Find Wolfy page. Check check check, soothe soothe soothe, numb numb numb. Go back and do it all again. Numb it all down to nothing but a blank sadness.

A box pops up, a Facebook message from my cousin, Maya, in California.

'Kate, are you there? Any news on Wolfy?'

I type a colon and an opening bracket. A sad-face pops up in the box.

'Kate, I have a friend who might be able to help you. She has done some awesome stuff for me in the past – maybe it's a bit way-out for you but she is what's known as an animal communicator and she's seriously good. I have sent her a

message saying I am passing on her info to you and that your
dog is currently lost. She's booked up months in advance but
she's a friend of mine. She will help you. If you think it is all
airy-fairy that's fine, ignore me. But I know from experience she
is good and may be able to help you in some way.'

Ping! A warm light springs into my chest. Hope! 'I will try
anything, Maya, I am desperate. I will definitely call her. Could
I call now? Where is she?'

'Her name is Anna Twinney. Look at her website,
reachouttohorses.com. She is based in Colorado but is English
and totally genuine in what she does.' She sends me her phone
number. 'I said you might call her.'

'I'd never have you down as someone who goes to psychics,
Maya, you're the most grounded person in the entire family.'

'I know it may seem way-out but it has worked for me
before. I have used her with horses and dogs – been amazing.
Make it happen, Kate.'

The warmth and light spreads a little. 'Thanks Maya. I will.
He ran off from Will's house so doesn't know how to get home.
As far as we know he is heading further away from Will's in the
wrong direction.'

'Hugs to you big cousin. Be brave. I know how horrific it is
when they run off. I know how you are feeling.'

I text Anna straight away. 'It's Maya's cousin. When can we
talk?'

CHAPTER TEN

Jayne Wallace runs a string of female psychics out of Selfridges' basement in London and Culver City in LA. She also has offices in Epping but you hear less about this now, since she's read for Kim Kardashian. I interviewed her earlier in the year for a story about energy vampires for Red magazine – you know, those people who make you feel like the life's been sucked from you after anything more than a few minutes in their company. I'd thought it would be fun to add a bit of cosmic witchy-woo to a story, fundamentally, about depressed and needy people.

She's a blue-chip psychic, Jayne. A half-hour reading with her costs £125, less than a top barrister but still, more than a decent haircut. Right now, I've got no moolah for this. As I wait for Anna Twinney to get back to me, I am hungry for magic. If I can't have the miracle of Wolfy coming home, psychics will have to do.

That's how I wake up on 5 November, with a need for answers and instant gratification.

There's no way I'm asking Charlie for money for a psychic. Having to use his money robs me of my power, and having to use his money for *psychics*? I can forget my dignity too. There's no surer way of being consigned to the second-sex dustbin than by succumbing to paranormal commerce.

Castor comes padding up the stairs looking for love and for once I pat the bed and invite him up. I've booked him in to doggy daycare for the rest of the week. The walks, the rolling, the showers are a daily torment of remembering and regret and I feel bad for how neutered all my doggy affection is now.

The slender, gentle dog lays his head on my thigh while I focus on how to get access to Jayne. I need to make up a bogus reason to interview her. If I can find one I could probably get to her right now.

One of the pieces I have to write this week is about hangover cures. I've got a professor of genetic epidemiology commenting, and a nutritionist to showbiz caners and mental workaholics like Charlie. I've quoted P. G. Wodehouse. Why not Jayne; why not a psychic cure for a clang? She'll add a bit of spirit and sparkle, I tell myself.

She's game, and has a slot at 11.30. I am standing in the study when we talk. It takes her no more than five minutes to relay a cure, a pink angel crystal and psychic energy clearance. I'll remember that one, I think; after, that is, I've done 400mg of ibuprofen, 1000mg of paracetamol, a double espresso, a litre of Berocca and a bowl of porridge.

As we wind up the interview with thanks and quick pleasantries, I jump in. She's busy, Jayne, she's got soothsaying shit to do.

'Hey, Jayne, before you go. Can I just ask you something seeing as I have you here? It's just my dog has gone missing and I wondered if you could tell me anything?'

You don't need to be a clairvoyant to spot immediately that the premise for the interview was a weak cover for the real reason I am on the phone to her. Barely a beat and she says, 'He's all right. He's inside with an older man with a bad leg, he's being well looked after, he's safe.'

I'm not so hungry for magic that I want to hear something I don't want to hear.

'Oh.' I'm ashamed already of piggybacking my lost dog trauma on the back of this interview, so I don't ask any more questions. 'Thank you. Thanks so much. How can you tell, though?'

She's a kind person, Jayne, but she's got that Essex bluntness. 'Can I give you a piece of advice, Kate?' she says, her accent making her sound fierce to my pussy middle-class ears. 'I've done a lot of readings for people who've lost their dogs. I did one woman who had an Alsatian lost for six years and she never let up looking for him. It was her whole life.'

'It's only six days,' I whimper in a flash of fear as I realise the eternity of sadness that could lie ahead.

She talks straight over me. Businesslike. 'I told this lady that he was living with people in Scotland, that the garden looked over a big field where he went every day to run and to play. I told her she had to let up looking for him and accept he was happy in his new home. Let him go.'

I want to tell Charlie about Anna Twinney. Anna isn't like a psychic sister; she's an ex-copper and gives huge conferences on what she does. OK, so what she does may well, ostensibly, be the same, but the package is way less woo-woo.

My ace card is Maya. Anna comes recommended not by Kim Kardashian but by my shy and extraordinary cousin. She was Monty Roberts's right-hand woman for years, the guy who invented a system of animal communication known as horse whispering. This in turn was bastardised into bestselling romantic schmaltz in a novel called *The Horse Whisperer* and then a Hollywood movie with Robert Redford.

She is a brilliant rider and a woman so tethered to reality I can feel hyper and silly in her presence. I know Charlie respects her. Maya is the real deal countrywoman. She has worked with horses all her life; she loves them but she has also shot them, lots of them over the years, because that, generally, is how old, sick and insane horses meet their end, not lying on a giant bed eating sugar lumps and carrots. (I know a farmer, too, who kills his own dogs. Quietly and with no fuss. Bang. They're gone. It's over.)

Maya told me once that if horses are in pain and suffering you don't wait for the vet to come. She lives on a ranch with thousands of cattle and hundreds of horses that all roam free over hundreds of thousands of acres. She is 15 miles from the nearest tarmac road. When they lose horses she calls Anna to try to work out where they are. When she couldn't work with a horse as a horse whisperer, she would use Anna to go next level in the human–equine communiqué.

Charlie has a furious dislike of psychics and thinks that even if the magic is real, they can cause untold damage. He has his reasons for this; they are sad and personal and not for me to share. I totally understand his phobia.

But Maya is not a brainless bunny hugger, and now it is hell night – Guy Fawkes Night. Fun for all the family, except the dog. The fireworks will start this evening and carry on right through to the big formal displays at the weekend. They are an immense added worry in an immensely worrying situation. Right now, I will do anything to get him back, including psychics.

Around lunchtime, Anna gets back to me. 'Hi Kate, send pictures of the dog. I will try to find time to talk to you tonight or tomorrow.'

She is six hours behind. Her tonight could mean three in the morning here. I have to go to Sexy Fish tonight to get lots of juicy colour for my piece, which needs to be in by tomorrow. I pray that it is soon; as every informationless minute slips by I'm banking on Anna more and more.

I rush down to the shit pit and sit naked at my desk rifling through my files of photos. It hurts more acutely to look at him than just to think of him. I send them to Anna.

I fumble around the kitchen trying to think about feeding myself. Charlie appears. 'It's impossible in the office, listening to people's petty moaning is driving me insane when I just want to find Woofs. I'm going to work from home this afternoon.' He has an odd new energy. 'I'm going to get coffee,' he says. 'Want one?'

'No, no coffee.' I hold up my hand. I haven't had a coffee since Saturday morning, when I picked one up with Wolfy and Castor on my way over to Will's. Now, when I drive up

Blenheim Crescent it's with only the left eye open, so the stretch of Portobello where our six legs spent so much time together caffeinating, begging for biccies and vegetable shopping isn't visible. If I don't see the visual triggers, the memories won't flood back so painful and fresh. Sludgy, all-pervading, stale misery is the best I can hope for in this dog-lost world. It's possible I will never go into Coffee Plant ever again. It's not only that it is 'our' place, it's the practicalities. The staff will ask me, 'Where's Wolfy?' and I will have to tell them he's gone.

It's been the same with Rita and Janice. I've ducked, avoided and ignored them as I speed down the alley. Can't face it. Can't face the explanations.

'I'm fine with tea.' I pour hot water over a bag of Assam and let it stand until it is black. When I add the milk, it's a tooth-staining shade of brick.

Charlie's standing scrolling through his phone and reads out a message from one of the DogLost ladies: 'If he is happy at home, he should have come back by now.' Another one of those theories complete strangers have. 'Grrrrrr. "If he is happy at home" – what the fuck! She's implying he might have legged it because we don't care for him properly.

'Don't take it on board. Take the good, ditch the bad. If we listened to everyone we'd spend our lives hunting for him in kebab shops.' Instead we talk about our plans. I say: 'Back to Finsbury I suppose, back to Will's.'

I relay the opinions and movements on Twitter, he deals with more tangible authorities and rescue centres. In between, we both work. Sometimes I cry. He doesn't.

'I'm going to Battersea Dogs and I'm going to do that Parkland Walk. It's the old railway line between Ally Pally and Finsbury Park that's been turned into a nature reserve. Lots of people have suggested it,' he says, 'as a place a dog might go.'

Fiddling about on the laptop, I see that Parkland Walk starts on Florence Road. 'He was seen there. He was seen on Florence Road.' Briefly I am animated, a new possible world appears. 'And, and ...' I scroll backwards through my tweets – 'And someone saw a dog a bit like Wolfy in Alexandra Palace, remember, the gingery one that wasn't him. Well, perhaps it *was* him, let me dig it out. He could have gone into Parkland Walk and come out the other end.'

'It wasn't him, Kate. Don't bother. We know what our dog looks like.'

With no sightings of him later than Sunday, we've been drifting further into the realms of the hypothetical. Or in my case, the metaphysical.

Jayne. This is information of sorts. I need to share it. I don't want to keep secrets.

He rolls his eyeballs in an amused sort of way. 'Go on.'

'I spoke to a psychic this morning. She says he's with a man with a bad leg.'

He starts laughing. It's Charlie's special hollow, mocking laughter. No one's gripping their sides with mirth here. 'Man with a bad leg. God help us. Didn't a Dutch clairvoyant predict that the Yorkshire Ripper was a 27-year-old washing-machine mechanic living in Aberdeen, a profile that did not fit Peter Sutcliffe in any way? Madeleine McCann is alive and well, apparently, and studying in Minnesota. I hope you didn't pay for that.'

Definitely do not mention Anna to Charlie now, I think to myself. 'No, I didn't, I blagged it. I'm low on cash actually. Can you lend me some money?'

'It's ridiculous. This is costing us a lot of money. I notice you've got another parking ticket. It all adds up.'

'Can we put a price on the dog's life?'

'Look, Kate. I feel as bad as you but I can't help thinking it's pointless to look any more. To hunt on constantly is a kind of madness. We aren't going to turn a corner one day holding a cooked chicken or shaking a jar of Woof nuts or during a seance with Doris Stokes and see him there waiting for us with a waggy tail. He's gone. He may well turn up; he may not.'

His tone is not uncaring, it is defeated, it is pragmatic and it is as close to tears as it gets with Charlie. The thing is, I don't disagree with him. In solid, grounded moments, I know that hunting all over London is irrational. Just an area of one street squared would hold countless spots a dog could slink off to and hide, never mind a whole postcode, or borough.

'But to do nothing is an impossible ask; and there's people on there ...' I say, dipping my head towards the laptop. I have it open on Twitter, typing my latest post about Charlie's plans to check Parkland Walk, '... who don't think we are doing enough.'

'Fuck them. This isn't about them. We don't even know who they are. It's about you, me and Wolfy. And we're exhausting ourselves running across London like this. I love Wolfy as much as you do, but he's either going to turn up ...' he pauses, 'or he isn't. He's an animal, Kate, not a child; they live and die by different laws. We have to accept he may well be gone for good. He may be alive, he may be dead, we may well never know.'

His sadness is turning to anger. If Wolfy was here he'd back out the back door and sit in the garden until it was all over. I don't push it. I know what is happening. Charlie is living with his own sadness and the way he feels sadness is anger.

A sane, dependable part of me stands back watching how obsessively the magical-thinking me is checking emails, anxious to make contact with Anna. Thoughts of finding him mooching about with gypsies and Travellers have gone from my mind. It's all about the psychics now.

Mum lends me the money to pay Anna; she is relieved, I think, to be able to do something to help. I make a mental note not to punish her for my pain, like a big baby. She does not deserve it. I promise to pay it back.

I am on the phone to her when a weird mobile number interrupts the call. Another hoax, another dog that looks like Wolfy seen by the army of dog walkers co-opted into our cause.

'Gotta go, Mum.' I switch the calls immediately and offer an urgent 'Hello' to whoever is there. 'I've just seen your dog in

Waterlow Park,' they say. 'Call the park ranger now, he's there. He was looking at me from the entrance, the gate down the bottom by Swain's Lane. Do you know it?'

Charlie has taken the car to do Parkland. I get up and run into the street, looning about left and right, looking for a taxi, too impatient to wait for an Uber. One of my neighbours comes out to ask what's wrong. 'My dog. Dog. Must find. Hampstead. Now.'

The neighbour does nothing, is thinking, I suspect, Avoid, Avoid.

I calm myself. Stop, breathe, order an Uber. Now, how do I contact the warden, which borough is it ... I ring the town hall, they don't want to give me a number, I call again, same story. Third time, they do.

I ring the number they give me and the voice at the end of the line tells me I need to ring another number if I want to talk to the warden. My heart rate is cranking up and up again. I want to scream when the warden doesn't pick up. Then the warden does pick up. The warden isn't on site. The warden gives me a mobile number of someone who might be able to help. Tick tock. I speak to someone on site. 'OK, we will alert everyone to look out for your dog'. By now I'm well on my way.

The approach to Waterlow Park on its Swain's Lane side tracks the eastern wall of Highgate Cemetery. Overgrown, broken down, it is a great place for a dog to hide: sheltered, leafy, hard for man to get in but plenty of holes in the old masonry for a dog to press himself flat and wriggle through.

Wolfy was seen at the entrance to the park.

I had never heard of Waterlow Park before. Its ornate gates look gloomy and Gothic in the Great British mizzle that envelops me as it floats down slow and moist from the thick grey sky above. The remnants of the stately garden it once was are evident and the smell of box and yew is painfully reminiscent of happy childhood days at my grandmother's house. The gates are only half open. I walk through the park, wondering what should I do. On Twitter, someone said sit down with a roast chicken and wait for him to come to you.

I don't have a roast chicken. All I have to lure him is my voice. 'Wolfy!' I whistle, call, 'Woooooolfy.' As people pass, I give them a flyer and I ask, 'Have you seen a dog?'

Inside the park two gardeners in blue overalls are digging over a large raised bed pegged off behind some hi-vis netting. I assume they have been briefed about the missing dog and launch straight in with my questions and logistical issues.

Of course, they have not been briefed about any lost dog. They look at me, blank. 'You what?' one says. The other carries on digging, uninterested. 'Lost your dog; have you? Sorry about that.'

'Did you see him?'

'No.' He's not interested either.

'If you see him …'

'Yes,' he says. It's not a promise, it's just a fob-off.

I call the person who originally rang me. What did he look like, describe him. 'Medium-sized, pale brown, nervy but not running …'

Is it him?

After I have walked around for an hour or so, the enormity and foolishness involved in the task of looking for him overwhelms the hope that I might find him. I head back to where 'he' was last seen. The gardeners have gone now.

My phone dies. I crunch through thick piles of brown leaves, while peering through the black railings into the cemetery, calling until I arrive back near the exit where the railings are obscured by a yew hedge. I'm engulfed by a wave of nausea-like sadness. I need to escape public view. I'm like Wolfy when he wants a shit and scurries into the bushes to void his bowels hidden and safe from harm. Only, it's my tear ducts I want to void. I wedge myself between the hedge and the railings and stand, poker-straight; like Lot's wife I'm turned to salt and salty water.

The tears go on. How many locations have I done this in now? It's embarrassing. An angel, draped in stone cloth, is bent in eternal supplication over the grave of a person long dead. I start to sing in a thin, pathetic, faltering voice to the *Scooby Doo* theme tune, 'Woofy Woofy Woo, where are you?'

I sing it over and over until the tears have dried up and I've wiped all the snot on my sleeve.

Walking out of the park, I see two women and offer them a flyer. They have knapsacks and sensible walking shoes on, and a handful of homemade Lost Dog posters.

'We're here for the hunt. Are you the owner? We read your tweet.'

'Wow. Thank you.'

'There's a lot of us out here you know. Everyone's looking.'

This is humbling. It spurs me on.

I walk around from the cemetery further down Swain's Lane, where there's a gated community of large suburban-looking mock-Tudor semis and ye olde blocks of half-timbered flats called the Holly Lodge Estate. I wander in here, for want of anywhere else to look, and walk up and down its private, quiet roads taping posters up on residents' noticeboards. Leaving via the Parliament Hill exit at the top of Highgate Road, where Will and Steph walked Castor and Wolfy on Saturday, I approach a middle-aged woman.

Holding one of my remaining crumpled flyers, she tells me I have her sympathies. Her dog died last year. 'I couldn't get out of bed for a week, it was worse than when my mother died.'

We talk for a while longer, marvelling at the hold these animals have on human hearts. I thank her, and move on.

There's an old spit, sawdust and sausage rolls real-ale pub not far from here called the Southampton Arms. I feel lonely; it's a thin, cold feeling, not plump with the satisfaction and poignancy of the aloneness I have relished with the dog. For a moment, I consider going there to sit in a dark corner and get hammered. I want to escape. I want medicine.

Who can I call? Friend? Family? Charlie? I text Emma Pratt. 'Could I ask you a question?'

'Of course.' The phone is answered by a pleasant-sounding lady, no discernible accent to distinguish her class, her ethnicity, her colour, her haircut or her taste in shoes. She is just disembodied female human kindness.

She asks how I am. 'My heart is breaking. I miss him. I was crying the other night and my boyfriend told me to pull myself together. I don't even know if my sister-in-law is talking to me, I feel like I've fucked up their lives. I feel like this whole thing is just a massive inconvenience for other people.'

'Don't think that. I'm sure it's a difficult time for everyone. Maybe your sister-in-law feels bad that the dog ran away from their house.'

'Maybe, maybe.' The old stew of mistrust and cynicism is churning. Through all my whining and crying, a voice in the back of my head has been constantly going, Would you do all this for a complete stranger?

'Why are you helping me, Emma?'

'Something about that picture of him looking so nice in such a beautiful place and then the desperation in your original post, I think. I just couldn't not help. I had given up going on these hunts because it's so devastating when they have an unhappy ending but—' She stops herself, realising what she's just said.

I clock this. Not going to let a worst-case scenario slide like that. 'What do you mean, unhappy?'

Emma doesn't react. 'Another reason was, I was sure he's alive. He's out there. We just have to keep looking. Don't give up on him.'

We talk a bit more. She tells me she has been in touch with Brett, the tweeter I call the midnight jogger. We've exchanged some direct messages on Twitter. Brett has esoteric exercise habits and this is why, he explains, he is my most ace ally in the hunt. His bio says he is an ultra-endurance athlete and inventor.

'I exercise at night, the roads are clear for cycling and running, the pollution is low. It's like I own the streets. The wildlife I see. If he's out there, you'll find him at night.'

The other night he stopped a man on the street in Archway and asked if he could take a picture of his Wolfy-esque lurcher, just in case it was stolen. The man was very reasonable; turned to him and said, 'It is a new dog. My wife just died, you see. The dog is keeping me alive at the moment but sure, go ahead ...'

Charlie has spoken with Brett on the phone. 'Odd chap. Seems pretty bright, though.' I'm too wretched to think about Brett's eccentricities much; I accept them gratefully for the help they can give us. Not even Emma would set out to look for the dog at 3 a.m.

Brett recently sent me an encouraging article from a Yorkshire newspaper about a lurcher surviving in the wild with foxes for over a year. Based on a theory about Wolfy keeping the same hours as urban foxes, his plan is a crazy one: riding his bike round prime find-Wolfy turf at night with raw meat strapped to his mudguard.

Yes, Emma and the midnight jogger are offering a whole other realm of support.

At first I was confused by the more committed dog hunters on social media. Moonieman, I understood – he's an earnest, helpful, local amateur copper. BeautifulMumsie is clearly in profound emotional pain and through Twitter she tries to ease the pain of others who are suffering. This is the social media version of the wounded healer. For the dog walkers of north London, it's their turf, their specialist subject; they're out and about anyway, and the viral drama online gives it a community aspect that is probably quite jolly to participate in.

I say jolly, but people were genuinely sharing my pain. A cab driver in Mayfair messaged me saying he was having problems sleeping what with the worrying about Wolfy and all that and, as I hadn't sent a tweet for a while, could I let him know if there was any news?

A friend of Steph's texted to say she was thinking of me and that 'The kids are beside themselves, desperate to help #findwolfy. I've only been allowed to walk the dog on the Heath all week.'

Sasha, Cecil's owner, said the same: 'We've only been walking Cessy on the Heath all week, and putting posters everywhere. Thinking of you.'

Sammy, the wife of a guy I went to school with rang me. 'I just want you to know we are all thinking of you.'

My glamorous friend, Jack, tells me he and his husband Dan are taking their two kids up to Queen's Wood in Highgate straight after school to put up posters. I imagine Jack picking his way through the mulchy leaves in one of his pairs of lambskin Gucci loafers. 'I told them, "Now darlings, we must help find Katie's dog, he's like her little boy." Well, they knew all about it already, I don't know how. Darling, I know you're feeling utterly beastly but you're a cause célèbre!'

Even Timbo, canine hater-in-chief, gives me a quick call.

Why? Why were people helping? Yes, people truly are altruistic. Yes, there is compassion and kindness out there. I feel ashamed because there is so much suffering out there. Child poverty and malnutrition exist, not in Sudan or Somalia, Syria or Yemen, but in our own country. There are the desperate faces staring out of the papers at us, migrants stuck in the Jungle in Calais; the corpse of a small Syrian boy was recently washed up on a beach in Turkey.

What were we all doing looking for a bloody dog, my bloody dog? Give or take the odd Brett or Moonieman, this great bank of kindness has in its majority been delivered by women. A class of human that, with very few exceptions, whether friend, family, frenemy or foe, I've had a fractious relationship with since childhood. I toughed out all 900 pages of Simone de Beauvoir's *The Second Sex*, which changed my understanding of what it was to be female; even if I didn't understand it all, that book changed my life. Same goes for Naomi Wolf's *The Beauty*

Myth; my paperback copy is frilled with use and reference. Yet, still, I felt the passive threats of my own sex far more than I did those of men. I accepted men for what they were, women less so. They scared me and disappointed me. Men, they're just easy.

I couldn't be arsed blaming this on my childhood any more. I remember confronting my dad once, and it was only once, about those unhappy years, cut off from Mum, with my stepmother, who must have found looking after my mother's children a royal pain in the arse. We didn't see Dad much. He worked very hard. The NHS and poorly children owned my Daddy. And he quoted the first few lines of Philip Larkin's 'This Be The Verse' back at me:

> They fuck you up, your mum and dad.
>   They may not mean to, but they do.
> They fill you with the faults they had
>   And add some extra, just for you.
>
> But they were fucked up in their turn
>   By fools in old-style hats and coats,
> Who half the time were soppy-stern
>   And half at one another's throats.
>
> Man hands on misery to man.
>   It deepens like a coastal shelf.
> Get out as early as you can,
>   And don't have any kids yourself.

I'd become obsessed by the poem. Though I remained a bit of an Eeyore at times, and was fairly certain I'd learnt this in childhood. Forgiving my parents, seeing them as humans, not meddling imperfect Gods, was empowering. We focus so much on where our parents went wrong, we forget to celebrate all they got right. Those famous first lines are only part of the story. The next two stanzas made the bleating and tears in therapy over the years feel silly. Between them, Larkin and the French Lacunian lady psychotherapist in Highgate sorted my head right.

Larkin taught me one thing, and the dog finished the job. Wolfy had helped me uncover how much love I had to give. The dog had taught me what an unequalled joy it was to love and be loved with no conditions, even by a dumb animal. He'd saved me. The dog saved me from myself.

I have to get the dog back. We have to find him.

Charlie is home when I get back, sat at his laptop on the sofa working. The dog would be lying next to him if he was here, squeaking occasionally if he fancied a tummy rub. His absence makes his presence felt everywhere. It is truly the epitome of ghostly.

At my desk in the shit pit, I sit down to 'work' some more. Meaning I prowl Twitter and Facebook for love and information. I catch sight of myself in the mirror. My hair is glued to my head in an extreme side parting, skin matt and grey with lack of care. I haven't washed properly since the dog went. I circle cleanser into my face. The thought of dressing for this Sexy Fish thing tonight makes me feel like my feet are nailed to the floor. The restaurant's going to let me sit quietly and anonymously at one of the counter seats so I can watch the hot folk congratulate themselves on being in a new hot place on the hottest night of the week.

I've got £20 in my pocket and there's probably about eight quid in cash in the change pot on top of the fusebox. It's all the cash I have in the world. Credit cards will sustain me til I next get paid. It's madness to spend my last pennies on a blow-dry but I'll go to the cheap Brazilian hairdressers by Avondale Park. If I meet other people's expectations of who I am, hiding how I am feeling inside will be easy. Dress the part of the groomed, together, sleek Londoner even if you aren't one.

My phone is ringing. I dive on it, desperate. It's one of the Sexy Fish maître d's checking I am still coming in. Not long after, it rings again, I answer in a foggy drab monotone, like I'm about to blow a hole in my head. 'Hello.'

'I spoke to you earlier today on the Holly Lodge Estate. Look, I've just been talking to my husband about your dog. There's something you need to know. I'd forgotten all about it but we could both hear this dog howling and running back and forth below the window in all the leaves down there.'

'When?'

'Last night, probably around midnight, one maybe. I went back to sleep, but my husband said he lay there listening to it. At first he thought it must have been one of the neighbours' dogs locked out in the garden but the leaves, the rustling ... The dog was running up and down, it must have been outside. Maybe it's not helpful, but I thought ...'

I reassure her that it's very helpful and that this is just the sort of information we want to hear, before rounding off the call with the usual round of insane levels of gratitude.

Clocking this, Charlie comes rushing in. 'What! What?'

I repeat back the call as I rub moisturiser into my face.

'He's there, he's living there. We've been looking in the wrong places. I know it. I'm going back. Give me the address.'

Charlie drives back to Swain's Lane in Highgate, back to where I just came from, all talk of leaving it to fate forgotten.

Anna messages me to say she can fit me in for an animal communication session in a short break in her teaching schedule. The time slot doesn't fit with my work but Maya has made me promise not to go to anyone else. She says that while a lot of people claim to be able to do this telepathic Doctor Dolittle thing, very few people can.

'Anna's the best.'

Anna's only available time slot today is after her morning classes at 12.30 p.m. I count this off on my fingers. 12.30 p.m. Mountain Time is 5.30 p.m. here. She makes it clear she is doing this as a favour. I cannot say no. But I'm meant to be at Sexy Fish then.

There have been a few Tweets questioning why I wasn't pounding the pavements of Finsbury Park 24/7, and I have wondered that myself. Is it laziness? It's not for want of his return; the madness of worry and longing is barely contained and in private moments leaks out constantly from my eyes. Six days in, like a granny, I'm learning never to forget my hanky.

My professional and financial situation is hardly 24-carat gold; it's barely tin plate. Toss in that the writing economy is much shrunk generally. Before Johannes Gutenberg brought the printed word to the people in about 1440, a book cost as much as a house. Printed words were incredibly valuable, a real luxury. In the information age they're stacked up in Poundland, by the out-of-date gingerbread. We've got words spewing from every electronic orifice.

In a crowded market I have to tap-dance and wave my pen-calloused jazz hands to get enough to eat (and to buy those nice scented candles I like). If I stop, the work stops. Start throwing in the towel and I am what's technically known as proper fucked.

Sexy Fish has to make this week's issue. Tomorrow's chip wrappers to you. A cheque in the post for me. The show *must* go on.

I tell Anna, 'Twelve thirty Mountain Time is great. Speak then!'.

How do we identify ourselves, and how do we satisfy other people's expectations of our identity? In my job, hovering on the edges of the high life, trying not to scare anyone while poking about in their business means I, a fairly scruffy bugger, as my stepmother accurately put it, had to fit in. I often borrowed clothes I'd never be able to afford and wrote notes up my leg with biro in the ladies' for want of a bag that looked expensive enough to put a notepad in. Sometimes I thought I belonged there, among the money and the yachts, motor racing, diamonds, art, ski towns for the super-rich and beach clubs for the idiots who wanted to copy them.

I really need a blow-dry.

'Where is dog?' The Brazilians in the salon by the flat are used to me coming in with Wolfy, who sprawls across the white tiles or shambles about greeting everyone as they come in. The owner is my age, probably, with a hard, not unkind, but unreadable face surrounded by ludicrously youthful, bouncy honey-coloured hair. She always has a little Portuguese love-in with him. 'Mmmn mmmmn' – they are nose-to-nose – '*Meu docinho de coco ... mais fofo.*'

I'd like to sit in silence, but the others, who speak no English, are all busy so there's no escaping her. 'The dog is gone? *Seis* days? You don' know where is he?'

I hear the rustling of the leaves as Wolfy runs up and down, howling. I think of the imaginary man with the limp who is becoming more and more real in my mind. I see the corpse of a dog curled up under a bush. I see Wolfy peering through the gates of Waterlow Park.

'He cannot hear you or see you but his ...' she struggles to find the English word, '*âmago*, you know? Open your heart. Let your heart find him. His *âmago* will find your *âmago*. The dog is a survivor. Now, you want tongs or brush?' Eh? 'The hair,' she says, pointing a comb at me. 'You want loose waves or big curls?'

Walking home, I hear the crack of the evening's first fireworks and sing again the Scooby song from Waterlow: 'Woofy Woofy Woo, where are you?'

CHAPTER ELEVEN

Here on the sofa to call Anna Twinney. I think this was Wolfy's favourite spot. I'll be sitting on skin cells and microorganisms that lived on Wolfy's body, a tiny ecosystem that lives on despite his being gone. Here it is easy to connect with him, like when I climbed in his nest, but less mental.

I slept in my grandmother's empty bed the night after she died. I hated the smell of death and old age but I wanted to be close to her residue, to breathe it all in and not waste a molecule, so I slept on the deflated air mattress on her death bed, the sort with bars and sides and electronic positioning, which had been moved into her room when she came home to die.

My aunt walked in the following morning to find me curled up like a child in a cot and had screamed in alarm. 'Oh my God, it's you. You gave me such a fright, I thought you were Mary.'

'No, Mary's gone, Granny's gone.' We had watched the matriarch slowly die and by the time she was gone it was like we'd been weaned off her presence. I was not relieved, I was just ready for it. I made jokes about stealing her morphine with the funeral director's assistant while his boss and the vicar talked to my mother and uncle about immediate arrangements for her corpse and soul respectively. I sang like an ebullient chorister at the funeral. I beamed as I read the grim Victorian death poem that Will and I shared at the funeral, while my cousin broke down and couldn't finish his. No Robbie Williams's 'Angels' for Granny. She got Matthew Arnold's 'Requiescat'. RIP. It was time to go; her meat body had failed her. Near to the end, the only writing she did was binary. Filling the crosswords she had once done so quickly with only two characters, 1 and 0. Turning the pages of the newspaper without reading. She stopped talking altogether. Her eyes closed. I never grieved, or cried; even at her graveside, as my mother sobbed I did not.

That's why the dog going has hit me like a madness. He's still vital and alive in my mind. I don't have the inevitable misfortune, yet, of comparing this loss to a greater one.

The sitting room is usually lit with lamps. I don't like the miserable one-dimensional light of the overhead, but lately I don't care. I snap the ceiling light on and sit down. I call Anna Twinney at the precise time she requested and sitting in Wolfy's spot, looking towards the fire and the bookcases either side. 'Are you sitting down, are you comfortable?'

The way she speaks is plain, practical and she has a slightly hard intonation, stern, perhaps, confident to the point of egotistical. She fills me in on the thousands of readings she has done, the successes and the experience she has. Not just horses and dogs, elephants, sloths and anteaters too. It is all to preface this point: 'You need to know, if I make contact with him he may or may not be alive. If he has only recently died I cannot be sure, as the spirit lives on for a few days after the body has died. He may be in transition, you see.'

I don't really see; it feels like a Get Out of Jail Free card for psychics. I feel foolish for paying money for this. 'There's more – lost animals are often frightened and disorientated, the further they've run the more confused they are. It can be hard to get any clarity from them.'

'How do you communicate with him?' I ask.

'He will communicate to me in images, visions, body feelings, tell me if he is hungry, thirsty, in pain, and it's up to me to interpret them for you. I'm just a translator.'

OK, understood.

'Now, Kate, Wolfy is obviously very precious to you. Not all dogs, like not all horses, are the same. Some dogs are very shallow, all they need is to be walked, peed, fed; others help us evolve as people and see life differently.'

'I feel that Wolfy saved me,' I say. 'I don't know if anyone really understands how much. Maybe my boyfriend does. He's been a great dog, he has brought love and peace and back to our lives.'

'Understood, absolutely. I do a lot of work with Gulf War veterans and it's the same with horses. Some have the ability to cure veterans of PTSD, some are just normal, even annoying, like some people are.

'But there's just this one other thing you need to be ready for. Some dogs run because they want to leave, and some might bolt in shock or something, but once they are on the move, they like it. They don't want to come home. Be ready for that.'

'I'm ready.'

'Just try to connect with Wolfy yourself. Think about him. I need to ask you not to speak unless I ask you a specific question or you could break my connection with him. I am going to go quiet for a minute. I am shutting off all my senses to I can open myself to him.'

The distinct sounds of the city outside slow, blur and muffle together into one solid form that cloaks the windows like lagging. The room is changing. I can see the light, dull and granular, sitting around my physical body while my spirit scratches at the door trying to get out to find my soulmate.

She begins. The line goes quiet.

It stays quiet for maybe five minutes. I breathe, I wait.

With a sharp sucking intake of air she says, 'I've got him and ... he's alive. He's definitely alive. Oh isn't that great. I'm asking him to describe his home, I want to make sure this is right. I'm seeing a lot of stairs. Stairs up to the house, stairs inside, a lot of steep stairs. You can speak – is this right?'

'Yes.'

'I'm asking if he likes it here.' More quiet, then: 'He's telling me he likes lying somewhere looking along a corridor with stairs at the end.'

I think of his spot in the bathroom where he likes to lie on the cool floor, away from the action but with a good view of it and, ideally, with a pile of smelly washing for him to rest his head on. There at the furthest end of the flat, he has a prime view up the steps in the kitchen, and the steep wooden stairs to bed.

'He's allowed to sleep on your bed. That is his favourite place. It's a very big bed. That's where he wants to be now.'

I think of how still and empty the bed is at night as we both turn over to sleep. The conversation when we bought it went, 'Let's get the biggest bed they've got.'

'Goes without saying,' Charlie said.

'He's not with anyone. He is alone. He is in a very busy, urban place, hundreds of legs passing him by. There is a strip of shops and a lot of brown and black faces around. He's staying hidden away, peeping out. He is staying away from people. He is not with anyone. He's hiding. He wants you to know that he is OK but he doesn't understand why you haven't come for him yet. He's frightened.'

Anna asks if I want to say anything to him. I hadn't expected this. 'Be a good boy. Find a human, Wolfy. Find a friendly human. Come home. Good boy. I Love You.'

I feel stupid.

The call is coming to a close. She checks I have transferred the money to the right account. And ends with the words, 'Get out there and find your boy.'

I notice I have written down everything she said in my awful shorthand, yet I have no memory of moving a muscle.

Dazed, I sit for a while staring at the wall and then I get up, mechanically dress, put on some make-up and leave for the bloody Fish place.

'I saw your dog on Tuesday, please call me.'

I hurtle off the tube before it goes underground at Paddington and call the number. 'Hello. Hello! It's me. Yes, it's Wolfy's owner.'

'It was on Hampstead Lane by Kenwood House. He was running all over the road, zigzagging and weaving through the traffic so fast no one could stop him.' A lurcher is good at turning, I think, in a flash of pride. 'I'm so sorry I didn't contact you sooner but I've only seen your poster now.' Which way was he going? 'I don't know for sure. Down,' she says. 'Maybe down towards Parliament Hill. The bottom end of the Heath on the Highgate side.'

'Swain's Lane, do you mean? Could he have been headed down towards Swain's Lane, round the cemetery, because someone thought they saw him there on Wednesday.'

'Oh yes, definitely, that's the direction he was headed, there or Highgate Road. Is that helpful?' she says. I pant words to the affirmative: 'God yes.'

'I hope so, and good luck finding him. It's so good to be able to tell you this.'

I can't stop saying thank you. 'Thank you, thank you.' I say it until I am out of breath.

It's no distance. Wolfy can rack up a mile in ten minutes at a relaxed trot.

Late now, I rush past the windows of shops for the rich. Mayfair: past expensive art, the finest porcelain at Thomas Goode, Rolls-Royce, Harry's Bar, Sautter for fat-cat cigars, Mark's Club, Tim's flat, jewellery, Celine and Goyard, the French trunk-maker where a couple of dog bowls in a leather carry case cost £5,000. There is nothing in these windows that I would trade for my dog. Not even the £10 million Cy Twombly painting sitting in the window at Phillips. No amount of money in the world could make me stop wanting him back.

My spirit is on an astral plane floating through Kenwood. It can smell the autumn, hear the crunch of dry leaves and gravel; it's moving across the Holly Lodge Estate, the rustle of the leaves towards the sanctuary of Highgate Cemetery, via a small hole in the wall on the corner of Swain's Lane. It moves like a wraith among the graves under the dark of the trees and emerges to peep through the gates of Waterlow Park. I am briefly with him. Emma Pratt is right: my dog is alive. 'Hide yourself away tight Woofs. Don't be afraid of the fireworks. I am coming …'

Full of longing and pain, mingled with adrenaline and the metaphysical ecstasy that he might be safe and alive, I arrive at Sexy Fish. Like we're in a decompression chamber, two handsome doormen in peaked caps and frock coats open two heavy gold doors one after the other and I burst from the bubble of magical thinking into something else entirely. The roar of a packed and popular restaurant.

There's a lot of faces in. Minor royals, major-league restaurant critics – two aren't even reviewing – Clauds, with a wild-looking and (whispered) *very collectible* female artist and two imperious, snobby gallerists, Hollywood actor at four o' clock, retired supermodel at two. Billionaire family get-together at midnight and, ooh, what's this, in the far corner at about eleven on the clock there's a major famous-guy alert on table one, the hottest, darkest, most discreet table in the house, where he is sitting glued to a famous heiress. Other women sit at the table but it's her he is close to. An affair. Without a doubt. She's half his age but when did that ever stop a guy. So the whispers are true. His marriage must be over. All these are educated hunches. What is absolutely certain, though, is that they're sniffing coke at the table. It's pathetic how obvious as they bend down under the table and spoon the white powder into their noses. Do they think we can't see? What a car crash of entitlement and stupidity.

This perch I have at a countertop by the open kitchen is an absolute winner.

As the general manager, Paul, passes, I mouth, 'Thanks, great spot' and we chat for a minute before he has to glide off in his Saint Laurent tuxedo and Givenchy patent leather gentleman's opera pumps to hover and swoop over his 150 diners. A PR powerhouse walks past me. 'Do I know him', asks Paul the GM. 'I don't; he's too important for the likes of me', I say, in a thick Bristol accent for comic effect. Charm radiating out of every cell and through his sparkling white teeth, Paul says, 'No one is more important than you, Kate.' We both laugh. We know it isn't true but somehow it still works and makes everyone he says it to feel incredibly special. 'You know what, he lost his dog once, perhaps you should talk to him.'

I'd never have imagined this guy had a pet; he's cold-blooded, I assumed. He won't talk to me for longer than 20 seconds. I have had interactions with him before and I think the word 'deign' describes his attitude to conversation with anyone less than an authentic somebody. I ask him quickly, before he rushes off to give continental kisses to all the editors, critics and movie stars, 'How was losing a dog for you?'

'Like losing a child minus the helicopters and press conferences,' he says, and walks off.

I go to join Clauds at her table. She's in a good spot, in between the billionaire family outing and the retired supermodel. Her friends all shuffle round and I squeeze in between her and the bonkers artist, who is wearing an enormous pair of Gucci sunglasses. 'Can you see me through those?' I ask.

She goes straight in with a hug. You have to love the Yanks for the emotional displays. 'I hear you lost your puppy, you poor baby girl, you must be mad suffering right now honey.' I nod. She tells me how much she loves her own dog and I nod some more. I don't want to talk about it. Instead I whisper to her and Clauds about the very famous guy and the heiress, nose down on table one.

'Not any more, doll,' she says, and we watch as Paul sedately walks very famous guy to the door, leaving his coterie of women to sit wondering whether they really want to give up the hottest table in London tonight.

They wave over a waiter and order more drinks. Clearly they aren't that bothered that their elderly coke-sniffing pal has exceedingly discreetly been kicked out.

We're all enjoying this delicious moment of restaurant theatre when my phone rings. It's a woman and I'm struggling to hear her. I get my head right under the tabletop and what she's saying starts to become clear. 'My friend saw your dog this morning. Someone was trying to catch him but he ran off.' I ask her to repeat what she knows several times, then write the address she gives me in my notepad and sit back up.

'The dog. Someone saw him.'

'Go. Just go. Take my driver. I'll get a taxi home,' says Clauds. 'He's round the corner, run, I'll tell him you're coming.'

We can redistribute the wealth tomorrow. Tonight I need a chauffeur to help me find Wolfy.

As I get in the car Ernie starts to make sympathetic noises. 'Sorry to hear about dog, Kate.' His English is good – better certainly than my Tagalog – but the problem is he talks quietly, in a muffled murmur, and as I paw and scroll around maps on my phone trying to locate this Harvist Estate and put it in context with all the other Wolfy sightings, Ernie's voice is just a soft steady sound coming from the driver's seat.

It appears to be in the shadow of Arsenal's Emirates Stadium, next to a train line. It's highly likely that this sighting is real. The Harvist Estate is just off Hornsey Road, which is the last confirmed place he was seen on Saturday and miles, I reflect mournfully, from the Hampstead Lane sighting on Tuesday or the Waterlow Park one this morning.

Ernie drives, and mutters to me, while I rock back and forth between the maps on a small screen in the dashboard and the ones on my shattered old phone. How close is this place to where he was last seen? I call Charlie and he says he is coming; I call my brother, who says he's had a drink. 'Don't worry, Will, I'll collect you.'

Anna said a lot of people, a busy place; she said there were hundreds of legs passing by him. She said there was a row of shops and lots of dark-skinned people around. Swain's Lane and Holly Lodge are enclaves of white wealth and privilege. You don't see so many dark faces on the street round there.

As we drive onto Camden Road, the main road round the back of Will's, I settle down enough to hear what Ernie is trying to tell me in between my directions to Will's front door. 'Idolatry, Kate.' He keeps repeating my name. 'Dogs are not meant to have the human love. Kate, you should not love your dog so much. I hope you find him but turn to the Lord, a dog' ... mutter mutter ... 'You know Kate you need to find real happiness in your life.'

Religious orthodoxy and its dislike of dogs is something I'd only ever ascribed to Muslims and stuffed away, my 'virtue-signalling wet' afraid of the implied Islamophobic overtones. Ernie is redressing the balance and reminding me that Christianity is pretty babyish too.

Will jumps in the car, bringing the brash energy of the street into this hermetically sealed pod of comfort and wealth, and Jesus. His enquiring look says, What the hell you doing in a limo; he actually says, 'Sweet ride. Pay rise?'

Ernie stops talking about dogs and God and drives in silence for the remaining five minutes, which takes us in a fairly straight line from Will's to the Harvist Estate.

I shower Ernie with the usual effusive insincere thanks for the ride and the interesting sermon. Will has already left the car when Ernie starts to tell me it is too dangerous for me to be here. I ignore him and dive out after my brother.

Will looks up and around at the four lumpen, grubby and cheap-looking tower blocks. I am already scoping for corners and dark places where a dog could hide. He asks me, 'Where do we start?'

I don't know. I'm grateful he is here. We give each other a brief hug and set off on our own ways, walking and calling around the concrete paths that snake around the 23-storey buildings. I wander and call, looking under bushes and back to giant wheelie bins. Anyone I see, I stop. I don't care.

Will and I, and Charlie, just arrived from west London, briefly convene around a short strip of shops inside the estate's boundaries. The young man working in the corner shop is just leaving as I approach him, but he unlocks the shop and puts a poster up without questioning it, and says he'll give one to the chemist tomorrow. The kid working in Domino's Pizza says no.

'Why?'

'It's the rules, head office.'

Pointlessly, I rail against a corporate authority that doesn't allow a local shop to put a missing-dog poster. I look around us at these bare containers for housing people who can't afford to live in this city. 'And some corporate turd in Buttfuck American Midwest is going to make your decisions about what is right, and what is wrong for this community here in your corner of London?'

'I don't know mate but it's the rule, I could lose my job.'

I kick the blue chair.

'Sorry, mate, she's a bit upset,' says Charlie, patting my arm and steering me out of the shop.

'Kate, that was ridiculous. You're like the vigilante who only beats up OAPs and kids.'

I go back into the shop and apologise. 'Yeah, no problem. Yeah. Hope you find your dog, yeah.'

We look around together for a while, poking our noses in the gardens of the low-rise houses that surround the estate on the Hornsey Road side before heading back to these blocks that look like something Khrushchev knocked up with prefabricated Soviet Lego. The paths between the blocks are empty save a few small clusters of young men leaning on walls and lamp-posts. One group wearing rock band T-shirts are disappointingly white – perhaps he isn't here – and stoned off their gourds, nattering at us in gibberish while swigging on giant cans of cheap caffeinated fizzy pop called ROCKST★R. The next guys are a mix of black and Asian-looking, possibly stoned too, or just very relaxed. They're polite. I can feel Will and Charlie thinking how pointless this is. We move away from the basketball court.

I look at a cluster of wet leaves in one corner and wonder, Has my dog pissed here, have his paws come this way?

A neat woman with a tote bag, businesslike, returning from work, stops to listen to my lost-dog query. She is black; Anna's rubric has formed in me a heightened awareness of people's skin colour.

Nodding and listening, polite and interested, she interrupts me when I show her the flyer. 'There's a man in there got a dog like that,' she says. 'He's not had it long, I saw him with it the other day. He usually only has one dog, but he had two, and this other, new one, well, he was struggling to control it.'

She readily agrees to take us to the man's front door and we follow her into Citizen House.

As we climb the stairs behind her the atmosphere in the search party becomes more adrenalised; we walk up two flights of an open stairwell up to the second floor, where we press through two glass doors, and she points to the flat directly in front. 'There. Good luck.'

We stand in a wide corridor with old shiny red lino on the floor and wooden doors spaced 20 feet apart along the wall. My first thought is what an immense waste of space this hallway is, given how poky the flats inside must be. No light shows under the door. Charlie and Will are mumbling to each other, joking nervously about getting the crap beaten out of them. There's an energy now that only comes from the feeling of being in danger.

The hunt for our dog has brought me to a stranger's door in a north London tower block at eleven on a Thursday night. I rap on the door. Gentle at first. Then sharper and harder. After five minutes a tall man, big as in strong, not fat, pulls the door open with an irritable 'Yes!'

His salt-and-pepper hair is awry and the skin under his two-day beard crumpled with sleep. I go into a genteel and effusive round of apologies and explanations, during which he looks remarkably like he'd like to smash us all on the tops of our heads like boiled eggs.

During this exchange I can see his dog asleep in a basket behind him. It's a skinnier version of Wolfy, definitely a lurcher. His wife comes to the door of what must be the bedroom to ask what's going on. 'I heard you had two dogs,' I say. 'Could we see your other dog?'

'I don't have two dogs.'

I press on, 'One of your neighbours ...'

This denial passes back and forth, with me dropping an obsequious apology here and there to avoid him coming out and punching our lights out. I implore him, as a fellow dog owner, to understand that I just need to know for peace of mind that my dog is definitely not with him.

'Tell her about the other dog,' the woman calls from back inside the bedroom.

'I had another dog like that one but I got rid of it last week. It was no good ... I gave it back.'

'Can you tell us where the dog is now?'

'I want you to go. You wake me up, get me from my bed, disturb my wife.' The conversation, on his part anyway, is drawing impatiently to a close.

The woman calls from the bedroom, 'Good luck finding your dog.'

The door closes.

'Fuck! Did anyone notice if he had a limp?' I say.

Our detective skills having been found lacking, we turn back to the wider estate. Charlie and Will make noises about going but I can't bear to leave. I know the dog is here. His fur brushes against the skin of my imagination. Anna's words, 'he doesn't understand why you haven't come for him yet' ring in my head.

Roaming beyond the estate into a London-brick development of modern townhouses, I wander aimlessly, calling and calling between choking on tears. A young black guy, maybe 16, comes towards me on a mountain bike and I stop him. Has he seen this dog? I wave a flyer under his startled face. He's perfectly polite – 'I ain't seen it, sorry' – and he goes to pedal forward and away from me. I clock the crumpled mound of tenners spilling from his inside pocket. 'Take this, please.' I thrust a flyer in his hand.

The boys are right. We have to go home. I walk back towards the exit of Citizen Road where Wolfy was, allegedly, last seen down by the railway at the junction with Hornsey Road.

When we drop Will home I get out and give him a huge hug. 'You OK?' he says.

'Mmmn.' I give a non-specific response to his shoulder. 'Send my love to the kids.'

Back in the car driving west, I keep tapping Google Maps, postulating theories. Someone wise on Twitter told me that in order to find his way back to where he first ran from, he'd circle around and around until his nose took him back. My eyes are itching with weariness and I'm finding it hard to match logic with the variety of theories, metaphysical and solidly practical alike. 'If we add up all the places he's been seen they are all within about a mile radius of Will's house. Perhaps he's moving back and forth between the west and east sides of their place.'

'I can't believe he'd want to stay there.' Charlie says this with a shiver.

'But maybe that guy really did have him. There's meant to be loads of rabbits around Kenwood. Maybe he was hunting with him up there and Wolfy escaped this morning.'

'The only thing I know for sure is I'm not going back to that place again.'

Maybe I will wait to tell him about Anna.

CHAPTER TWELVE

Charlie sits on the sofa and I jump up and down in front of him to adequately act out the drama of the Twinney conversation. I don't necessarily believe her telepathy or clairvoyance with the dog is a fact, but I have added her reading to the phone calls and the sightings and I feel surer than ever that he is alive.

'Near a busy place, with a lot of dark-skinned people. He is hidden away, he is avoiding people even though there are so many around. She says he peeps out from his hiding places. He won't make himself known. He's afraid. He isn't with someone. It's Harvist, it's the estate from last night. I'm going back.'

'Why have you called up these cranks and spirit-dealing goons? It's like drugs, Kate, just escapism from reality, a way of twisting the world to the shape you want it to be.'

Repeating back to Charlie the experience with Anna has been immediately polarising. 'This shit is unhelpful. And I am not going back to that fucking estate, we don't belong there. It's dangerous. Knocking on that man's door last night could have got us hurt. We were lucky it didn't turn into a fight. He was angry. And big. I was a bit scared. He wouldn't have thumped you, it'd have been me or Will that got it.'

He looks at me, then stands up and walks to the kitchen. It's not far, a couple of cat swings, but it's designed to make a point. As he's walking away from me, he says, 'You are starting to scare me.'

Sadness ripples across the surface of his frustration with me. I can feel it. Gently, I say, 'Sorry, sorry I opened this Pandora's box, but I'm desperate, I want him back. Every minute he isn't home I want to be out there, looking.'

'I believe it more than ever now. He'll either turn up somewhere, or someone's got him, or he's dead.'

I have no rational reason to disagree with him, but a few irrational ones. 'It's just what Anna said: "he doesn't understand why you haven't come for him yet".'

He clutches his head as he crouches down by the wine rack, rummaging for a bottle that isn't port or crème de menthe. 'He's a dog, he can't fucking talk.'

'But Ray Winstone ...' I try to lighten the mood.

'I'm having a big drink and I am driving nowhere. I'm knackered. If you want to drive off on a fruitless hunt for a needle in a haystack, you knock yourself out trudging around miserable estates all night. I've had enough of this madness.'

Picking up the car keys and my bag, I suck any dark emotion deep inside and paper the cracks with humour: 'I'm going then. Byeeee!'

'Bye,' he says flatly as he cracks the cap on some screw-top Shiraz I bought for chucking in a stew.

I filed the Sexy Fish piece at four and now I can breathe into the Wolfy hunt fully. There are no more pressing deadlines now for a few days. Emma and I talk on the phone while I drive from Notting Hill to the Emirates Stadium. She has been at the Harvist Estate tonight putting up posters with her kids. Her son is excited to be hunting for a dog, while her husband is there because he doesn't want her wandering alone with their son. 'Emma,' I ask her, like I do every day now, 'do you think Wolfy is alive?'

'Yes, I do.'

I tell her about Anna. 'Oh I see. That's interesting.' The inflection in her voice says she has no comprehension of this witchy business.

Harvist is deserted, lights on at the windows but no one in the streets. The corner-shop guy was true to his word. There is a lost dog poster in the chemist. In Domino's Pizza, they still say no. Had to ask, didn't I. I wander over the road to another estate by a big lumpy building called the Sobell Leisure Centre. This estate is low-rise and dark, with corners of the blackest black. I walk around calling and calling. I imagine him trotting round the corner, him just being there. I imagine him sitting in the dark, not emerging.

My sense of longing is so desperate that I press my body flush up against a wall, feeling the cold rough brick pressing into my skin. Has the dog really been here in the arsehole of Finsbury Park, or is he curled up and safe in the leaves on the graves at Highgate? Where are you? Where are you?

Being alone feels unbearable. I call my friend Kim, who comes to meet me. Together we walk and call the dog's name in the shadow of Arsenal.

After watching me talk for ten minutes to a stinking street drunk, the weathered, dirt-brown kind who looks like they've been out here for years, she steers me away and into a pub.

We sit opposite each other with big glasses of thick and fruity pub red and she says, 'Are you all right, Katie?'

'No, Kimmy, I can't bear it, I miss him so much.'

'That's understandable, babes. You've been having a love affair with Wolfy.'

I recoil at this. 'Don't say that. It sounds too close to bestiality.'

'Of course I'm not saying you're shagging your dog, but I think we've both had enough love affairs to know what one feels like.'

'Yes.' I puff out a little laugh. Discussing the frustrating and unsatisfying dynamics of pairing with the male human is a constant for us. It's how we met each other. Fifteen years ago, after circling each other like a couple of wary cats, we eventually bonded over our love/hate of the same toxic bachelor. We are both battle-scarred veterans who stopped counting a long time ago and we are good friends. And the man in question? Long forgotten.

It's the calmest I have felt since the dog went missing. 'Wolfy made me happy, he showed me a very simple sort of happiness. You know what I was like before, Kim, I was all over the shop.'

'You weren't *that* bad.'

'I can't bear to think of him suffering.'

'What about Charlie? How's he doing?'

'I don't know. Isn't that terrible. I don't know. We'll cope, we always do. It's not like it's a child, it's just a dog.' I look down and we sit in silence.

'I saw that dog.' A loud bloke appears. He's waving a pint of Stella Artois over the stack of Wolfy posters and flyers in the middle of the table. 'I'll never forget it, ever, in my life, it was running so fast, faster than the traffic. Last Saturday, it was.' The guy's hammered, but obviously telling the truth. This is immensely reassuring, we are in the right place. He's been here. He may well still be here, tucked away and scared, but, as Anna promised, alive and alone. The guy continues. 'Fucking mental. It's been on my mind all week. I hope you find him mate, coz you got yourself a wonderdog there.'

Around one in the morning we walk back to the car that Charlie calls the glorified dog bed on wheels.

'Have you eaten anything today?'

'Not really.'

'Let's go to Maroush on Edgware Road on the way home for a posh kebab.'

'And Lebanese wine.'

As we sit there peeling back the flatbread inhaling the garlicky chicken. 'Thanks for being kind, Kimbers. You're a brick.'

'That's all right, it's what friends are for.'

'Mad, isn't it, that I'm so uncomfortable with it. Friends and help and all that.'

'Tiz a bit, yes.'

At home, I fall into bed and Charlie mutters, 'How was it?'

Moving closer to him, I speak into the warm skin on his back. 'Usual.'

'You?' I ask.

Apparently a dog that looks like Wolfy has been picked up in a remote London borough and taken to Battersea Dogs Home. Charlie was alerted on the DogLost website and it's already spread across Twitter. A woman in the #findwolfy crew went down there tonight to bang on the door and claim him. The staff sent her away, saying if she wasn't the owner she couldn't check him out.

Charlie says, 'I'd better drive down there and check it's not him in the morning.' Resigned and tired as he is, he's still got skin in the game, if that's not a ludicrous way to describe participation in wacky races around London after a third-hand lurcher. These hurtling drives and dashes to anywhere the internet or callers point us feel absurd, but to do anything else with our time feels somehow obscene.

'Coffee?' he asks, when he rings on his way back from Battersea the next morning. He's already confirmed what I already knew – that the dog wasn't Wolfy. No. Still no to coffee. It's impossible not to dwell on this-time-last-week type thoughts. Seven days have passed.

Saturday is my first full day of hunting since last Sunday. I have to confront the zero-liquidity issue. Every pocket is turned inside out; every bag, upside down. Twenty quid is all that turns up. The money, my money, has run out.

Charlie brings a stack of plastic folders to put posters in so they aren't destroyed by wind and rain. He has drawing pins to tack them to trees, Blu-tack for windows, Sellotape. The tools of the dog-hunting trade. He's despairing of the cost of losing the dog, again so I don't dare mention I have only £20 in my bank account. I'll have to wing it.

I set off for the Saturday hunt on my yellow pushbike. It's heavy and old-fashioned and there are more hills in north London than I am prepared for. As the day proceeds I get tired and that particular type of stressed that comes from winging it with hardly anything in my bank account. I print out more posters in a strange copy shop with a sad rack of dusty greetings cards and a few food items like ginger nut biscuits and Angel Delight. It's like they've been there since the seventies. There are four men in there; one obese guy with a ponytail is sweating over an old grubby computer terminal and the other three are clustered in the back of the shop eating Pot Noodles and drinking instant coffee from mugs. It is one of the seediest internet cafes I've ever found, but it has a big printer and I print off 50 posters and 100 flyers, which I will guillotine down to size.

A tall skinny mean-faced guy in a leather blazer comes out to serve me. His breath stinks of instant coffee. I order a cup of tea to drink while I do the posters, which he serves in the worst possible way, sour-faced weak and milky. Any attempts at friendliness on my part are assertively rebuffed. The other two guys stare at me from the back room. It's like I've walked through a shabby portal into a malevolent all-male world. I think of Coffee Plant, with its regular parade of all Notting Hill's human life from the film directors to the regular lunatics; there's the odd junkie pops in to use the toilet there after an NA meeting, and the artist mum who brings her two girls in to run feral round the place and give Wolfy tummy rubs. From the tough black guys saying 'innit' and smoking rollies outside to the laconic playwright chain-drinking espressos and chatting up the compact French ex-ballet dancer, it's a distillate of the place I call home.

I want my dog back because I love him, but I also want to take my life back.

As I do the printing I talk to the obese guy. His body is straining against his clothes. I tell him all about my dog, and he tells me that he hasn't seen his daughter for ten years, that her mother won't let him near her. He is peculiarly vulnerable in his friendliness but there's something not right about the place.

When I come to pay I have badly miscalculated the cost of the posters and am £14 short. The skinny guy stands and looks at me with contempt. 'What are you going to do about it? The cost is £34.'

I start to flap about and try to call Will, who is the only person I feel comfortable asking for money at this point. My phone dies. It's a mess. I need to get out and hunt for the dog. The stress is making me feel sick.

The obese guy says, 'I'll pay for it.'

The skinny guy says to him, 'Don't do that, John. You don't even know her.'

'The girl lost her dog, Colin, have a heart. I'll pay.' He slips £20 out of a wallet tucked up somewhere near his armpit in his brown polyester jacket. 'Don't worry about the change.'

I've grown enormously suspicious of all these guys while I have been hiding out here. There's an atmosphere of secrecy that makes me imagine some dark scenarios. But this weird, childlike, obese guy has saved my bacon. I accept the kindness of strange strangers without shame. I take the money, keep the change and get the fuck out of there.

The midnight jogger calls me as I attack Archway Road, the long steep hill that goes from my brother's place up to Queen's Wood, an ancient patch of old oak woodland. He has a new plan and wants to meet me. He can't do tonight though. Tomorrow is fine, I say. He speaks fast and with great enthusiasm like a kids' TV presenter, but without the modulation of emotion that indicates a shift in the conversation. So we have moved from our meeting tomorrow at the Palmerston pub just up the road from Will's house to the real identity of my beloved tweeting police officer: 'That Moonieman. I tracked as far back as I could in his Twitter and there's some dodgy stuff. I am not sure that's what a community policeman would put up. Is he what he says he is?'

This, I admit, is a blow. A blow because thinking confidently that you have a copper, even a volunteer one, on your side always reassures any human, we all want the police on our team. Be they an armed robber or a frail little old lady. On the other hand, the #findwolfy story has moved on. I don't need to keep using him as an emotional prop. The wheel of hope, or hopeless hope, keeps cranking away with the help of psychics and many kind-hearted people. I can do without Moonieman, the Porno PC.

It's not like I've lost Emma, and Brett's still there, midnight jogging for Wolfs. Onwards. As I climb the hill, I grind my way down through the gears until it's low enough to cope with the unfamiliar North London terrain. Onwards.

In the afternoon I hunt for the dog with a woman I know, but not very well, a minor celebrity who lives in the area. She's kind and I'm grateful, but I'm getting kind of paranoid. Whatever my body is overdosing on in this stress state – is it adrenaline? – is starting to have the same effect as a mixture of speed and cheap student hash. Out of the corner of my eye, I catch her looking at me as I repeatedly leap across a muddy cricket pitch in Queen's Wood, thrusting flyers at everyone I see: 'Have you seen my dog, have you seen my dog.'

In the moments when there is no one to assail with the Lost Dog story, we walk and talk. 'How's your lovely man Charlie?' She's always applauded me for making a sensible choice in a man. 'You did well there. Wish I could.'

I sympathise. 'Took me til forty to realise the things that drive you wild about a man will pretty quickly be what makes you hate him, or him hate you. I reject my type and look at us, We're doing OK. Ish.' Why can't I just say something like 'I love him' or 'I'm lucky'? 'It's always very ish, isn't it.'

I wonder where Charlie is. He went to Hampstead today, chasing a sighting, pinning up posters. He's probably long home by now. If it were me, I'd have dropped in at Will's, but Charlie won't do that.

I tell the minor celebrity I don't know where he is, that I have had no charge in my phone since it died in the Pederasts' caff, which is how I described the creepy print shop to her. 'You cannot say that!' She's outraged.

'Is paedo cafe better? It's only for me, I'm not putting it on Trip Advisor. It's not for a guidebook. It's for a list called "things that only happen when you lose your dog". That place was *dark*.'

Before, I would never have spent time with her anywhere other than some party, clutching a free glass of champagne and batting back and forth short spiky gossipy sentences. In my edgy state, there's a nervous frankness – I don't have the emotional wherewithal to censor myself. We share information with each other about our lives. She's a good egg, despite the fact that she vamps around on red carpets in lovely borrowed dresses; she doesn't do *Hello!*, so I'm probably being unfair calling her a minor celebrity, with all the naffness that suggests.

We are walking down a wide north London street lined with mature trees. This is now way out of my comfort zone; I don't know where we're going. She cuts off down a pathway that tracks a long line of allotments on our left. It's getting dark. Why am I even looking here? It's two miles from Will's and so far no sighting has been further than about a mile away.

Shouldn't I have gone back to Harvist or Highgate Cemetery?

We walk past a tennis club where a fireworks party is just getting going and I curse the bloody things. 'Ahhh, not another one.'

'Yes,' she says, deliberately misunderstanding, 'I hate tennis clubs too. Horrible institutions full of dog whistles of the patriarchy.'

'A different kind of horror to the Groucho though.' We share an eyeball-roll about Tim. Everyone knows Tim; the world's worst best friend if you're trying to kick drugs. 'I can't tell you how many times I have deleted his number from my phone,' I say.

'Sympathies, babe.' She's been clean for years, and has the sort of superhuman strength that only damage followed by recovery brings to a woman.

'I've always found you utterly terrifying, you know,' I say.

'Pot. Kettle,' she says.

'I'm so crap with women. They either scare me in their strength or disgust me in their weakness.'

'That's horrible. I see women as my allies in a world full of old crap systems designed by men to bully and subdue my power.'

'Yeah and that too,' I say, wishing I hadn't said anything.

I hold out a pack of Marlboro Lights. 'I'm smoking, sober. Something else to add to the things you do when you lose your dog.'

'Go on then.' We stop and cup our fags to the lighter.

'But in a way,' I go on, 'the fact that men don't really bother me means that I have handed all the power to women already. If I hadn't handed them all this power they wouldn't be able to hurt me as much as they do.'

I leave her at her house, pick up my bike and ride towards my brother's. It's all downhill, which sounds better than it is. I don't have any lights and the pavements are covered in wet brown leaves that make me skid if I use the brakes. I come off, and go sprawling across the pavement, grazing my knees as I tear through my wool trousers.

Throwing the bike onto a patch of grass and trees, I sit on a low wall around a concreted seating area by the side of the road. It's shaken me up even more; my pretence at calm with the minor celebrity is gone. I'm a big panting, flapping, teary mess.

In this state, I read a text from an old university friend telling me a mutual friend has died suddenly. I respond. She follows up with a call, she wants to discuss it.

'I can't talk or think right now, I've lost my dog and I'm in a state.'

'You think losing your dog is worse than Dan dying?' She is appalled.

'No, but I can't connect to Dan's loss. I hadn't seen him in twenty years. I spent every moment with my dog. It's proving very hard to handle. I'm cracking up.'

The phone call ends badly. She tells me I'm 'pretty sad'. I tell her to fuck off. I don't care. I don't care at all. I sit on the wall in the murky dark under the trees, away from the street lights. Wherever the hell I am, I will limp my bike down the hill and walk into the nearest pub and get drunk.

Thank God, the next pub I see isn't a bad one. I reviewed St John for the *Evening Standard* back in the early noughties. It's a bit more corporate now but the wine list isn't too dull. If it had been a proper crap boozer with swirly carpet and the sort of red wine that gives you a blocked nose *and* a headache, that might have felt more fitting for my desperate mood, more authentic, but I'm relieved the first pub I come to doesn't require me to drink shit wine.

'Do you have a cold-climate Pinot noir, a phone charger and any pork scratchings?'

The bartender charges my phone and brings me a goldfish bowl of posh pub red and long strips of home-made crackling in a glass. The crackling is gone in 60 seconds. I sling the glass back at him. 'keeps 'em coming.'

As soon as I have 10 per cent battery I call Charlie and tell him I've fallen off my bike, my heart is breaking and I'm getting smashed in St John's Tavern on Junction Road. 'I'm coming,' he says.

Charlie and I talk, we laugh. 'Hey, I haven't told you the news. This French woman rang to tell me she definitely saw

Wolfy on Camden Road on Wednesday morning. Sounds like he was quite near the back of Will's. There, that's good. Another sighting. Cheer up, Foxy.'

We stand up off our stools and hold each other for a really long time, and then he digs in too, and starts drinking. 'It's OK,' I say. 'I'm back here tomorrow on the hunt. I'll pick up the car.'

We've been drinking an hour or so when a call comes in. 'I've seen your dog in East India Quay.'

What? That's Docklands. Miles away.

We run to Will's in Tufnell Park, where he and Steph are sitting over dinner and a bottle of wine with their friend. I post the sighting to Twitter and two people say they are heading there immediately. It's ludicrous. 'That's ten miles away from where he was last seen. Should we even go?'

'Yes, go, go,' says Steph. 'I'll stay here with the children.'

Will says he will drive us and we all pile in his car. He has on a pirate radio station and the combination of the alcohol and the music makes me think, Yes, *now* we are going to hashtag find Wolfy.

As soon as we get there I go to meet the woman who called me. I can't escape the sneaking suspicion that she is on something. She seems totally sober, looks, dare I say it, a bit boring, but she describes the dog having red eyes, like it was really tired, like it was a devil, and wearing a bandana. A tired devil dog wearing a neckerchief.

But the hope is there in me, also like a drug. I search on through the estate by the Thames.

We are hunting for the dog in a bland development of brand-new, triple-glazed, yellow brick condos. They are starter homes for the young professional who isn't too fussed about ideas of community and just wants 'amenities' and 'facilities' and to be not too far from work. This isn't a place with the breadth of all human life on its doorstep. I expect they are advertised as executive Thames-side residences. It's soulless, more so than the Harvist Estate, and aside from pools of rusty lamplight, it's dark and it's deserted. The Thames is on one side, the busy eight-lane Aspen Way rushes by on the other. As we split up in our usual Scooby style, I am overwhelmed by an aimlessness, of having no clear purpose in the way I hunt. Yet, still, images of his head popping round the corner of the human hutches taunt me to move on, still calling.

'Wolfy. Woooolfy.'

Two hours later: 'Ever get the feeling you're on a wild goose chase,' Will asks tentatively as we drive back north to his place.

'Yes,' says Charlie, 'a lot. That was a joke. That woman was having a fucking laugh at our expense. Red devil eyes. Please. I'm reaching the end of my patience with this.'

The sensation of being laughed at had occurred to me too as I called around the blocks in the development. 'I thought it was hopeful,' I said.

'And how does that place gel with Highgate. Or Harvist?' Charlie isn't being cruel, or brutal, just utterly practical.

'It's the circling theory, you know, that he's moving around Will's, trying to track himself back.'

'Sorry, still don't understand – how does that explain Docklands?' Will motions to the blur of traffic outside the car. 'There is no way a dog could get across some of these roads.'

Will's not usually gentle. Normally a sardonic inflection touches his every utterance. But there's none of it now. We are rational and debating whether to keep pushing out into the city looking for the dog, or not.

A text from Emma Pratt: 'You say Wolfy seen by canal Camden Wednesday. Canal comes out at Limehouse Basin, not far from where he was seen tonight. What do you think?'

'It's the canal. The canal! The Regent's Canal comes out just below yours and comes out the whole way to Docklands at Limehouse. I'm coming back tomorrow, I'm going to walk from here to Docklands along the canal.'

'Really,' says Will. 'That sounds a bit mad.'

I hear Charlie mumble in the front.

'What's that? I didn't catch it.'

'I said that's it. I'm done. You can keep looking, I still believe he will either be found, or not.' He's raised his voice, like a patronising care worker talking to a deaf old bat.

'Will? Will? What do you think?'

'I agree, Kate. Steph and I were talking about this last night. It's hard to say, but I don't think we can change the outcome of this.'

'But Steph doesn't give a shit, she's just thinking of this whole Wolfy thing as an inconvenience to the family, of course she thinks that.'

'Kate. Steph is beside herself. She hasn't got a clue what to say to you and she's like me. She's devastated the dog ran off on our watch. She doesn't think it's an inconvenience, she knows it's a total nightmare for you. All we can compare it to is if you lost one of our kids. It's the same, we know that. I'm sorry if you feel we don't. The fact remains, though, that I think we've done everything we can. It's out there, people know what he looks like. We can keep putting up posters. But all this running around? I dunno, it's wearing everyone out, it's fucking stressful, and it's actually kind of dangerous. We could have got badly messed up at Harvist the other night. Kate, Charlie is right. You've got to leave it. It's in the lap of the gods now.'

What gods?

CHAPTER THIRTEEN

The midnight jogger has asked me to bring him a load of my smelliest clothes – knickers are probably best, he says, and sweaty things, socks, sports gear. He wants to explain his plan for luring Wolfy out. The carting of a carrier bag full of dirty laundry across London does not feel problematic. It feels logical, given that dogs live in the Buddhist realm of smells. What feels perverse is handing it to a complete stranger, and a man at that. But he has a plan and, eight days in, I'm too desperate to be coy. Charlie knows half the truth, the half with socks and a smelly T-shirt. The other half with the dirty knickers I keep from him.

I leave the flat early on Sunday morning. I want to hunt for as long as possible, stick posters up all along the canal, stop and talk to people. If a person can feel committed to something on a cellular level then that's me and today's Wolfy hunt. Back to Docklands to where we were last night, then a good six miles up the canal and on to meet the midnight jogger with my smelly laundry basket stash.

Charlie tells me again that he isn't going out looking today. For him, from here on in, it's fate that takes care of our dog. He's been saying this for several days now. This morning, though, there's real steel in his resolve.

'Go, do what you planned, but come home this evening, please. I've got a rib of beef from the butchers. Let's get a decent bottle. I'll cook. Come home, we can eat together, watch a film.'

It feels like punctuation marking the end of the hunt for Wolfy. The feast at which we hand ourselves over to fate. I promise him I will be home by six.

It takes me a while to get to Docklands, and make no mistake, no matter how perky and smiley I may appear to the people I stop, I am in a state of perpetual low-level distress. Meaning? I make mistakes. I lose the car keys. I drop money. On the Docklands Light Railway this morning, I had got off at the wrong station. Crossing over the platforms, I got myself into a tourist-like confusion, and popped up several times in the wrong place. Eventually I had to stop and try to pull my feverish self together.

Charlie texts: 'Dog seen on Hampstead Heath again'. Here he inserts an emoji rolling its eyeballs. By the time I call him he is already jogging across the Heath and talking to me with that mix of excitement and cynicism that only someone hunting for a dog will understand.

I sit and wait for him to call with my eyes closed. Canary Wharf DLR station is new and sterile, in contrast to a lot of the battered old Underground stations. But with its weekend calm and grand steel and glass elliptical roof it feels like being in church. It's calming. When the phone rings I allow myself the brief luxury of thinking that he has found the dog.

He has not. Having met the walker who saw 'Wolfy', the two made off after this golden shaggy lurcher, only to catch up and find that it was following behind its owner, who was on a run. 'No, it's still not Wolfy,' the guy said. It obviously wasn't the first time this had happened.

I travel on. Heavy-hearted and in need of perpetual motion. In the 20 minutes it takes me to get back to East India DLR, Charlie has obviously been on the phone to his mother. She calls me. She's been very kind and reassuring before, but now her tone is sharp and impatient. 'Who is this chap you are going to meet? Have you met him before? Are you meeting in a public place? How do you know he's a good person?'

I placate her with lies. The truth is I only trust the midnight jogger because he's an endurance athlete and he invented an energy bar.

'OK, well, if you are sure. But promise me this is your last day. Do what you have planned today and then go home to your boyfriend. You can get another dog. You won't get another Charlie.'

'You can get another dog.' These words sweep through my body, prickling and panicking. I can't cope with the idea.

That's it, more tears. 'I don't want another dog, I want Woofs back.'

'I know, I know, and he may well still come back but you need to get some normality back in your life. You are making yourself ill.'

This conversation clearly won't end until I make her a promise.

I constantly make and then break promises to editors about getting things in on time. If it's a promise she wants, I can give it to her. I'm good at pretending. I pretended to be OK when I lived with my dad and stepmum because appearing upset just made everyone pissed off. I've got this. As I take the steps from the DLR down to the street, I say, 'OK Christina, I will just walk the canal from Docklands to Camden and then I will go home to Charlie and stop looking. You're absolutely right. Promise.'

As soon as I put the phone down I start blubbing again, right in front of a homeless guy. It's getting embarrassing, all this crying.

'Hey, hey, hey. What's wrong? What you crying for. Look at me, I've nae teef.' He shows me a gummy smile. 'At least you're not a useless old junkie like me.'

What a dreadful big baby princess cunt I must look in my old fur coat and Parisian Stephane Kélian trainers. I crouch down on my haunches opposite him. 'I'm a dog addict. I've lost my dog. I loved him, love him, so much, maybe too much ...' I offer him a cigarette.

'You're all right, I've given up.'

'So *had* I,' I say, taking a puff. 'Sorry I haven't got any money, for real, I have *no money.*'

'Aye, looks like it. I don't want anything off you, now fuck off.'

He laughs.

I laugh.

'Thanks for cheering me up.' I smile and I mean it.

The rendezvous I was going to make with Emma is nixed by my grief-addled bumbling transport errors. As I arrive she is leaving. She too has been to East India Quay this morning, with her son.

We coordinate by text but I still want to ring for our soothing daily 'Do you think he's alive?' chat, in which she reassures me to hunt on is not the act of a soft-headed fantasist.

'Yes,' she says, as she always does, but for the first time since I started talking to her, I doubt she's being honest.

'You sound unsure, Emma, why can I hear doubt in your voice? I trust you. Tell me.'

'Sorry Kate. I know how distraught you are. I sit up at night waiting until you've sent your last tweet to the #findwolfy followers because I never want you to feel alone in this. I've barely slept this last week. I want you to know I've fallen in love with Wolfy. It's like I am feeling your pain.'

'It's called empathy, I think, or is it sympathy, either way I am really sorry to foist my suffering on you. It's so wrong.'

'No, no, I'm sorry.'

'No, you aren't allowed to be sorry. I forbid it. I owe you such a huge drink, you've kept me sane this week, or as sane I could be.'

I feel like she is leaving me, I feel like I'm being dumped. She must have sensed my fear. 'I'm having a hard time at home with my daughter. She's revising for her GCSEs and she thinks I should be at home with her, not out hunting for a dog I've never met.'

I throw a load more sorrys at her. 'Sorry, God, I'm so sorry. You absolutely must go home to your daughter, please put her first.'

'I wanna keep looking, Mum,' I hear a boy's voice in the background. 'We are going to Find Wolfy.' He says it like it's a quiz show slogan.

'Sorry, I've got to go,' says Emma. 'My husband's just pulled up in the car.'

I say sorry back once more.

So ends a very apologetic and British conversation about dogs.

Emma's wavering confidence is a blow. Despite the careening about chasing leads, there has not been a strong and plausible sighting of the dog since he was seen twice on Thursday. The surge of interest and supporters of the first week he was missing is starting to wane; of course it is. A missing dog. That's not a long player. Is it? Every day I'd have a moment when I'd wonder if it was possible to feel less distraught, approach this whole situation from a more easy come, easy go perspective. Like Pat had said, 'They do run sometimes.' And Anna, 'Some dogs, once they are on the move, they like it.'

I try that attitude on for size but it doesn't fit. Keep looking.

In my desperation, I ring the *Daily Mail* and wonder if they'd like a story about a sad childless middle-aged woman who has lost her dog. I paint the sort of picture they want in order to gain access to their millions of readers. I don't care.

When he woke up, he'd sometimes walk up the top of the bed and sit above me looking right into my eyes. He'd sit there for a bit and then he'd collapse with a big whumpf into a comfy position to lie close to me, still looking directly into my eyes. His neck would stretch forward and he'd say good morning by giving me two tiny licks on my nose with his tongue. It was a moment of such sweet focus and nothing would break it – unless he heard Charlie cooking sausages downstairs or rustling a packet of biscuits, obviously, in which case he'd launch himself down the lethal-to-lurchers stairs and wait.

You cannot rationalise love. It's not just a load of oxytocin; at some point there's some magic, a spirit that weaves its way through the chemistry and that no one can explain. Love isn't just neurotransmitters, is it? It's not just dependency. It is our route to something beautiful, mysterious and transcendent. Without it, life is a hollow set of functions and, frankly, pointless.

From this part of south-east London where we were hunting last night, it takes me not far off an hour to walk to the canal's entrance at Limehouse Basin. It's then another six or so miles from there through prime hipster country on the canal to just before the Kentish Town lock, where I will exit onto Camden Road, near Will's and near where the dog was seen by the French woman earlier in the week. The plan has a modicum of logic.

We have already skimmed the borders of east London in early searches around Clissold Park in Stoke Newington. People have told me they put up posters in Victoria Park too, which is proper east, an area we haven't even considered. It's a blinder of a day as I start the second week of his absence. I am grateful for an azure sky and I am relieved the canal walk offers a straight line to follow. I walk the 200-year-old artery of the Industrial Revolution; the information superhighway of its time, with its brickwork and bridges black with the patina of industry and time.

I stop passers-by. Like a charity chugger or a politician I am recruiting people, ever more, to the cause. People are kind, there's a steady generosity of spirit. Londoners in all their shapes and sizes are good people. They care. When I stop for a cup of tea somewhere near Dalston the waiter refuses to take my money when he sees the stack of Lost Dog posters at my side. I bump into two photographers I have worked with in the past and they both give me warm hugs.

I keep a smile stretched across my normally hangdog face, which is unusual for someone used to strangers' jeers of 'Why the long face?', 'Cheer up, love, it might never happen' and 'Give us a smile.' This is a face that says, 'Like me. Listen to me.'

After four poster-pinning hours I arrive at Camden Road. My legs feel like lead. But to move is better than to stay still. There are several points where the dog would have had to leave the towpath. Would he have carried on following the canal, or been redirected into the streets at these points? If indeed he has been here at all. I imagine him trotting along the path, perhaps moving at night so no one sees him.

When I scrolled through the lost dog stories, it was plain that dogs often turned up dead on train tracks or in canals. If he's followed these routes, has he survived? The questions are infinite. I let them in one ear and out the other as the next unknown shuttles up the queue.

Back at Will's my nephew's birthday party is in full swing. There are kids aeroplaning around the house and a woman called Snakey Sue draping eight-year-olds in fat boa constrictors. I had forgotten this, and have no card or present for him. Normally when I come here all I want is a drink and a good gossip. What I really want this time is decent paper map of London.

Will makes a good show of looking before I let him off the hook. 'You get on and enjoy the party. I'm going to the pub to meet this guy.'

'Not sure "enjoy" is the correct word. Old Snakey Sue here seems a little too relaxed with her snakey pals.'

If I can't bring a bit of joy to proceedings then I am extraneous. Quietly I bugger off to meet the midnight jogger at the Palmerston up the road, on my way out dropping a freshly smelly T-shirt from my stash, and hiding a pair of pants among it for luck, in the pile of Wolfy-luring smells outside Will's front door.

Christ I'm tired.

Charlie mum's words, 'You can get another dog,' are gnawing at the back of my mind. I don't want another dog. It's way too early for such talk. It's made me quite angry, in fact. I stride on up the road looking ahead, fists plunged into my pocket, in no way ready to give up the fight.

If I have to – and it looks like I will – I will seek on secretly.

As soon as I get to the Palmerston I fall on my phone's cracked screen and try to put together a theory about where Wolfy is. I draw mental lines along train lines and towpaths. Try to see patterns in what sightings we have had. I know there is some logic somewhere but my brain can't see it. It's just my gut, really, my gut and the sightings that keep my faith alive.

I'm itching for a drink. I hope this jogger character fancies one too.

'Are you Kate?' a tall, grey-haired but vital-looking man calls from the next table. It's the midnight jogger. He has been there all the time. In all the returning to his Twitter page over recent days, wondering if he is mad or, since Moonieman's outing, even real, I have only ever seen him dressed for ultra-endurance pursuits. I didn't recognise him without his wetsuit and swimming hat.

'Would you like a drink?' I ask. He orders a green tea. I urge him too keenly to have a proper drink and he says he is teetotal. When someone is about to go out of their way to find your lost dog it's probably best to appear sober and serious, I think, standing waiting at the bar I repeat to myself, 'order tea, order tea,' while longing for the soothing mallet to the skull of a dose of thick jammy pub red. 'Merlot. Just a small one.' The bartender says the smallest glass they do is a medium, 175ml. I nod, too tired and distracted to quibble for a 125ml. I won't have my favourite pedant's argument about the logical impossibility of a medium glass of wine being the smallest. How can I ever moderate my drinking if the first glass is big enough to get me on the way to pissed? As I expected, I guzzle the wine too fast and the combination of wretchedness, no food and alcohol hits me like a sledgehammer. I fast feel blessedly squiffy already.

'My wife isn't happy,' he admits. 'She says I shouldn't be getting involved in other people's lives.'

I wonder what Charlie would do if I started hunting for stranger's dogs? In gratitude that the jogger's absurd levels of altruism exist, I spill my guts to him about how people are giving up on the hunt and my family are telling me to stop looking. 'Why are you going to so much effort to help me?'

'Because I lost my dog once in the park. It wasn't for long but I didn't know that at the time. And what I remember of it is feeling so desperate and asking people to help me and no one did. No one cared. I will never forget that feeling of helplessness.'

My phone is ringing. It's Charlie. 'Where are you?'

His voice is tense with stress and barely disguised desperation. With an artificial brightness I answer, hoping to deflect any expectation that I come home. 'With that nice man Brett. He's got a great plan. I'll be back soon, I promise.' I put the phone down. I'll deal with smoothing things over later.

So what is his plan? We have yet to discuss it.

It's complex and tests my stressed brain with its logistics. He takes all these fetid clothes and sets up a nocturnal nest of smells and enticing carnivorous foods within Parkland Walk, where, he is convinced, 'He will go because it's by far the safest and quietest place a dog could live, plus you have the sighting there last week.' Wolfy will follow the scent. There I will set up a number of CCTV cameras that will allow us to spot the dog.

I don't get it, which I am not about to tell him. Instead I give him the edited highlights of Anna Twinney's reading – the dark skins, the high footfall at Arsenal: 'Wasn't there a match yesterday?'

The antipathy, or disgust, that he feels about the psychic information shows on his face. 'I'm not interested in that.'

'Even if he is there, won't the foxes get the food before Wolfy does?'

'All scavenger and carnivore animals will be attracted there, but the scent will be so strong that eventually Wolfy will make his way there. I'll just keep buying meat if I have to.'

'Oh. I'll pay,' I say, wondering how.

I'm not sure about it as a plan. But to reject support of such a significant level seems counterintuitive.

Charlie rings again. There's a desperation in his voice that I have never heard before. 'Come back now. Please. I don't feel good about you meeting this stranger.'

'I'm with him now, he's nice, don't worry.'

'Come back now. Come back, Kate.' The desperation in his voice ramps up.

'I will. Soon.' I put the phone down.

He rings again. I switch the phone to silent.

'So why do you figure he's on Parkland Walk and not somewhere else?'

'It's the sightings, there's a pattern . . .' He pulls out a plastic document wallet containing a printout from Google Maps and we both settle over it as he shows me his theories.

'You see, I've been thinking about the routes he could be taking that we as humans can't see.'

My phone vibrates. Charlie's mum. I ignore it. As soon as it has gone to voicemail, she rings again. And again. I put my phone in my bag.

When the midnight jogger gets up to leave I hand him the bag of dirty laundry. It's like we are doing a shady deal. He does not smirk or make a single joke about anything.

Charlie's mother has rung ten times in the hour I was at the Palmerston. As I walk out I brace myself for the call. 'What are you doing?' Her voice is shrill with fury. 'Stop these mad schemes and go home now to your boyfriend. He is sick with worry. If you go on like this you will end up in the loony bin. You are losing your mind. Wolfy was lovely but he was an animal, Kate. Go home to your boyfriend, now. You're going to lose him. You're making yourself ill.'

'I am, I am.' I smile as I say it, laughing with nerves, or am I laughing like a mad woman in a Victorian novel? 'I am going home now.'

I walk in the door and Charlie has roast potatoes and a big rib of beef cooked and a bottle of claret already open. I don't think I have ever seen him so vulnerable. My angry man is utterly exposed, truthful; for once his pain is not hidden behind pragmatism or anger. He is pleased to see me. He holds out a slotted spoon. 'Will you make the gravy?'

He loved the dog too. We have both lost something that was precious only to us.

'Oh God.' I move towards him and hold him tightly. 'I'm so lucky to have you. I love you.'

'You too Fox, it's all right.' We stand in the kitchen, me leaning against his chest, him stroking my hair. Two scratchy, odd, hurt humans in a rare moment of straightforward love. I kiss him and we say nothing, not a word, about the dog.

He has lit the fire. We eat and talk. I am ravenous. The beef is delicious. My enthusiasm for everything is abnormally bright. I try to tame it. 'This is great, thank you. The wine is so good.'

'I dropped a bit extra.'

'I can tell. It's brilliant. Something a bit …' I take another sip and pretentiously wash it a round my mouth like a pompous twit at a wine-tasting. 'Mmmn, what is it?'

'Erm, is it grapes?' Charlie says it in a dullard's voice. It's an old standard we two use a lot when I'm being a wine ponce.

'It's sort of salty and smoky.'

Ostensibly, this is normality.

I put the plate on the floor. No dog comes over to try to lick it. My mobile phone rings in the kitchen and I go to answer it.

'Hello.' A child's voice, gruff, faint, early teens maybe. 'Are you the person that's lost their dog coz I seen it.'

'Where?'

'It was lookin' out under a bin, I saw its eyes.'

'Where? Where? Which street?'

'Near Brecknock Road, I don't know.'

'Which street?!'

'I can't remember. I seen your poster on the estate.'

'Where do you live?'

'Colley House on the estate.'

'Was the dog near your place?'

'Yeah.'

'Is this a wind-up?' I say it gently so as not to scare him away.

'No, I seen it.' There are no manic giggles. 'He looked frightened.'

I believe him.

I come off the phone.

'Who was that?'

Brecknock Road is behind Will's house. 'No one, one of the dog-walker lot, wanting to know news.'

I don't say anything, I don't send a tweet. I act like nothing has happened. Inside hope springs round my body like a rubber ball. The heavy sludge of longing is in every cell of my body, weighing me down, but there's something else. There's more hope than I've ever felt in my life, and there's tomorrow.

I tell Charlie I love him again. 'Love you too, Fox. What are you doing this week?' I can feel his relief at the safety of having the routine conversations of six years together.

'I've got a lot of writing to do, I'm going to work at the London Library. You?'

All the experiences of the last nine days concertina into one powerful surge of energy. When we go to bed I lie there sending messages to Wolfy. Stay safe, stay warm. I'm coming. I see him curled up, peeping out under his shaggy brows from his spot under the wheelie bin somewhere near my brother's house. Stay there, stay safe, stay warm, don't die Woofles. Tomorrow.

*

In the morning I pack to 'go to the library', meaning I put my first pee of the day into an old Evian bottle and tie a few pairs of my and Charlie's smelly socks to a long cane that usually holds up the honeysuckle in the scrappy yard at the bottom of the steep metal steps. I take the tube to Tufnell Park and I walk the streets behind Will's house.

I go into every deep dark corner, I step down into every basement entrance to a flat. At the top of Corinne Road there is a deserted house and I walk around every corner of it, and take care to squat and pee, just to ram the point home.

Why didn't I do this before, just fill the streets around Will's with scent that could draw him back to me in his blind and confusing world of smells.

As I travel around these maybe six streets and the estate where the boy said he lived, I squirt my scent on the wall at dog nose height, dragging the cane behind me and looping back to the gate of Will's place. Wolfy has been here enough times, he knows the smells. He's near here. I know it.

Walking down Corinne Road, I bump into Will on his bike on the street. 'What are you doing? I thought you were at work,' I say.

'Bah, I don't need to be there til ten-ish. I've just been out shaking some of the cat's food,' he says, holding up a jar of brown beans. He looks down at the near-empty Evian bottle. 'Is that pee?'

I wave the sock at him. 'Scent trails!'

Will cycles on and I carry on round the streets alone with my wretched faith.

At 10.30, thereabouts, Charlie calls. Someone has called him to say they have the dog.

'It's probably a con but I'm on my way there now. Do you want to come and check it out? Can you get here, from the library?'

He gives me the address, a garage no more than a mile from where I am now. I flap briefly. Should I walk, or wait to spot a black cab, try an Uber. I try Uber, the wheel turns on the screen as the app promises to find my driver. I can't wait. I can't rely on a black cab passing. My heart is beating so weirdly I feel nauseous. I drop the stick, socks and Evian bottle in the first bin I see and start to run to the minicab office in the parade of shops by the Irish pub on Dartmouth Park Hill. The Lost Dog posters are still there in the newsagent, the barber and on the glass that I am talking through. 'Do you have any cars, do you know the M&A Coachworks on Highgate Road?'

'You can walk it in ten minutes.' The woman's phlegmy response echoes the strong smell of stale cigarette smoke drifting through the hatch.

'I'm in a hurry.'

'Alright love. Outside. White Toyota.'

A driver is waiting on the kerb and I jump into the grey synthetic pod of body smells and Magic Tree fragrance with a suggestion of illicit Silk Cut. The same type of chariot that had shuttled me round London at dawn in my partying days was taking me to my saviour. Maybe.

Minutes later I meet Charlie as he jumps out of the car. He is confused: 'How did you get here so quickly from the West End?'

'I'll explain later.'

The garage is in a series of railway arches and it's not clear where we should go. There's a security guy at the entrance. 'We're here about a dog?' I say hopefully.

'No dog is here. Do you have an appointment with someone?'

There's Porsches everywhere, packed in the small spaces like cattle in a truck. We keep walking on with the security guy cautiously escorting us, to the back of the first arch and a reception desk with two suited ladies sitting by telephones. I stand there with my hands in my pockets. I'm wearing a different coat, one I haven't worn since the dog ran away. There is a small bone-shaped biscuit in one pocket. I turn it over and over with my fingers. 'You have our dog here. A man rang us about a dog.'

'You're here to see a man about a dog,' says the older of the two, harsh-looking with her solid helmet hair, cynical. 'No dogs here Madam. You've got the wrong place.' It's a wind-up. I can't take it. I should have known after all the hoaxes and false alarms. 'Do you want to try the pub next door, maybe?'

I remember – the Southampton Arms; I'd stuck a poster there the other day. Drunken hoaxers. How dare I get hopeful.

Then a man emerges from a doorway leading to the next arch. 'Yeah, come with me. I think it's this way.' Charlie and I follow, through these immaculate white shining arches crammed with a jigsaw of Porsches, pink, neon green, black, old ones, new ones, half a Porsche, a Porsche jacked up two metres above the ground, punctuated by the odd Bentley. We emerge from the arches into a small rhombus of tarmac with a drop 20 metres on one side to the train tracks. The overland train rumbles above our heads. Over and over, I turn the biscuit.

Sound warps and bends in my ears. When I'd sat speaking to Anna Twinney the world shrank around my shoulders and it feels like this now. The hope is gone, the yearning is gone. Time stops. I am pure energy. Pure love. Outside I can hear the twittering sound of my own voice, pointless and polite. Inside it is like meditation in a state of high arousal. And the biscuit turns through my fingers. 'Where should we go?' asks Charlie. A polite tic because, short of launching ourselves onto the train tracks, there is only forward.

We weave through the expensive cars, trashed and broken, a red Carrera with its back completely stoved in, the rear end of a vivid blue 911. In places we have to turn sideways, they are so close together. Blokes in liveried overalls turn as we walk by. A couple of them fall in and follow us. The tarmac dips into a huge brick garage, free-standing, open, tiled and bright white. To the right of us a thick bank of brambles. The biscuit dances on my fingertips. A cluster of men, white overalls rolled down to their hips, are waiting in a semicircle, arms folded, serious.

'Where is he?'

We walk into the garage and turn left. There, sitting in the corner with electric flex tied round his scuffed brown collar, is a grubby, wide-eyed, polite shaggy lurcher.

'Here you go. Here he is.'

It is Wolfy.

The dog limps over squeaking and feebly letting his tail wap his whole today. Charlie and I both fall to our knees. Wolfy burrows deep into my body, making tiny bleeping squeaks. I fold around him, my forehead on the top of his skull. He smells deeply richly terrible. 'Oh my God. Wolfy. Wolfy. My boy. Wolfy. Oh my God.'

What is time now. I can't feel it moving, I can only feel relief and love. I rest back on my heels and Wolfy goes to Charlie, his whole emaciated body moving in a ripple of physical delight.

And after a few minutes Wolfy walks over to one of the guys in overalls and leans very firmly against his leg.

'Did you find him?'

'Yeah, yeah I did,' he says, stroking the sides of the dog's ears.

'He's saying thank you to you.' I want to bark, howl and cry with happiness.

Another of the mechanics says, 'Don't think we need to check whether they're the owners. I've never seen a dog so happy.'

Wolfy comes back to me. I look at him. He is thin – the arc from his ribs up to his tummy and down around his haunches is exaggerated – but he doesn't look awful. We've probably overfed him a tad but in the circumstances that doesn't seem such a bad thing; it meant he survived. We walk out of the garage back to the tarmac. As soon as we are clear of the building Wolfy lets out a long thick stream of dark brown pee. He doesn't cock his leg, he simply stands and lets it go. 'Hey, don't worry,' says one of the mechanics, anticipating my apology.

'What happened? Where did you find him?'

'I got in early and I was just getting changed when I heard this howling. It was so faint I couldn't work out where it was coming from. I ignored it for a bit, but it sounded so sad and low, it was pathetic, you know. So I came back here, looking up and down, and then I saw his face right back there.' He points deep into the thicket of brambles beyond the high steel railings with their 'Property of Network Rail' sign. These are keep-out railings in no uncertain terms, six foot high, spaced barely an inch apart and with razor-sharp points at the top.

'I thought it was a fox at first but I could see his face was white. He looked shocked and scared. I told him I'd get him out, and went off to get a drill. When I came back he was at the railings, trying to scratch his way through, digging and biting. The railings are close together, dug deep into the ground, but there is one steel post hanging loose from its screws and pulled to one side. He squeezed through by himself. As soon as he was through he came and leaned on me, it really felt like he was saying thank you. Yeah, it really did. He was so happy to see me, you know, and then seeing him with you ...'

He's a quiet guy, soft-spoken.

Another of the mechanics, stacked and muscular with a shaven head: 'It's nice to see a happy ending. We lost our dog last week, he was old, he'd been ill but nothing prepares you for that feeling. So I know how you must have been feeling. How long's he been gone? Nine days did you say?'

Someone appears beside me holding a box of cheap dog biscuits. 'One of the boys went and got them from the shop. We knew he must be hungry and thirsty. Take them.'

We say our thank-yous, practically bowing as we back away. We walk out the way we came, the poignant difference of the fizzing lightness in every step we retrace. Wolfy trots along beside us.

There's a deep grumble as the next overland train passes
above. Next stop, Upper Holloway, the station he was seen running into last Saturday. Where has he been? I will never know.
For all I know he has been living in the dense thicket of brambles
between two railway lines for a week.

The dog is not strong enough to leap into the car, so Charlie
puts his arms under his hindquarters and lifts him up. Wolfy sits
on the back seat and I climb in with him and he collapses down,
using my thigh for a pillow.

I pull the biscuit from my pocket and hold it out to him
between my thumb and finger. His mouth nuzzles it from my hand
like he's done a thousand times before with a thousand biscuits,
the stodgy uncooked centre of a croissant, an offending crust of
a sandwich, a sinewy scrap of beef. Normal service is resumed –
almost – this time the crunching is cautious. His mouth is red and
sore from trying to chew through the steel fence.

As we drive back to west London, I call everyone, Will,
Steph, the parents, Emma. I send the midnight jogger a text –
'Throw my dirty laundry away. He's back.'

While we wait in Notting Hill Vets I take a photo and share
it to every corner of the social media we turned to for help.
'Wolfy is found.'

The reams and reams of responses are ecstatic and relieved.
Steph tweets, simply, 'Wolfy is found. Good things do happen.'

His tail is broken and bloody, and his gums infected, but
other than that he is fine. The vet prescribes him antibiotics.
The Aussie veterinary nurse crouches down as we weigh him.
He has lost three kilos. 'Ah Wolfy, you been eating like a
student, mate?'

Charlie lifts him into the car again and points us homeward
in the direction of Notting Dale. One more stop. We buy beef
mince from the butcher.

Wolfy expels the contents of his intestines at great force in
the yard; a week's worth of anguish in the form of chocolate
bum milkshake. Inside he goes to his favourite spot and watches

us as we wonder what the hell to do next with our adrenaline-addled human selves.

A shower, obviously. I strip naked and wash the dirt of his adventures off him. He stands hunched and patient while Charlie holds his broken tail out of the way. There's a bottle of Krug in the fridge, and no more fitting time to drink it. I pop and pour while Charlie lights the fire.

The three of us settle fireside on the shaggy Turkish rug. Wolfy sprawls, his head turned and one ear resting contented on a paw. Gradually his fur returns to golden as it dries. Us two humans sit either side of him, sipping this ambrosial champagne and feeling a calming of the alarming mix of neurotransmitters that only people who have lost a pet will comprehend. Our bodies' internal pharmacies have been working overtime. The story ends where it began, really: me, on a comedown.

What's different now is how happy and grateful I am for this life I have. I'm grateful for the awkward bastards club, Charlie and me, and the more or less happy family we have found with the addition of a third-hand lurcher called Wolfy.

'Can you hear something outside?'

'Yeah, what is that?' I get up and go to the window. 'There's a bloody great Sky News truck out there. What the f—?!'

'Oh no, I'm not getting involved.' Charlie disappears upstairs to hide while I watch the journalist go to my downstairs neighbour Annabel's front door.

'You need to go round the back,' I shout through the window. 'We don't have a front door.'

Wolfy and I make the six o' clock show in the upbeat 'And finally' slot. The anchorwoman Kay Burley, an early recruit to the Find Wolfy cause, interviews me live. We even get the rolling banner at the bottom of the screen. 'Lost dog Wolfy found after viral social media campaign.' Wow! We are like real news.

I look horrific. My hair is stuck to my head like an Elastoplast and as I talk I dementedly stroke the dog sleeping in my lap.

Not long after we come off air dear old Timbo calls. 'Marvellous news about the dog. Though I must say, seven minutes on Sky News, bit excessive isn't it? After all, it is just a dog.'

EPILOGUE

Not long after Wolfy came back my father's dog, Moby, died. He was an old dog but of course Dad was heartbroken. I'd taken these tearful calls from both Mum and Dad over the years when their dogs died. Now, I could see they had both been carrying on love affairs with their dogs all their lives. I'm glad they've both had that love through their own struggles, which define our passage through life.

That Christmas when I went to stay every walk we took together felt poignant and precious. My dad looked lonely without Moby at his side. I felt so lucky to have Wolfy back. The body of my friend Lisa's dog, Olive, who had gone missing around the same time as Wolfy, had recently been found on the railway line near where Wolfy was found.

In another very possible world, I could have lost him not for nine days, but forever.

He's a scientist by nature, my dad, not one for the magical thinking. He's always telling the more airy-fairy of his six kids off for believing in 'mumbo-jumbo'.

One evening we sit together by the fire after everyone else has gone to bed. There's a space at his feet where the old liver-spotted springer would normally have lain. Now my stepmother has gone upstairs, Wolfy has snuck up on the sofa.

'I can't make sense of it Dad. Where does all this love for Wolfy come from? Is it a sort of madness in me? Is it just oxytocin?'

I might be nearly 50 but I still think my daddy has all the answers.

Dad pinches the bridge of his nose behind his round gold-rimmed specs. He's welling up. 'I'm sure there are scientific attempts to explain it. But I don't know, darling, I don't think anyone has ever adequately explained the bond between mankind and the dog. It's one of the great mysteries.'

ACKNOWLEDGEMENTS

Will, 'Steph', Sam, Bay, Arty, my beloved family and all those friends and frenemies whose lives I plundered in order to write this book, thank you. Think of yourselves not as defiled and used but as 'patrons of the arts'. Mum, Martin, Ginge, Mark, Yogesh at the newsagents and Devlin's Portobello fruit and veg stall for all your interest free credit over the years. Patrons of the arts, the lot of you.

Mum, Dad. I hope you skipped the book and went direct to here. Thanks for everything and especially liking each other long enough for me, Tom and Will to be born. Don't be offended, just be relieved I got a f***ing book out.

Robert Caskie, to many more years of, 'I am taking my agent out for lunch'. Thanks for believing in me and my ideas. Robyn Drury, my publisher at Ebury, who can reference Adrian Mole and Samuel Pepys in the same sentence without turning into Melanie Oxbridge. Sarah Bennie, Steph Naulls, Lucy Brown, Rae Shrivington. You went above and beyond.

I stole the expression 'hopeless hope' from the artist Jake Chapman. If two words sum up the experience of searching for a lost dog then it is those.

The dog hunters at DogLost.com, when a dog goes missing they make it easier to cling to the hope in hopeless hope.

The countless friends, strangers and traders who lent their energy, support and shop windows to the #findwolfy cause. My belief in humanity and Twitter is born again.

Hugh. I'm sorry you aren't here to disapprove of my book. شكر

Most of all I'd like to thank Charlie, crisps, wine, and Wolfy.

AUTHOR'S NOTE

The owner of Lewis Hamilton II is Nicholas Burton, one of the last people to be pulled alive from Grenfell Tower on 14 June 2017. His 'boy' was killed that night, along with 71 of his neighbours. The following January, his wife Maria Del Pilar Burton, Pily, died in hospital as a consequence of the tragedy. Nick's ability to bring light into a room despite his great personal loss is astounding. He is a wonderful, warm man.